Harald Sophus Leonhard Weitemeyer

Denmark

Its History and Topography, Language, Literature, Fine Arts, Social Life and Finance

Harald Sophus Leonhard Weitemeyer
Denmark
Its History and Topography, Language, Literature, Fine Arts, Social Life and Finance
ISBN/EAN: 9783743433083

Manufactured in Europe, USA, Canada, Australia, Japa

Cover: Foto ©ninafisch / pixelio.de

Manufactured and distributed by brebook publishing software (www.brebook.com)

Harald Sophus Leonhard Weitemeyer

Denmark

DENMARK

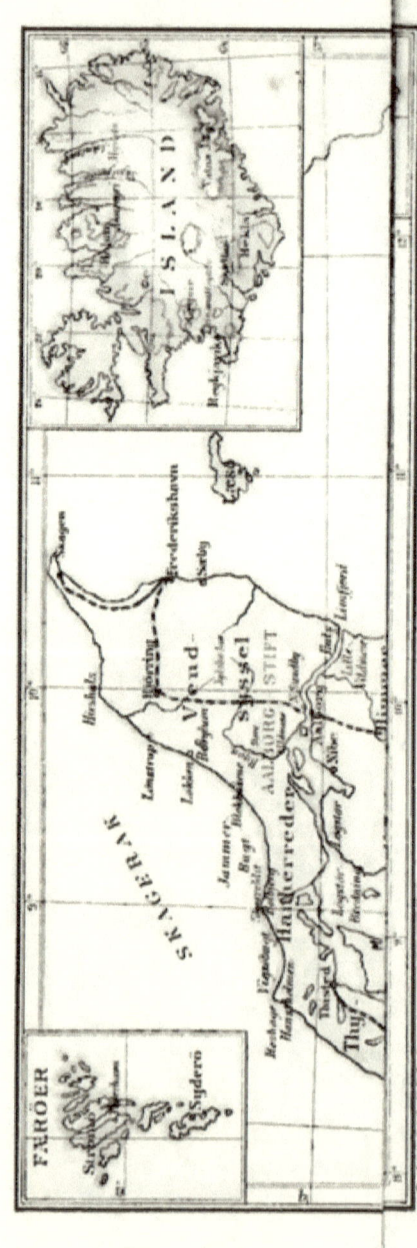

DENMARK

ITS HISTORY AND TOPOGRAPHY
LANGUAGE, LITERATURE, FINE-ARTS
SOCIAL LIFE AND FINANCE

EDITED BY

H. WEITEMEYER

WITH A COLOURED MAP

LONDON
WILLIAM HEINEMANN
COPENHAGEN: ANDR. FRED. HÖST & SON
1891
[All rights reserved]

COPENHAGEN -- PRINTED BY GRÆBE

Dedicated

BY GRACIOUS PERMISSION

TO H.R.H. THE PRINCESS OF WALES

PREFACE

What is the work here offered to the reader? It is, in a few words, a book with no claim to say anything new, and which yet hopes to be something new; it treats of Denmark and a great variety of things Danish, and yet it does not speak the Danish tongue. Without pretending to teach the Danes anything, it addresses foreigners in the three languages of the world. Strangers feeling an interest in our country will find here a well, whence they may draw a goodly draught of intelligence concerning to the soil and the people, its more important institutions and intellectual movements, seen as it were with Danish eyes. It is to be hoped that in this way foreigners will become acquainted with a little kingdom, sharing, as far as its limited sphere and means will allow, in the great civilisatory currents of our time. They will also acknowledge that, in spite of the hard trials it has undergone, the nation has courageously stood firm, and both mentally and materially struggled with success to keep its own rightful place among the states of Europe.

The general plan is an old and favorite idea of my publisher, Mr. *Christian Höst,* and is in fact but a continuation of his former attempts to make known abroad Denmark as she is, and also to give an idea of the scientific progress she has made. When he proposed that I should help him in carrying out this plan, I saw at once the difficulty of the task. As far as possible there should be a oneness of labor throughout the whole, and yet each section was to be written by a separate individual; so also, the specific Danish should be seen and heard in the foreign garb, and yet without doing violence to the language in which it was to be written. Difficulties like these it was not always possible entirely to overcome, but the will to do what could be done has never been wanting.

A word as to the orthography of the proper names. It is undoubtedly most correct to allow the names of places keep the form which they bear in their own country. People are seldom so absurd as to alter names of persons. But why should not also place names be generally respected? Instead in this manner, the method in vogue is often mere caprice. Sometimes the word remains unchanged; sometimes it is only slightly modified; in other cases it is twisted out of all resemblance to the original. All this chaotic spelling should be held in check, especially where Geography is concerned. The reader ought to know what the name is in the country itself, however common such forms as "Copenhagen", "Funen" and "Elsinore" may be. Where the foreign and home spelling — as in the case of "Schleswig" and "Slesvig" — may be equally admissible, I have naturally preferred the latter. Still, for very good reasons, I have only carried this out more or less consistently in the geographical chapter, "Country and people"; elsewhere the current orthographies are commonly not interfered with.

Finally it should be said that the bibliographical notes following each of the larger sections, do not lay claim to completeness. Yet it is to be hoped that they may be sufficient not only to introduce the foreigner to Danish literature, but also to give him some idea of the copiousness of this literature.

H. Weitemeyer

A SHORT SUMMARY OF DANISH HISTORY

Denmark until 1660

Denmark, in all probability, ranks among the oldest kingdoms in Europe. Its authentic history, however, goes back only about a thousand years; for during the time preceeding A. D. 800 we know but little of the country and its inhabitants. To supplement this deficiency we must have recourse to archæology, the youngest of the sciences; for it is only through the study of the remains of antiquity, and of folk-lore, that any light has been thrown on the obscurity of these remote ages.

After the country had risen from the depths of the ocean and assumed somewhat the form it now has, it became covered from an early age with great forests, apparently of coniferæ; the aborigines dwelt chiefly on the coast, where they sustained life by hunting and fishing, their imperfectly constructed implements of wood, stone, and bone being inadequate to clearing the woods. It is especially the "Kjökkenmöddinger" (kitchen middens or heaps of refuse from meals &c.); the "Stendysser" (dolmens), and the "Jættestuer" (barrows), the latter sepulchral chambers formed of colossal blocks of unhewn stone, that throw light on this most ancient period of Danish history — the Stone Age — of which, together with its inhabitants and their origin, we are otherwise in utter ignorance. It may, however, be probably assumed that the race of people who in the prehistoric period formed the population of Denmark, as also of most of Scandinavia, namely the Northern tribes, were masters of the country very early in the so-called stone age, having reached a more advanced stage of civilization and driven out the former inhabitants. A new period then began, the Bronze Age, thus named because the arms and tools were chiefly of that metal. An attempt could now be made to clear the woods, and penetrate into the interior of the country, and the soil was cultivated. The progress of certain kinds of industry during this epoch may also be traced, in the arms and jewels found in the tumuli, in which were deposited in urns, the ashes or unburned bodies of the dead. Communication with the civilized countries towards the south was, however, but limited at that time; and it is only about the Christian era that the influence of Roman civilization asserts itself. But centuries before, a new period had commenced, the Iron Age, in which the people learned the art of working this metal, and now made their arms and other implements of iron. Large ships were now built, the horse was taken still more extensively into use, and the oldest known Northern letters, the Runes, made their appearance. Later on, Roman ornaments in gold and silver were imported and imitated. Important remains, throwing some light on this period, are to be found in the tombs, bogs, and marshes. This, in short, is what archæology reveals to us with regard to the past of Denmark.

The historic period has as its precursor the heroic age, the records of which are handed down to us in the Icelandic Sagas, written in the 11th and 12th centuries, as also in the work of the Danish chronicler Saxo, who lived about the year 1200. This period abounds in accounts of the expeditions of the petty kings and chieftains, the so-called Wikings, to the coasts of foreign countries, as also of their valiant and heroic deeds at home; but, as is the case with the dawning historic life of all races, it is difficult to distinguish fact from fiction. All we know is, that the mythology and the social institutions of the Danish people of olden times have the same characteristics as those of all the Northern tribes. The people were divided into two orders, freemen and serfs, and the government was wholly patriarchal, the father being the head of the family. By degrees several families formed themselves into tribes, each with its own chieftain, and thus Denmark was soon divided into a great number of petty states, at the head of which were kings, who however, beyond the influence their own personal qualities commanded, had but slight authority, the freemen meeting at the national convocation (Thing) and settling public affairs. The most notable of the royal seats of these petty states was Leire in Sealand, and among the kings of Leire, Frode, Roar, Helge and Rolf Krake occupy a distinguished place in legendary lore. Another celebrated royal seat was Jellinge, in Jutland, where the most famous king was Vermund den Vise (the Wise).

Tradition may be said to be our only source of information far into the 8th century, and only then does it begin to give way to the clearer light of history. Ancient authors relate almost nothing about the Scandinavian countries; the only one who especially mentions them is Pytheas, the merchant of Massilia, who lived about 300 B. C. The first authentic account of the Danes, forming an introductory link to the historic ages, is to be met with in the writings of the Anglo-Saxon and French chroniclers, who furnish ample details of the piratical expeditions of the Wikings to the coasts of England and France in the time of Charlemagne. When this prince had subjugated the Saxons in the north of Germany, and extended his empire to the Eider, the old southern boundary of Denmark, he had a feud with Godfred, king of Jutland, who was however killed before the war actually broke out. His successor, Hemming, concluded peace with Charlemagne, on condition that the Eider should be recognised as the permanent boundary. Shortly after, Christianity made its way into the country; Harald Klak, king of Jutland, supported by Louis the "Débonnaire", son of Charlemagne, was baptized at Mayence, and brought back with him the monk Ansgar (St. Anscharius), the

"Apostle of the North", who as Bishop of Hamburg and afterwards of Bremen worked zealously for the propagation of the new doctrines until his death in 865. But it took some time before the new creed, and with it milder practices, became prevalent among the people; the Wikings long carried on their piratical expeditions, and the country was still divided into petty kingdoms. Towards the year 900 however, the province of Jutland, the Danish islands, and the south of Sweden, were united under Gorm den Gamle (the Old); he showed no toleration to Christianity, notwithstanding the fact that his queen, Thyra Danebod, whose memory is still cherished for having built the Danevirke rampart to protect the southern frontier, was a strict adherent of that faith. It is only during the reigns of Harald Blaatand (Blue Tooth), Svend Tveskjæg (Sweyn Forkbeard), and Knud den Store (Canute the Great), kings of his own line, that the new doctrines were widely propagated and firmly established in the country; especial merit being accorded to the last named king by the Church. Knud was indeed justly entitled to bear his surname, for during his reign Denmark became a great power; he not only annexed Norway, but he also reigned over England; a conquest, which had already been begun by his father, Svend Tveskjæg. After the death of Knud however, the three kingdoms became once more independent of each other, and on the decease of Hardeknud, his son, all connection between England and Denmark was finally severed; indeed Denmark itself for a few years came under the dominion of Norway.

In the year 1047 a new dynasty, originating with Svend Estridsen, a grandson in the female line of Svend Tveskjæg, ascended the throne of Denmark. It continued for over 300 years, a time rich in glorious memories, but also not devoid of periods of lamentable relapses into degradation and barbarism.

Svend Estridsen (1047—1076) is especially renowned for his patronage of the Church and the clergy, both under him attaining great prosperity. He regulated the ecclesiastical affairs of the nation, erected several new bishoprics and began to build churches of stone, among others Roskilde Cathedral. Of his five sons who ascended the throne successively after him, Knud den Hellige (the Saint) and Erik Ejegod (the Goodnatured) are the most celebrated. The former was no less zealous a friend to the Church than his father, and became later the tutelary saint of the country; but in point of fact, he was of a turbulent nature and as a king by no means beloved. He met his death at the hands of his own subjects, at Odense (1086); where the shrine containing his relics is still to be seen in St. Knud's church, which was erected shortly afterwards. Erik Ejegod obtained for the country an Archbishopric of its own, with the see at Lund, and he also engaged in a successful struggle against the Wends in North Germany, along the shores of the Baltic, where they carried on their piracies in the same way that the Danish Wikings of old had harrassed the coasts of other countries. This warfare was continued with great spirit by his son Knud Lavard (Lord) during the reign of Niels, the last of Svend Estridsen's sons and a man of but little capacity. But after the death of Knud, the Vandals took advantage of incapable rulers and the civil war carried on between the three competitors for the throne, Svend Grade, Knud, and Valdemar. The latter came off victorious in 1157.

With Valdemar den Store (the Great), 1157—1182, begins a new and brilliant era for Denmark. Not only were peace and order reestablished in the country under this wise and powerful monarch, but war was waged energetically against the Wends; a war in which Valdemar was powerfully assisted by Absalon, Archbishop of Lund, a friend of his earlier years and the founder of Copenhagen. Summer and winter the Danish fleet ravaged the coasts of the Baltic, the island of Rügen with the fortress of Arkona falling into Danish hands, 1169. Knud VI (1182—1202), Valdemar's son, also assisted by Absalon, pursued the struggle with equal success, his conquests extending to Mecklenburg and Pomerania, so that he was finally enabled to add to his other titles that of "de Venders Konge" (king of the Wends or Slavs). Under his brother Valdemar II Sejr (the Victorious), the whole of the Baltic coast, from the Trave to the gulf of Finland, was conquered by Denmark; but of all the exploits of this prince, the most celebrated is undoubtedly his expedition to Esthonia, and the battle of Reval (1219), from which dates the adoption of the Danebrog flag as the standard of the Danish army. Denmark, now at the height of its glory, was the most powerful kingdom of northern Europe. But suddenly this proud edifice crumbled into dust; King Valdemar being surprised and made captive on the Island of Lyö, to the south of Funen, by Count Henry of Schwerin; the conquered countries revolted, and the German Emperor took advantage of this opportunity to regain possession of his former territories. Valdemar recovered his liberty only by relinquishing all his conquests, with the exception of Rügen and Esthonia. Nevertheless, shortly afterwards he made an effort to regain his lost lands; but after the decisive defeat he sustained at Bornhöved in Holstein, in 1227, he renounced his ambitious plans and devoted himself to the improvement of the internal administration of the country, especially by making laws; an achievement which has won for him as glorious a name in Danish history, as any he acquired by his famous wars. The law given by him to Jutland ("jydske Lov") in the year of his death, 1241, begins with the well known words, "Med Lov skal man Land bygge" (Law shall build the land).

After this brilliant era of the Valdemars, during the next hundred years, all through the reigns of the sons of Valdemar Sejr, Erik Plovpenning (Ploughpenny), Abel and Christopher I and their immediate successors, there followed a calamitous time for the country, — a time rife with civil wars and contentions between the State on the one hand and the dignitaries of the Church and the nobles on the other. These higher orders, who had formerly been the mainstay of the throne, now became its bitterest enemies. The conflicts between the great vassals and the princes of the Church, so well known all over the great civilized countries further south, where warfare of this kind had raged for several centuries, only now penetrated to the north. During the reign of the above-mentioned Christopher I began the struggle with the Church, Jacob Erlandsen, the arbitrary Archbishop of Lund, being at its head; a struggle all the more dangerous to the royal prerogative on account of the contest then being carried on with regard to South Jutland or Slesvig, which had been given as a fief to Abel's family, and thus for the first time separated from Denmark. At the same time, the strife with the nobles broke out; Erik Glipping, Christopher's son, falling a victim to a conspiracy among the leaders of the nobility at Finderup near Viborg, in 1286. Under his son Erik Menved, the struggle was still carried on against the nobility — "regicides" as they were called — and the Church; the latter being represented by Jens Grand, the violent and despotic Archbishop of Lund. During this king's reign the dispute about Investiture ended in Denmark, as it had done all over the world, in the triumph of the Church. The calamities of the country finally culminated during the feeble and incapable reign of Christopher II, who was forced to purchase his crown by signing the so-called "Haandfæstning" (Charter); a document in which he granted considerable privileges to the dignitaries of the Church and nobles, and which descended as an inheritance to all his successors in turn, until, in the 17th century absolutism put an end to aristocratic power. At Christopher's death, in 1332, it was found that the whole country was mortgaged to Danish and foreign magnates; an expedient to which his brother, Erik Menved, had also had recourse, in order to supply himself with money to carry on the war with the regicides and to gratify his luxurious tastes. Denmark was now on the verge of ruin; an interregnum of eight years followed, during which there was no leader at the head of affairs, and the mortgagees had an opportunity of oppressing the citizens and peasants and generally doing much as they liked; the Hanseatic Towns had meanwhile checked the advancement of the citizens by their monopoly of the entire commerce of Scandinavia, and the peasants fell more and more under the yoke of the powerful landed proprietors.

But brighter days were in store for Denmark; the most powerful of the usurping lords, Count Geert the Bald of Holstein, was killed at Randers by the Knight Niels Ebbesen. The country however was still far from being saved, and it was only by the ability and shrewdness of Valdemar IV, a son of Christopher II, made king in 1340, that a catastrophe was averted. During the next 20 years, with laborious and indefatigable energy, employing force and artifice by turns, he succeeded in collecting the scattered factions of the kingdom under him, and eventually won back the ancient boundaries from the Skaw and Götaelv on the north to the Eider on the south. Thus through the energy of this prince, perhaps the greatest of all the Danish Kings of the Middle Ages, did light once more dawn upon Denmark; he has, on this account, been surnamed Atterdag ("Day once more"), though, by his contemporaries, who were weighed down by heavy burdens and repressed by his iron hand and arbitrary policy, he was called "the Bad". Unfortunately Valdemar did not rest content with these achievements, but seized the Swedish island of Gotland in the Baltic. This led not only to a breach with the neighboring kingdom, but also caused dissensions with the Hanseatic League, which had made that island their principal port of commerce in the Scandinavian countries, and in this case Valdemar had the worst of it. With him the race of Svend Estridsen died out in the male line, in 1375.

We now come to the last section of Danish history appertaining to the Middle Ages, namely the "Union". It is in many respects a fresh era of greatness for the country, but it is also a time fraught with disappointments and defeats. It is inaugurated by Valdemar's daughter Margrethe, one of the grandest characters in the history of the North. First as Regent, during the minority of her son Olaf, and later on after his death (1387) as sovereign Queen, she reigned over Denmark and from the year 1380 also over Norway, which had devolved on her at the death of her husband King Hakon. Thus was effected a union between these two kingdoms destined to last for over four hundred years. But Margrethe did not stop here; shortly after, by the decisive victory of Falköping in 1389, she added to her two crowns that of Sweden, thus becoming sole mistress of the Scandinavian countries. To strengthen this union, she convened an assembly of the notabilities of the three kingdoms at Kalmar, where measures were concerted for the joint election of their monarch, and for the settling of affairs common to all three kingdoms; she at the same time had her nephew Erik of Pomerania appointed as her successor. These events are known in history as the "Kalmar Union", and although this union went no further than the preliminaries above-mentioned, and never was legally ratified, it was and remained a great achievement for Denmark. Notwithstanding the animosity of the Swedish nobles, Margrethe by her superior ability was able to keep the union with Sweden intact duringh er lifetime; whilst Norway, weakened by centuries of civil war and crown intrigues, was utterly incapable of offering any resistance. But after the death of Margrethe, in 1412, matters took another turn. The union of the three kingdoms was frequently broken and again renewed, her successors being far from equal to the task imposed upon them.

This was proved in the reign of her immediate successor, Erik of Pomerania, who besides the difficulties which beset him in the north had inherited the complications with Slesvig, which province Margrethe had been on the point of uniting more closely to Denmark. The struggle in the south ended by Erik, after peace was signed at Vordingborg in 1435, being forced to cede Slesvig to the Count Adolph of Holstein, who had formed an alliance with the Hanseatic Towns. In Sweden disturbances broke out under Engelbrekt Engelbrektsson, and in a few years affairs were so embroiled that the country took matters into its own hands and elected a Regent ("Rigsforstander") in the person of one of its own noblemen, Karl Knutsson Bonde. Meanwhile Erik had no better luck in Denmark; he had excited so much discontent among his own nobles, that he was obliged to flee the country, and was deposed in 1439. Under his successor Christopher III of

Bavaria, the three kingdoms were again united, though the king was not chosen by delegates from each realm, as had been originally determined at the Kalmar Union, but was elected separately in each kingdom. At his death in 1448 the union was once more dissolved, Sweden taking the opportunity to elect Karl Knutsson as its king, whilst the Danish Rigsraad (Council of State) chose Count Christian of Oldenburg, who thus became the founder of the Oldenburg line of kings, which for over 400 years occupied the Danish throne.

Christian I (1448—1481) began his reign as king of Denmark and Norway, but he by no means overlooked the fact that it was his right, and consequently his duty, to re-establish the Union; an undertaking in which he was successful, making himself master of Sweden by the expulsion of Karl Knutsson in 1457. Moreover, by the death of his uncle, Adolph of Holstein, he shortly after acquired not only Slesvig, which now reverted as a fief to the Danish crown, but also Holstein by the convention of Ribe (1460), and thus became one of the most powerful princes in Europe. The union with Sweden however was but of short duration; the extravagant expenses of the Danish rule causing much dissatisfaction, not alone among the Swedish nobility, but also among the clergy, who were otherwise well-disposed towards the incorporation of the three kingdoms. Karl Knutsson was re-called and re-elected king, and the defeat sustained by the Danes at Brunkebjerg, outside the walls of Stockholm in 1471, at the hands of Sten Sture the Elder, Karl Knutsson's successor as regent, deprived king Christian of all hope of maintaining the union. Matters did not mend under his son Hans (1481—1513). Only after a period of 16 years did he succeed in subduing Sweden, and then but to have it again wrested from him after a short lapse of time. An unsuccessful expedition against Ditmarsk once more fanned the flame of revolt and restored Sten Sture to power, and disputes which arose with the Hanseatic League, together with disturbances in Norway, prevented King Hans from taking any further steps against Sweden. With his son Christian II

(1513—1523) the line of the "Kings of the Union" comes to an end. Like his predecessors he began his reign only as king of Denmark and Norway, whilst Sweden was governed by the regent Sten Sture the Younger. After several attempts Christian II succeeded however in gaining the mastery in that country; and Sten Sture being vanquished and mortally wounded at the battle of Bogesund in 1520, Stockholm opened its gates to the "King of the Union". But, by his cruel policy, Christian lost all that he had gained. On the 8th of November 1520, a great number of the nobility and many dignitaries of the Church, belonging to the first families of the country, were by his orders executed in the market place of the town. This event, known in history as the "Massacre of Stockholm", roused universal indignation against "Christian the Tyrant", as he was called in Sweden, and ultimately ended in the Swedes electing a king of their own, Gustav Vasa, in the year 1523. Thus was finally dissolved the union between Denmark and Sweden, but a foundation of animosity and hatred between the two nations had been laid, which for centuries displayed itself in long and bloody wars. One kingdom still remained to Denmark, notwithstanding the dissolution of the union. Norway, which had in times past been an independent country of considerable importance, with a Council of State of its own, decayed by the era of the Reformation into a Danish province, a state of things which lasted for three centuries.

King Christian II, in the meanwhile, met with an equally hard fate in Denmark. In maintaining the struggle he had undertaken with the object of improving the condition of the citizens and peasants, he had earned for himself the animosity of the nobles and the clergy, and the unfortunate course events had taken in Sweden gave these latter the ascendency. The same year that Gustav Vasa was proclaimed king, the nobles of Jutland threw off their allegiance to the Danish monarch, and made overtures to his uncle, Duke Frederik of Gottorp, at the same time offering him the crown. Christian abandoned the struggle and fled the country accompanied by a few faithful adherents. Among these were a

Dutchwoman of the name of Sigbrit, mother of the celebrated Dyveke ("little dove"), the king's mistress, who had died some years previously, and the Queen Elizabeth, sister of the Emperor Charles V, through whose powerful intervention the exiled monarch hoped to regain his dominions. King Christian II, in spite of his capricious temperament and violent paroxysms of passion — the latter almost bordering on madness — is one of the most interesting royal personages in Danish history. A testimony to his great mental endowments, and foresight for the welfare of his people, is to be found in the many judicious laws which he has left behind him.[1]

With Frederik I (1523—1533) is ushered in the Reformation. It was through men of the people, like Hans Tausen, the "Danish Luther", that the new doctrine was propagated. It was favoured by the king notwithstanding the fact, that in the charter which he signed at his accession there was a clause in which the monarch pledged himself to the clergy to watch over the interests of the Roman-Catholic Church. It was only under his successor Christian III, and after the civil war, the so-called "Grevens Fejde" (Count's feud), which lasted three years, that the Lutheran faith was recognised as the State religion by the Rigsdag (diet) in Copenhagen, in 1536. A period of greater enlightenment followed in the train of the Reformation; wholesale confiscation of Church property took place, with a part of which the government endowed schools and other educational institutions; especially the University, which had been founded under Christian I, but for lack of funds, fulfilled very inadequately the purpose for which it was designed. "Grevens Fejde", the feud already mentioned, led to most important results; it was apparently a struggle to decide who should be king in the land; for the lower classes, supported by the

[1] C. F. Allen, who has written a "History of Denmark", translated into French by E. Beauvois, Copenhagen 1878, has made him his historical hero; Allen's principal work: "De tre nordiske Rigers Historie under Hans, Christian II etc.", treats of this period.

citizens of Lübeck, whose privileges had been restricted by the nobles, were fighting for the re-instalment of Christian II, — then imprisoned at Sönderborg in the island of Als, after an unsuccessful attempt to regain his crown — but in reality, this feud was the last effort on the part of the lower classes to shake off the yoke of the aristocracy by armed force. The war ended with the victory of the latter; and the ascendency and political influence thus obtained by the nobles steadily increased; whilst the peasants, worsted in the struggle, were utterly cowed and reduced almost to a state of slavery. The citizens and clergy were meanwhile excluded from taking any part in political life — for with the introduction of the Reformation, the power of the Church had come to an end, and the ecclesiastical offices, now of slight importance, were given to the sons of the citizens.

The following period, often called "Adelsvældens Tid" (the period of aristocratic autocracy), is full of disastrous wars with Sweden; for the fruits of the union were not slow in showing themselves. Peace, it is true, was maintained during the reigns of the prudent monarchs Christian III and Gustav Vasa, but under their young and impetuous sons Frederik II (1559—1588) and Erik XIV of Sweden, the Scandinavian seven years' war broke out; — a conflict which led to nothing but a retaliatory system of pillaging in both lands, though in it many noble Danes, among them Otto Rud, Herluf Trolle and Daniel Rantzau aquired great renown. On the whole, the nobility at that time may be said to have been justly entitled to wield the great power vested in it; all the talent and intelligence of the country were centred in its ranks, and to it Denmark owes one of her most illustrious sons, Tycho Brahe the astronomer, who died in 1601.

Under Christian IV (1588—1648) the wars were still more disastrous. The first, the "Kalmar war", with Sweden, ended however without any loss to Denmark. Far worse were the reverses Christian IV met with, when fighting on the side of the Protestants in the Thirty years' war in Germany. After the defeat sustained at Lutter am Baremberg (1626), Jutland was occupied by the imperial troops, and the enemy was only prevented from crossing over to the islands, by the intervention of the fleet, commanded by Christian himself. Peace was concluded at Lübeck in 1629, without, it is true, any material loss to the country; but the prestige of Denmark had received a severe shock. Finally came the last war with Sweden, brought about by the attempt of Denmark to check the advance of the Swedes in Germany during the Thirty year's war; King Christian indeed succeeded in maintaining the supremacy of the Danish fleet at the celebrated battle of Kolberg (1644), near the island of Femern, but at Brömsebro in 1645 he was forced to conclude a peaceon most disadvantageous terms, by which Denmark lost some of the northern provinces, which till then had belonged to Norway, and also the islands of Gotland and Oesel in the Baltic. Christian the Fourth's reign thus ended disastrously for Denmark, and yet he is the most popular and most beloved of the Oldenburg line of kings. His majestic figure is probably more familiarly known among the humbler Danish classes, than that of any other monarch. The blame of these misfortunes, doubtless, cannot justly be laid to his charge; they were mainly due to the domineering and insolent spirit pervading the aristocracy, whose overweening pride of race and arrogance had increased in the same measure as their abilities had deteriorated; and although they alone were in a position to assist the impoverished country by their wealth, they obstinately refused to do so, pleading their immunity from taxation in excuse. Discontent too was rife, and took distinct form in words among the citizens and clergy. The bow had been bent too far; it was ready to break.

But now the wise and shrewd monarch Frederik III (1648—1670), and his equally clever Queen Sophie Amalie, ascended the throne, and from the first resolved on turning to good account the popular feeling against the aristocracy. They were further greatly encouraged in their efforts by the turn events had taken all over Europe. It was the age of absolutism; France with Richelieu, Mazarin and

Louis XIV showing the way. The king was however obliged to go prudently to work, and above all carefully conceal his intentions until a favorable opportunity presented itself; at the very outset he was forced to sign a Charter with more rigorous conditions than had ever been imposed upon any Danish sovereign. Nevertheless, he succeeded shortly after in overthrowing the most powerful of the aristocratic factions, headed by Corfitz Ulfeldt, and subsequent events, as we shall see, combined to effect the realization of his plans. What contributed materially to this end was the unfortunate war with Sweden, in which King Carl Gustav, after landing in Sealand, forced Denmark at Roskilde (1658) to conclude the most disadvantageous peace that had ever fallen to her lot; a peace in which the important provinces of Scania (Skåne), Halland, Bleking and Bohus were ceded to Sweden, and the Sound became Denmark's boundary on the east. Shortly afterwards, Carl Gustav again recommenced hostilities, with the bold intention of completely effacing Denmark from the map of Europe; but fortune now forsook him, and at the storming of Copenhagen by the Swedes in February 1659 the citizens repulsed the enemy with great bravery, and soon drove them entirely out of the country. Denmark, however, did not recover the Scanian provinces by the peace of Copenhagen 1660. The maritime powers, England and Holland, did not allow her to retain the sovereignty of both sides of the Sound, thinking that Denmark had long enough monopolized the exclusive right to the entrance of the Baltic, exacting as she did the payment of the so-called "Sound dues", which at that time indeed constituted the principal source of the revenue of the country.

When the Rigsdag met in Copenhagen in 1660, to concert measures for ameliorating the condition of the impoverished and almost ruined country, the power of the nobles was entirely at an end. The citizens, who had acquired a high sense of their own independence since their successful defence of Copenhagen, with their famous Burgomaster Hans Nansen at their head, and the clergy with an equally clever leader, Svane, Bishop of Sealand, succeeded notwithstanding the opposition of the nobles in making Denmark an hereditary monarchy; and the King, to whom had been delegated the task of framing a new charter, and who it was expected would have accorded the delegates of the people the privilege of taking part in the government of the country, now by royal mandate, the so-called "Arveenevoldsakt" (Hereditary Autocratic Act), in 1661 assumed the whole prerogative himself. Denmark thus became an absolute monarchy, and the "Kongelov" (Royal Law) which was framed in 1665, but only made public in 1709 (when it was taken for granted that the people had somewhat accustomed themselves to the new order of things) became the Fundamental Law of the country, and remained so for nearly 200 years. The old Rigsraad (State Council) was done away with, and the affairs of State were assigned to Colleges, or as they are now called, Ministerial Offices, the King however keeping the reins in his own hands.

II

Denmark until 1848

We now enter the Age of Absolutism, which lasted until the year 1848. It must be acknowledged that in many respects this form of government weighed heavily on the nation, as it tended in a high degree to check both intellectual and material development and gradually made the people ignorant of public affairs. Notwithstanding all this, it must be admitted that matters might have been even worse. Although the Royal Law conferred so absolute a power on the king, a power such as was perhaps not vested in any other sovereign in Europe, the autocrats of the Oldenburg dynasty — good natured, upright and not more than ordinarily gifted as they were — exercised the prerogative, on the whole, with moderation and leniency, and the country had often reason to be thankful for the advantages secured to it during this period, especially when, among the royal Councillors, were to be found men of talent and capacity.

The nobility was necessarily the first to feel the difference between the state of things before and after 1660. Reference here is not alone made to the individual cases of those who specially writhed under the lash of Frederik the Third's autocratic government — notably Corfitz Ulfeldt, for whose fate but little commiseration can be felt, sentenced though he was to the forfeiture of property, life and honour for High Treason; but every one must sympathize with the fate of his wife, Eleonora Christina, daughter of Christian IV, who expiated her devotion to her husband by a hard captivity of 22 years, from which she was released only after the death of her most mortal enemy, the Queen Dowager, Sophie Amalie. But the position of the nobility underwent a great change after 1660. Displeased and mortified, they withdrew from the Court, declining by their presence to add to the splendour of a throne around which they themselves formerly had ruled supreme, and where they were forced to share the social privileges, to which their rank intitled them, with an aristocracy of counts and barons introduced from Germany.

The age of absolutism, however, inaugurated its reign auspiciously under Frederik III and Christian V (1670—1699); for besides consolidating their autocratic power by re-organizing the army and navy and surrounding themselves by a brilliant staff of officials,[1] they also carried out important reforms in legislature. A common law for the whole country was compiled, which was promulgated in 1683 under the name of "Christian the Fifth's Danish Law". It is true that these monarchs had the advantage of the assistance of

[1] Under Christian V the two Orders of Knighthood: the "Order of the Elephant", of which however there is an earlier proto-type under Christian I, and the "Order of Danebrog", were instituted.

one of Denmark's most eminent statesmen, namely Griffenfeldt (Peder Schumacher), an ardent admirer of the French monarchical form of government. He had taken a prominent part in the framing of the "Danish Law", and the "Royal Law" also partly owes its existence to him. In the management of foreign affairs, he displayed abilities of a very superior order, notably in the incorporation of the counties of Oldenburg and Delmenhorst with the Danish crown; but he certainly failed in hindering Denmark from taking part in the war carried on between France and Holland, in which Sweden was the ally of the last-named power. Indeed before the conclusion of this contest, Griffenfeldt's downfall had been accomplished; he paid the penalty of his devotion to king and country by an imprisonment of 22 years, extending almost to the time of his death. This fierce "Scanian War" (1675—1679), which as far as Denmark was concerned was only a struggle with Sweden, did not however achieve the object aimed at, namely the re-conquest of the much coveted Scanian provinces; for though the Danes met with some brilliant successes, notably the great naval victory obtained by Niels Juel in the bay of Kjöge (1677), Sweden's powerful ally France watched over her interests at the peace of Lund, and Denmark was obliged to content herself with barren honour. A final and serious attempt was made to wrest these provinces from Sweden under Frederik IV (1699—1730), when he took part in the "Great Northern War" against Charles XII, after the signal defeat sustained by this prince in Russia, in 1709; but the Danes after the unsuccessful battle of Helsingborg (1710) were soon driven out of Scania, and on the whole obtained but small success on land, though their naval heroes, with Peder Tordenskjold at their head, succeeded in maintaining their great reputation at sea. In 1720 peace was concluded at Frederiksborg, but not on particularly advantageous terms to the country. On the other hand, this war was the means of settling temporarily the knotty point of Denmark's policy towards Slesvig. A part of this duchy had fallen into the hands of a collateral line of the House of

Oldenburg, the Dukes of Holstein-Gottorp, who always took up a
hostile position towards Denmark. Christian V had endeavored
to come to some arrangement with them, and Frederik IV had, at
the commencement of the Northern War, tried to dispossess the
Duke of his sovereign rights over Slesvig, but Charles XII by the
peace of Traventhal (1700) had forced the Danish king to re-instate
the Duke in his rights. During the war, however, Denmark con-
trived to seize upon Slesvig (1713), alleging as a plea, the treachery
of the ducal government, which had admitted the Swedish army
under Magnus Stenbock into the fortress of Tönningen, and after
the peace of Frederiksborg the duchy as a reverted fief was incorporated with the Danish kingdom, under the guarantee of
France and England.

This was the last great fight in which Denmark was involved
during the 18th century. That the country escaped being drawn
into the great European conflicts, is mainly owing to the talent
and ability of the statesmen at the head of the government during
the most critical periods, notably the two Bernstorffs. Thus
it was owing to the efforts of Johan Hartvig Ernst Bernstorff
that Denmark avoided taking any part in the Seven Year's
War in Germany, which raged close to the Danish frontiers, and
entailed a costly outlay to the kingdom to keep up a standing army
for the purpose of preserving its neutrality. He at the same time
brought the Slesvig question to a successful termination, it being in
spite of all that had happened fraught with great danger, as long
as the House of Holstein-Gottorp — which by intermarriage with
the Russian royal family had ascended the throne of the Czars —
continued to maintain its claims. War was indeed within a hair's
breadth of breaking out on the accession of Peter III; his sudden
death alone averting the catastrophe. By his skilful statesmanship,
Bernstorff now succeeded in inducing the House of Holstein-Gottorp, under Katharina II, to forgo its claims on Slesvig as also
their share in Holstein, on the condition of receiving in exchange
the duchies of Oldenburg and Delmenhorst, this being the so called

"Oldenburg Deed of Exchange" of 1767. His nephew, Andreas Peter Bernstorff, steered with equal skill the course of Denmark's foreign policy during the American War of Independence; not only did he ensure her immunity from war — a great advantage to Danish trade and commerce — but together with Sweden and Russia he contributed to the formation of a league of armed neutrality, constituted for the purpose of putting a stop to England's aggressive attacks on the merchant ships of other nationalities. Later on, he displayed a superior order of talent, by the skill with which he guided the ship of state safely into port, through the dangerous shoals of the first wars of the French revolution; how far he could have succeeded with this policy in the long run, it is difficult to say; one thing however is certain, that on his death, in 1797, the era of peace was at an end. But of this later.

Denmark thus, during the greater part of the 18th century, preeminently enjoyed the blessings of peace, which afforded an opportunity for something being done to better the condition of the exhausted country. Among the improvements, which may especially be cited, were reforms in the Scholastic system and the Legislature, as also the efforts made to promote the Trades and Arts of the realm under Frederik IV and his successors Christian VI (1730—1746) and Frederik V (1746—1766). It was, however, principally Commerce and Industry which they sought to encourage, by protective duties and monopolies, as was the custom of the times; whilst nothing was done for agriculture, one of the most important sources of revenue to the country. This was entirely neglected, and how could it have been otherwise? The peasants were utterly crushed, both economically and mentally; they were in a condition allied to slavery as regarded the landed proprietors, especially on the islands, where the "Vornedskab" (villenage or tenure of land by base services) was in full force — a custom which reduced the peasant to the level of a living chattel, largely at the disposition of the proprietor. This state of things was certainly done away with, in the reign of Frederik IV (1702); but in the pietist and bigoted reign of Christian VI, another order of things was introduced, which rendered the position of the peasant quite as deplorable as before, namely the "Stavnsbaand" a kind of feudal system or vassalage which forced the peasant, during a certain number of years, to remain on the estate on which he was born, so as to enable the Lord of the Manor to furnish soldiers for the Militia, organised about that time; moreover the "Stavnsbaand" system held good for the entire country. These bonds were drawn still tighter during the reign of the pleasure-loving Frederik V; and only a few of the more enlightened men of the time — especially Johan Hartvig Ernst Bernstorff — recognising how pernicious this state of things was for the country, gradually came to the conclusion that serious reforms were required, not only as far as this question was concerned but also in many others. The Finances, for instance, were in a deplorable condition; and to this had contributed not a little the extravagance and insensate love of building (Christiansborg Castle and other costly edifices) which had characterized Queen Sophie Magdalene, Consort of Christian VI, together with the enormous sums expended on the armed forces organized to maintain the neutrality of the country during the reign of Frederik V.

The most interesting epoch of Danish history relating to internal reforms, is in the latter part of the century. It is ushered in by Johan Frederik Struensee's eventful ministry, under King Christian VII (1766—1808). In the year 1771, under the patronage of the young Queen Caroline Mathilde, he was raised to the high post of "Geheimekabinetsminister"(Minister and Member of the Privy Council), an office which conferred on him almost unlimited powers; but in the short term of sixteen months his downfall was complete. He was of the order of statesmen to which the Emperor Joseph II of Austria, also belonged; they highly favoured the new-fangled ideas then flowing fresh from the pens of certain advanced French writers, and being regardless of old blundering routine and prejudices, carried out their reforms on behalf of the people; but they went too rashly to work, heedless of the soil they had to cultivate. Struensee, a man of German extraction, estranged himself from the people, by his scorn and contempt for everything Danish and his utter lack of religious sentiment, and thus it was that many of his reforms, excellent in themselves, were of little benefit to the country. Of these changes may be mentioned the establishment of the liberty of the press, a better organization of the Finance and Law departments, especially the creation of the tribunal the "Hof- og Stadsret" (a lower Court of Justice in Copenhagen), the abolition of the torture, and a more equitable mode of conferring government appointments. The ill-will he had excited by his arbitrary way of proceeding, as also the relation in which he stood to Caroline Mathilde, gave the party hostile to him at the Court, with the ambitious Queen Dowager Juliane Marie, her son the Hereditary Prince Frederik, and his tutor Ove Höegh Guldberg at its head, an easy game to play. In January 1772 after a Masked Ball at the Court, Struensee and the Queen were arrested and put under restraint; the latter spent the remainder of her short life in exile at the castle of Celle in Hanover, Struensee was beheaded.[1]

Guldberg was now at the head of affairs, and during the next twelve years carried on a reactionary policy; the sole aim of which was to obliterate all traces of the measures planned by Struensee, whether good or bad, nor did he attempt to introduce reforms in other quarters; the sole point on which he deserves to be praised, is the thoroughly national feeling which animated his administration, especially characterized by the passing of the "Indfödsret", a law which precluded foreigners from occupying posts under government. In 1784, Crown Prince Frederik having assumed the reins of government in consequence of the illness of his father, there ensued a period marked by salutary radical reforms and national progress. Surrounded by able men, such as Andreas Peter

---

[1] An account of this important period of Danish history is to be found in the interesting book entitled "Struensee et la Cour de Copenhague 1760—1772, Mémoires de Reverdil, Paris 1858". Reverdil had been tutor to Christian VII.

Bernstorff, Christian Ditlev Reventlov and Christian Colbjörnsen, this conscientious and popular Prince set himself to his task. Many of Struensee's projects, especially the reforms in the Courts of Law and the liberty of the press, were adopted, but the matter most seriously discussed was the emancipation of the peasants, a question which had also attracted the attention of Struensee, though he had no opportunity of working out his scheme. After several amendments tending to but slight amelioration, the "Stavnsbaand" was abolished, and the enfranchisement of the peasants declared, June 20th 1788; the first step was thus taken towards allowing the peasants equal rights and privileges with the other sons of the nation. Among other laws testifying to the humanity of these times may be mentioned the abolition of the negro slave-trade in the Danish West Indian colonies, and the emancipation of the Jews.

The prosperity of the Danish nation rose to a great height during the remaining years of the century, commerce especially making great strides, while most of the countries around were involved in the Coalition Wars against France. The old controversy with England, which insisted upon examining Danish merchantmen to see if they carried contraband goods, alone gave cause for apprehension. But the new century opened with a series of disasters. The quarrel with England led to a new armed neutrality with Russia and Sweden; the upshot being that an English fleet under the command of Parker and Nelson arrived before the Capital; the battle fought in the roadstead of Copenhagen, April 2nd 1801, was honourable to the Danish fleet, under Olfert Fischer, but led to no result, Russia having withdrawn from the league of neutrality. During the following six years, the country again enjoyed peace, but in 1807 it became finally involved in the general war; and unhappily it must be said, that it was especially the vacillating policy of the Danish government which brought about the catastrophe; its sympathies inclined to France, its interests were bound up with England; and so as not to offend the susceptibilities of either side, ambiguous tactics were adopted towards both. When therefore Napoleon and Alexander agreed at Tilsit to force the smaller powers into co-operating in the continental blockade, and proposed to Denmark to deliver up her fleet for the purpose of her assisting in making an attack upon England, the latter country forestalled her enemies, and sent a fleet under Gambier and Cathcart to Copenhagen. The Danish government was taken utterly unawares; although it had had timely warning that England meditated a counter stroke: the Capital was as good as defenceless, for the few thousand men General Peymann had at his disposal were quite insufficient, and the greater part of the army with the Crown Prince Regent were in Holstein, guarding the frontier. After the terrible bombardment of three days in September 1807, in which a great number of public as well as 300 private buildings were laid in ruins, the town capitulated to the enemy (September 7th), who did not however take their departure, until they had either destroyed or seized upon everything belonging to the fleet and pillaged the Arsenal. After this aggressive attack, what other course had Denmark to pursue but to ally herself with France? But the war which was carried on for seven years with England, as also a two years' feud with Sweden, had almost entirely crippled the country: the fleet, which had been her only important defence against the attacks of her powerful enemies, had been wrested from her; finances were brought to a low ebb; and her trade and commerce were utterly ruined. Notwithstanding all this, Denmark even after Napoleon's overthrow in Russia, in 1812, remained his stanch ally; and as a natural consequence was at war with the greater part of Europe. After a short struggle, the country was forced to agree to the peace of Kiel (1814), by which Norway was ceded to Sweden. To compensate for this loss, a trifling concession was made; Swedish Pomerania and the island of Rügen being handed over to Denmark; but at the Congress of Vienna, she exchanged them with Prussia for the duchy of Lauenburg. With bitter mortification the Danish people received the tidings of their separation from Norway: still this rent must have come sooner or later; for already up in that rude mountain region signs of great discontent had begun to manifest themselves, the result of disregard paid to their interests and the deplorable state of subjection in which they were held by the Danish government for centuries. A feeling of independence, which prompted them to oppose their being incorporated with Sweden, had also awakened in them; and at Eidsvold in 1814 they declared themselves free from foreign yoke. After some wrangling, however, they elected the King of Sweden as their reigning monarch; and since that time, the two countries, enjoying equal rights, have remained united under one sovereign.

Denmark came out of the struggle utterly impoverished. To defray the enormous expenses of the war, the government had gone on issuing paper-money without having its corresponding value in hand; this led to bankruptcy in 1813, and the establishment of a State Bank; after five years this was converted into a National Bank, entirely independent of the government. During the years of peace that ensued, no stone was left unturned to recruit the weakened resources of the country, and prosperity by degrees once more began to reign. Commercial interests were promoted, reforms introduced — both in the internal administration and in the Law Courts — and the educational system was amended. This epoch was also marked by the progress made in Science and Literature, and the development of the national spirit. At the same time liberal ideas began to spread, and a desire to take part in public life seemed to be growing on the people; the liberal party however kept somewhat in the background, restrained by a sentiment of deferential feeling towards the popular old King Frederik VI, who in 1808 had succeeded his father Christian VII, and with vigilant and jealous eye watched over his sovereign rights. Denmark was naturally also to some degree affected by the agitation, called forth in Europe by the revolution of July 1830; and the government therefore, as a conciliatory measure, by the enactments of 1831 and 1834, gave the country Consultative Provincial

Chambers ("raadgivende Provinsialstænder"). The four provincial councils — for the islands, Jutland, Slesvig and Holstein — were composed of Members chosen solely from the higher orders of society, and their authority was limited: nevertheless these assemblies acquired some degree of importance, as they accustomed the people to occupy themselves with public affairs and to hear them discussed; at the same time they exercised some influence on the question of finance, as well as on Municipal legislature; they gave the first blow to the arbitrary principle of absolutism hitherto reigning, and formed a kind of preparatory school for the era of liberty then dawning.

It was however only after the death of Frederik VI (1839), that liberal ideas circulated freely among the people, and that the more advanced party, growing stronger and stronger, came forward and openly avowed the real drift of its pretensions, emboldened as it was by the hopes it entertained of being upheld by the new King, Christian VIII, a son of the Hereditary Prince Frederik, who has been already mentioned as having played a rôle in the conspiracy against Struensee. As a young man he had been Governor in Norway and had taken no inactive share in the stirring events of 1814; being an adherent to constitutional principles, he was elected King by the Norwegians, but was soon forced to resign his crown by the powerful intervention of Sweden, with the stipulation however, that the Swedish king acknowledged the constitution proclaimed previously by the Norwegians at Eidsvold. Great therefore was the disappointment of the liberal party to find, that King Christian had discarded the ideas of his youth, and was utterly averse to yielding up any of his power; nor was the general discontent at all allayed by his really good administrative reforms, more especially the order, hitherto unknown, which he introduced into the finances of the country. What however contributed much to strengthen the liberal party, was the growing national excitement provoked by the Slesvig question.

We have seen above, how Slesvig was incorporated with Denmark after the treaty of peace concluded at Frederiksborg 1720; but unfortunately neither the arrangement come to on that occasion, nor the subsequent Oldenburg Exchange in 1767, succeeded in bringing the question to a final settlement; and this was, to a great degree, owing to blundering on the part of the Danish government itself. Although from 1720 all possible efforts should have been made to encourage the Danish element in Slesvig — ancient Danish province as it was — just the opposite course was adopted; and the then incipient Germanizing was so favored that the half of Slesvig was German, when the revolt broke out in the duchies. Signs of this agitation had already manifested themselves during the reign of Frederik VI, who yet energetically made a stand against the pretensions of the Slesvig-Holstein nobles; but his decrees of 1810 and 1829, to maintain the prior rights of the Danish language, were of no effect. After the revolution of July, "Slesvig-Holsteinism" broke fairly out, the flame being fanned by a pamphlet written by Uwe Lornsen, in which the author demanded an independent Slesvig-Holstein, bound to Denmark only by a personal union (i e. under a common prince, but not under common laws). The faction appealed especially to the convention of Ribe (1460) which had adjusted matters by promising that the union between Slesvig and Holstein should "for ever be indissoluble", forgetting however the events of 1713, when Slesvig, owing to the treachery of the ducal government, had been annexed as a reverted fief to the Danish crown. The Danish government naturally dismissed the claims of the faction; but on the other hand showed some apparent favour to the movement, by according to Slesvig and Holstein, at the same time that the council of Provincial Representatives were established, a joint government and a joint Supreme Court, by which proceedings the duchies eventually stood in the relation of a single state to the kingdom. And the Slesvig-Holstein party, having thus reinforced its ranks, gained the ascendency in the "Councils", and became more and more audacious in its demands; particularly as Christian the Eighth's cabinet persisted in its conciliatory policy, which in the eyes of the faction was a sign of weakness. These concessions went so far, that the government in 1842 appointed as Stadtholder in the duchies Prince Frederik of Noer, a brother to Duke Christian of Augustenborg, the Prince selected by the party as their future ruler. If the government had counted upon winning over the Slesvig-Holsteiners by this yielding policy, events proved that it was altogether a false calculation; the party became at length so arbitrary, that they would no longer allow Danish to be spoken at the meetings of the Slesvig "Representatives"; and unfortunately the Danish government here, as on other occasions, to all appearance countenanced the innovation. When finally a change of policy was deemed advisable, and the government took the resolute measure of publishing the "Letters Patent of 1846", in which it declared that the order of succession was the same in the duchies as in the kingdom, it was too late. The Slesvig-Holsteiners protested openly and insolently against the Letters Patent, supported as they were by public opinion in Germany, which for years had been worked upon by the German press. The Danish government responded by removing the Prince of Noer from his post of Stadtholder, and appointing the energetic and loyal Count Carl Moltke in his stead.

The last years of Christian the Eighth's reign were full of disquiet and anxiety. At his death there was every reason to fear a violent breach with the duchies, and affairs were not much better at home; the persecutions against the press and the Liberals had alienated the affections of the people from their King, and they demanded loudly a more liberal constitution, one which would guarantee the safety and unity of the Danish monarchy. Thus opened the momentous year 1848.

III

The Slesvig wars; Denmark as a constitutional State

Christian the Eighth died on the January 20th 1848, and was succeeded by his son Frederik VII. From the first day of his reign the liberal movement took a decided character, issuing its sentiments through the press and in addresses to the King, and on January 28th appeared a rescript announcing a more liberal Constitution, to be enjoyed in common by the kingdom and the duchies. This document had been drawn up by Christian the Eighth, and contained among other clauses one instituting a common deliberative Council of State, to be composed of an equal number of members from the kingdom and the duchies, an arrangement which excited the greatest discontent in both parties; in the kingdom, because they considered themselves entitled to the right of sending a greater number of representatives, on account of the more numerous population, equality giving the Slesvig-Holstein party undue weight in the balance; in the duchies, because they would hear of no tie in common with the kingdom. The dissatisfaction on both sides manifested itself loudly and violently, but nevertheless kept within the bounds of protest. The revolution of February now broke out in Paris, overflowing Germany with its mighty billows, and with one stroke giving a decisive turn to the course of affairs in the duchies. The Slesvig-Holstein party now decided that the right moment had arrived for carrying their plans into execution; on the 18th of March, in an assembly convened at Rendsborg, it was resolved to send a deputation to Copenhagen to demand the establishment of Slesvig-Holstein as an independent state attached to Denmark by a personal union only, and furthermore the incorporation of Slesvig in the German Confederation, of which Holstein had formed part for some time. This news caused the most intense excitement in Copenhagen; after a stormy meeting in Casino Theatre, thousands of the citizens with the Magistrates and Municipal authorities at their head repaired to Christiansborg Castle, and petitioned the King to assemble around him advisers who would make it their first aim to preserve Slesvig to Denmark, and who would especially work to consolidate its closer union with the kingdom under a free constitution. King Frederik VII answered that he had already anticipated the wishes of the people by dismissing his Ministers, and that he now intended to select men who conjointly with him would work for the welfare of the realm. It was with the most profound enthusiasm that the King's memorable words were listened to, words in which he promised that "if they would repose the same confidence in him that he reposed in them, he would always be their faithful leader to honour and liberty." From that moment was laid the foundation of the affection with which Frederik VII was regarded by his subjects, and which followed him through life. At the head of the new and responsible ministry, formed some days later, was one of the King's old advisers, Count A. W. Moltke, but among its members were also some of the most powerful leaders of the former opposition. Thus Captain A. F. Tscherning became Minister of War, and the Rev. D. Monrad Minister of Public Instruction, and as Ministers without "portfolios" the advocate Orla Lehmann and Hvidt, President of the Municipal Council of Copenhagen. The first acts of this so-called "March Ministry" were to rescind all the harsh laws issued against the press under the last government, and to answer the deputation from Rendsborg to the effect, that the King had neither the right nor the will to incorporate Slesvig in the German Confederation, but that he would on the contrary consolidate its union with the rest of the kingdom, and that it was his intention to give Holstein an independent liberal constitution, as an incorporate state of the German Confederation.

Such were the stirring events of these March days, so fraught with important results, and forming the prelude to Denmark's admission into the ranks of Constitutional states. But before pursuing this theme, we will follow the development of affairs in the duchies, which more than anything else engrossed the attention of the Danish nation.

The insurrection had broken out, without the Slesvig-Holsteiners having waited for the Danish government to give an answer to the Rendsborg deputation. On the 23rd of March a provisional government, of which Prince Frederik of Noer was a member, had been formed at Kiel, and the next day he surprised and seized the fortress of Rendsborg; a few days previously Duke Christian of Augustenborg had repaired to Berlin to ensure the support of the Prussian king, who not only willingly promised him assistance but also encouraged the insurgents in their claims. There was nothing now left for the Danish government to do, but to quell the insurrection by force of arms; it was therefore the first and most urgent task of the March ministry to put the army on a war footing, a task which Tscherning accomplished with marvellous energy; but the government was powerfully aided by the attitude of the people, who displayed a spirit of unity and enthusiastic self-sacrifice which were a natural sequel to the auspicious turn events had previously taken in the Capital. At the beginning of April a Danish army of about 10,000 men was assembled in Slesvig under the command of General Hedemann, and on the 9th they defeated the somewhat less numerous army of the insurgents at Bov in the neighborhood of Flensborg; after which the Danes occupied the town of Slesvig. The insurrection would now have been at an end, if Denmark had struggled with the Slesvig-Holsteiners alone; for in the duchies the spirit of revolt had not hitherto been very strong; but Germany was in the background. Public opinion had for many years been worked upon by the press and the authorities in favor of the Slesvig-Holstein cause; besides, just at that period, when all Europe had been convulsed by the February Revolution, the German princes, and the King of Prussia in particular, found the moment most opportune to create a diversion by engaging in a war. So the King of Prussia redeemed his promise to the

Duke of Augustenborg, and an army of 20,000 Prussian and allied troops belonging to the German Confederation, marched into Slesvig and joined the insurgents, the German enemy now amounting to 39,000 men. Thus broke out the First Slesvig War.

A fortnight after the successful engagement at Bov, the little Danish army of about 11,000 men, after an heroic defence of the Danevirke, was defeated at Slesvig, on Easter Sunday, April 23d, and forced to retreat north over Flensborg across the peninsula of Sundeved, to Als, a little island lying on the east coast of Slesvig which, being separated from the mainland by the narrow but deep strait of Alssund, was admirably adapted to serve as rallying point. The insurgents and the Prussians, led by Wrangel, crossed the "Kongeaa" and penetrated into the southern part of Jutland, whilst the other troops of the German Confederation occupied Sundeved. The Prussians however, — thanks to the intervention of Russia — soon evacuated Jutland, and the Danes who, from their supremacy at sea, had been enabled to keep up communication with the Islands, now receiving re-inforcements, attacked Sundeved from Als, and two successful and glorious engagements took place at Nybel (May 28th) and Dybbel (June 5th). The unequal contest Denmark had to sustain excited the keenest sympathy, especially among the Norwegians and Swedes, which led to a number of volunteers from both these nations enrolling themselves under the Danish flag; and although the Swedish and Norwegian government abstained from any active participation in the war, and England and France (who in 1721 had guaranteed Denmark the possession of Slesvig) also observed neutrality, the Scandinavian nations gradually took up a menacing attitude towards Prussia, and it was in fact notified to that power, that any attempt to attack Jutland and the Danish Islands would meet with decided opposition from their side. A Swedo-Norwegian army actually did take up its quarters in Scania, and a division of the same was eventually sent over to Funen. All these circumstances combined to induce Prussia, on whom the weight of the war fell with additional force, owing to the fact of the German ports being blockaded by the Danish fleet, to conclude an armistice at Malmö, in August 1848. This ended the First Slesvig campaign.

But the suspension of hostilities was of short duration, the armistice was not adhered to by the provisional government in Kiel, and the Danes in North Slesvig were treated with the utmost arbitrariness. Matters were far worse than in open warfare, and the Danish government therefore had no alternative but to wish the armistice put an end to without delay. In April 1849 began the Second Slesvig campaign. It opened unfortunately for Denmark. The plan of action decided on was, that the main army, which had its head-quarters on the island of Als, together with a smaller force stationed north of the Kongeaa, under General Rye, should march simultaneously into Slesvig; but the German Confederate army, commanded by General Prittwitz, was this time far stronger than the year before, and in conjunction with the Slesvig-Holstein forces under Bonin forced the Danes, after a slight advance into the duchies, to retire once more, partly to the north of the Kongeaa, partly to the island of Als. To this check may be added the unfortunate issue of the engagement in the bay of Eckernförde, where the Danish line-of-battle ship Christian VIII was blown up, and the frigate Gefion obliged to surrender. Once more the Danes made a desperate but futile attempt to arrest the far superior forces of the enemy in their advance north of the Kongeaa, and a hand to hand fight took place in the streets of Kolding on April 23rd, the anniversary of the battle of Slesvig. After this the main army, at the head of which was General Bülow, intrenched itself in the fortress of Fredericia, which was now invested by the Slesvig-Holsteiners, while a smaller Danish force under General Rye retreated in good order to the peninsula of Helgenæs north of Aarhus, pursued by the German Confederate army.

The campaign must therefore be said to have opened most disastrously, and the Danish people were despondent and anxious as to the turn events might take in the immediate future. But now the sun broke forth from behind the leaden clouds, and rose on one of the most glorious days in the history of Denmark. Fredericia, which at this time was besieged and bombarded by the Slesvig-Holsteiners, could not from the superiority of the Danish fleet be invested, on the side open to the sea; profiting by this advantage the Danes, without the knowledge of the Germans, had been enabled to assemble re-inforcements, partly from the islands and partly from North Jutland, whence General Rye and most of his troops now joined the main army. On the July 6th shortly after midnight the Danish army, numbering about 16,000 men, made a sortie, and after six hours of obstinate fighting drove the besieging force out of all its intrenchments, and put it to flight; in scattered detachments the enemy now made a precipitate retreat, partly towards the north and partly towards the south. The heroic and oft repeated storming of the trenches however gave the Danes a dearly bought victory; about 2000 men were left dead or wounded on the field, General Rye himself being among the former.

Some time before the battle of Fredericia, negociations had been entered into with Prussia and Germany; it was again the blockade of their ports, as also the involved state of affairs in Germany, which inclined Prussia to listen to overtures of peace, and a few days after their defeat an armistice was agreed to. The great body of German troops, it was decided, should evacuate Jutland and Slesvig; but with the proviso that a small Prussian force should occupy the southern, and a Swedish-Norwegian corps the northern part of this duchy; whilst the administration of the country was to be carried on by a Commission, composed of a Dane, a Prussian and an Englishman. At the same time, pourparlers were commenced with the object of concluding a definitive peace with Germany. In the meanwhile the Danish government met with many difficulties in the management of Slesvig affairs, especially in the southern part; for though the Prussians had officially broken off all connection with the Slesvig-Holsteiners — who, much against their will, had been obliged to withdraw their army south of the Eider — yet in an underhand way they continued to abet the rebels to the utmost of their ability. At last in July 1850 peace was concluded at Berlin with the German Confederation, but the conditions drawn up were so vague — a cordial understanding was to reign between the German Confederation and the King of Denmark, both parties however reserving to themselves their former rights — that in reality it could not be looked upon as definitive. The only actual advantage obtained by the peace was, that Prussia undertook not to hinder Denmark in her efforts to suppress the rebellion in Slesvig.

The Slesvig-Holstein party had as yet by no means made up their minds to submit. On the contrary they had strained every nerve to ensure a successful issue to the decisive struggle now imminent, and supported by volunteers from Germany, especially officers, they had raised the number of their corps to 34,000 men. A few days after the peace of Berlin the Slesvig-Holstein army, under the command of the Prussian General Willisen and accompanied by the Duke of Augustenborg, crossed the Eider. The Danish government had also put forth their utmost strength, so as to crush the insurrection at a blow, and their army under General Krogh now consisted of about 39,000 men. The two hosts met at Isted, somewhat to the north of the town of Slesvig, where the insurgents had taken up their head-quarters; and after some sharp but unimportant engagements on the 24th of July, a pitched battle was fought the next day. It was a protracted and obstinate engagement, and at the same time the most bloody of the whole war; the issue was for a long time uncertain, until it was finally decided in favor of the Danes, who now marched on south and occupied the Danevirke; whilst the enemy in good order, and but feebly pursued by the almost exhausted Danish troops, retreated to the neighborhood of Rendsborg. The news of this victory occasioned great rejoicings in the kingdom, it being the general impression that the rebellion was now crushed. And in fact such was the case, for the encounters that followed were but hopeless attempts on the part of the Slesvig-Holsteiners. The first attack made by the insurgents took place at Mysunde on the Slie, where the left wing of the Danish troops bore the brunt of the assault; the enemy was completely repulsed with severe losses. No better success attended their assault on the right wing, which had taken up a defensive position supported by the fortress of Frederiksstad. After a bombardment of five days, during which a great part of the town was destroyed, the Slesvig-Holsteiners stormed this fortress on the October 4th; but after a desperate fight lasting for several hours, the Danes under Colonel Helgesen compelled them to retire. Thus was brought to a close the First Slesvig War.

In July 1850, immediately after the occupation of Slesvig by the Danish army, Tillisch, the Danish member of the before mentioned Commission, was appointed Administrator of the affairs of the duchy. He set to work energetically to bring some kind of order into the general confusion; a task which was now more easy of accomplishment, as he was able to act entirely on his own responsibility. His first endeavors were directed towards regulating the vexed question of the languages, which he tried to accomplish under guidance of the following principles: In the northern Danish speaking districts, Danish was to be the language employed in the Churches, Schools and Courts of Justice, while towards the south, where the German tongue prevailed, that speech should continue to occupy a corresponding place; the two languages should enjoy equal privileges in the intermediate districts, except that Danish should be the one taught in the schools. The Germans of course complained loudly of ill-usage and infringement of the rights of the German-speaking part of the population; but though blunders were inevitable — it was so difficult and complicated a question, that it would have been impossible for any government to have steered quite clear of mistakes — these were certainly fewer than could have been expected, and on the whole the arrangements made were both fair and equitable. How political affairs in the duchies afterwards were developed, is inseparably connected with the great changes which took place in the Constitution of the kingdom as a result of the events of March 1848.

The March ministry set to work immediately on the important task of giving a free Ground-law to the Danish people. A Constitutional Assembly chosen on liberal principles of elective franchise met at Copenhagen at the end of October 1848, and the draft of a Fundamental law was laid before it. The March ministry, it is true, went out of office shortly after, and was succeeded by the November cabinet; but this change was chiefly owing to a difference of opinion between the King and his Ministers, and concerned the conditions of peace to be concluded with Germany. The Ministry were inclined to make greater concessions than the King, and wished notably to negociate on the basis of a division of Slesvig, according to the boundary marked out by the language spoken. But the new Cabinet among whose members were such men as Professors Madvig and Clausen, as far as this important question was concerned, held the same opinions as the preceeding one. After long debates the "Ground-Law" was voted by the Diet, and the King's signature affixed, June 5th 1849. The most important clauses were as follows: Denmark is a hereditary and limited Monarchy; the Executive rule being vested in the king, while the Legislative is exercised conjointly by the king and the "Rigsdag" (Diet, Parliament). The king is irresponsible and his person inviolable; he wields his power through responsible ministers, who constitute the Council of State, over which the king presides; the king's signature is valid only, when accompanied by that of a responsible minister. The Rigsdag, which is to meet every year, and to sit for at least two months, is composed of two Houses, the "Folketing" and the "Landsting". The right of voting to the Folketing is free to every burgher who has attained the age of 30, when he is of good reputation, unless he is in private service without a household establishment of his own; every citizen is eligible for election, when he has attained the age of 25; the elections are direct and are valid for three years. The right of electing to the Landsting is possessed by every one who has the same right to the Folketing; the elections here, however, are indirect, electors being first chosen, who in their turn name the members of the Landsting. Every citizen who has attained the age of 40 is qualified for election to the Landsting, but must enjoy an income of not less than 1200 Rigsdaler (about £135) or during the preceeding year has paid an income tax of at least 200 Rigsdaler (about £22); the election to the Landsting is valid for eight years. All laws require sanction by the Rigsdag; both Houses have equal rights to propose or to pass a law; the Budget ("Finanslov") must first be laid before the Folketing; no taxes can be collected before the Budget has been voted. If both Houses are not agreed on the passing of a bill, a joint committee can be appointed, whose propositions must be submitted to both Houses and settled by each separately. The king has the right to prorogue the Rigsdag, but only for two months in each session; and to dissolve either one of the Houses or both; but must in that case convene a new Assembly within two months; he has also the power of absolute veto. The Cabinet has access to all debates in the Rigsdag, but the right of voting only when they have been chosen members of the same. The Ministers, with regard to their administration, can be impeached both by the king and by the Folketing before the "Rigsret", a tribunal composed of Assessors of the Supreme Court of the kingdom, and an equal number chosen from its own members by the Landsting. Judicial power is vested in tribunals, the judges being nominated by the government. Among other important clauses in the Fundamental Law, may be mentioned those which provide for freedom of conscience (in religious matters), liberty to hold public or private meetings and liberty of the press; also those securing that no imprisonment of persons, except in pursuance of a legal sentence, can take place; that industry is open to all classes; and that all privileges or favoritism to special classes are abolished.

This (till somewhat modified, see p. 60) was that Ground-law, which the Danes obtained so easily; it had been preceeded by no struggle, as had been the case in so many other countries, and indeed perhaps Denmark obtained liberty too easily for it to understand or appreciate it. In the meanwhile there was general rejoicing, and but few misgivings. What caused most anxiety, was the state of affairs in the south.

According to the conditions of the treaty of Berlin, the German Confederation was to undertake the task of restoring order in Holstein, and in spite of the reluctance and jealousy of Prussia, Austria assumed this office and sent an army into the duchy. The insurgent government was dissolved, their troops disbanded, and the administration of the country provisionally entrusted to a Commission, consisting of an Austrian, a Prussian and a Dane. The Austrian regiments did not evacuate Holstein, but remained behind to await the issue of the negociations pending with the Danish government, concerning the future position of Slesvig and Holstein in regard to the kingdom. On the part of the Danes the opinion was, that the Fundamental Law ought to be extended to Slesvig, and that it would thus bring the duchy into closer connection with the kingdom, while the union with Holstein, which formed part of the German Confederation, would necessarily be far less strict in its character. But the German powers would by no means agree to this: they would not have a Ground-law which embraced only those parts of the kingdom extending to the Eider (Eiderstat), but wanted one which should include all parts of the kingdom (Helstat). In other words, they would not allow Slesvig to be more closely united to Denmark, nor indeed to have any share in the great political rights secured by the Fundamental Law. In these negociations Denmark, being supported by neither France nor England, was obliged to yield more and more, as the constant change of Ministry testifies. Finally, Bluhme, the Minister for Foreign Affairs, succeeded in bringing negociations with Austria and Prussia to a temporary conclusion. The result was, that the new

Cabinet, which Bluhme was called upon to form, published the Manifesto of January 28th 1852, by which it was settled, that Slesvig and Holstein should each have its own Assembly of representatives for the administration of internal affairs, whilst the kingdom should retain its Rigsdag. Moreover, the Danish government agreed to the proposal of a Helstat, promising a Constitution to every part of the monarchy, in all matters concerning their joint affairs. Thus it will be seen that Frederik VII had discarded his former advisers, the men of 1848, and had surrounded himself with the old statesmen, who adhered to the principle of a united state; among these was Carl Moltke, who now became a member of the Cabinet. Slesvig was thus not allowed to share in the privileges of the Fundamental law, but on the other hand all union between it and Holstein was put an end to — notably the administrative and judicial law of 1834, which had been in force in both duchies — and this from a Danish point of view could not but be considered a great advantage. The German Confederation declared itself satisfied, and the Austrian army evacuated Holstein.

At the same time another matter, which had played a weighty part in the insurrection, was settled. Doubts had been raised as to the order of succession in case the male line, then upon the throne died out, for Frederik VII was childless. It was therefore necessarily of great importance to solve this question, should the project of a united state be carried into effect. For some time negociations had been going on concerning the point at issue, and by a treaty concluded in London on May 8th 1852, the Great Powers, with Sweden and Norway, ratified an agreement made among the members of the royal house of Denmark, by which the person nearest to the throne, according to the text of the Royal Law, Prince Frederik of Hesse, a nephew of Christian VIII, ceded his rights in favor of his sister, Princess Louise, married to Prince Christian of Glücksborg, who thus became heir apparent. This decision roused a violent conflict in the Danish Rigsdag, the members of which considered it a serious matter to set aside so important a clause of the Royal Law as the order of Succession, and it was only after the dissolution of the Rigsdag and the formation of a new Ministry, at the head of which was Anders Sandöe Örsted, that the Law of the order of Succession was passed in June 1853.

The opposition became most serious, when the proclamation of January 28th 1852, relating to the Joint Constitution, came under debate. The Rigsdag declared itself willing to authorise all alterations absolutely indispensable to the establishment of a Joint Constitution, but would by no means accede to changes, aimed only at restricting the political liberty sanctioned by the Ground-Law. Indeed the project proposed by the Örsted ministry, for modifying the Fundamental Law, went much farther than was necessary for the establishment of a new Constitution. From this moment the struggle with the Ministry assumed an acute character: the Rigsdag passed an address of "want of confidence", and the government in answer dismissed from their posts three of the most highly esteemed members of that assembly, namely Hall, Auditor-General, Professor Andræ and Bishop Monrad. Meanwhile the persecutions against the press were again begun, as in the days of Christian VIII. These proceedings could not but rouse the people to a state of exasperation, which increased day by day. In July 1854, in the midst of the general dissatisfaction, the decree concerning the Joint Constitution was promulgated, and its text was in striking contrast to the chief clauses of the Fundamental Law. Among other things the "Rigsraad", the assembly appointed to investigate common affairs, was to exert legislative power only in matters relating to the levying of new taxes, or in the alteration or abolition of the old ones; in all other matters it should have a mere deliberative voice; at the same time the Rigsraad, as a body, was most inefficiently constituted. When therefore the Rigsdag met in October 1854, the language used by the opposition was unmeasured, and a resolution was passed to impeach the Ministry before the "Rigsret", for infringement of the

Constitution. At the same time an address was sent to the King. The only response made by the government to this, was to issue a decree dissolving the Folketing. But with the new elections the opposition was returned more numerous than ever, and the King then decided, in December 1854, on dismissing the detested Ministry. This was the first serious conflict between the government and the Rigsdag.

The new Cabinet, which among others included Hall and Andræ, soon came to an understanding with the Rigsdag. The government made such considerable alterations in the proposals laid before the House for the modification of the Fundamental Law, that they were agreed to without any further debate, and the Joint Constitution of October 1855 was promulgated shortly after. It was far more in accordance with the principles of the Ground-law; above all it was strictly constitutional, the Rigsraad obtaining legislative power in all matters relating to taxes and law affairs, and the Assembly itself was composed altogether more advantageously, as regarded the kingdom. The matter appeared now finally settled, and at first the political horizon seemed to brighten, for no opposition was offered in Holstein, and the elections for the Rigsraad took place without further obstacle. But the rejoicing lasted but a short time, the discontent in the duchies being too great, while in the kingdom itself, but little confidence was put in the new Constitution.

Shortly after the Rigsraad met in March 1856, eleven members from the duchies proposed to send an address to the King, petitioning that the new Constitution and Law of Suffrage should be laid before the Council of representatives of Holstein and Slesvig and the nobles of Lauenburg, and that their deliberations should then be submitted to the Rigsraad; because, as they said, it was unfair that the duchies had not been consulted in this matter, as had been the case with the Danish Rigsdag. They simply overlooked the fact, that the Joint Constitution had not been originally submitted to the deliberations of the Rigsdag, but that it had only been laid before the members for their information. The spokesman for the eleven was Baron Karl Scheel Plessen, Mayor of Altona. The Rigsraad rejected the motion, but the Slesvig-Holstein party had no intention of yielding, knowing that all Germany would be on their side, especially Berlin and Vienna; the latter was obliged to follow suit, if for no other reason than the fear of being outwitted by her rival. It was not long either, before despatches were sent to the Danish government both by Prussia and Austria, who ranged themselves on the side of the "Eleven" and threatened the intervention of the Germanic Confederation. And from this moment there was no end to the constant interchange of notes, — a diplomatic struggle in which Denmark was continually compelled to yield, particularly as she found support nowhere; the powers which had signed the treaty of London restricted themselves to sending proposals of arbitration, or else well-meaning advice as to making concessions.

The attitude adopted by Germany becoming more and more threatening, the Danish government, which from May 1857 had been under the leadership of Hall, now offered to lay before the Holstein delegates the draft of a new Constitution for the home government of the duchy. But the delegates would not hear of this, until the document had been revised according to their wishes; they demanded that the various parts of the kingdom should be represented separately in the said Constitution, and that each nationality should have an equal number of members in the Council of State. In the autumn of 1857 Lauenburg complained to the Diet of Frankfort of this grievance, the Joint Constitution, and at the same time Prussia and Austria called upon the Diet to take under consideration the position of Holstein as to the Danish monarchy. As a matter of course, the Diet pronounced judgement against the new Constitution, as being absolutely opposed to the rights and privileges of Holstein and Lauenburg; to make matters still clearer the Diet shortly after, on the part of Holstein and Lauenburg, called upon Denmark to abstain from all legislation based on laws contrary to the constitutional rights of these provinces. The Danish government continued to give way, while the German members in the Rigsraad determined to push matters to extremities, feeling themselves sure of the support of the Diet. Nor did Germany desert them; in May 1858 the Diet demanded from the Danish rulers a positive declaration, as to the mode of proceeding they intended to follow in regulating the affairs of Holstein and Lauenburg; if this were refused, more energetic measures would be resorted to. It was of no use that the Cabinet in Denmark expressed itself willing to regard the Joint Constitution provisionally abrogated, as regarded both Holstein and Lauenburg; the Diet threatened military intervention, and Hall now decided that it was necessary to yield. On November 6th 1858 a Manifesto was issued, declaring the Joint Constitution of 1855 null and void, as regarded Holstein and Lauenburg, while at the same time the Holstein deputies were summoned to meet in January 1859, to deliberate on the question of the Constitution.

The Holstein representatives showed themselves from the very first utterly intractable, closely following their old policy, whilst the Prince Regent of Prussia, afterwards King William I, promised fully to support them in their claims; and Prince Frederik, son of Duke Christian of Augustenborg, protested against the law of Succession of 1853, notwithstanding the solemn oath taken by his own father, pledging himself not to put any obstacles in the way of its execution. During the debates on the new proposal brought forward by the government, the Holstein deputies openly revealed the drift of their desires; they wished the administrative and legislative union between Slesvig and Holstein re-established, attacked the enactment concerning the regulation of the languages in Slesvig, and finally proposed the establishment of four Legislative Assemblies — one for the kingdom and one for each of the duchies. They at the same time demanded that the common right of nationality, enjoyed alike by the kingdom and the duchies, should be abolished, which would have resulted in a sharp distinction between Danish and German elements. Such exactions as these no Danish government could possibly think of discussing; in Letters Patent dated September 1859 it was notified, that the Danish government would work steadily for the consolidation of the union of Holstein and Lauenburg to the kingdom, as offered previously; and in November it moreover proposed to the Diet, that the controversy should be settled by a commission consisting of eight members of the Danish-Slesvig Rigsraad and eight members of the Holstein States General. After a few months of comparative tranquility, diversified however by several changes of Ministry, a new Cabinet was formed with Hall at its head; and the Frankfort Diet thereupon, in May 1860, agreed to the proposal of forming a Commission, on condition that it consisted of members chosen from the Danish Rigsdag, and the Slesvig and Holstein States. It was the first time since the insurrection, that the Diet once again drew Slesvig into the controversy. As a matter of course Denmark protested strongly against this interference; but Prussia asserted boldly that the Diet had the right to interfere in the administration of Slesvig, after what had taken place during the negociations of 1851—1852; while the only result of the mediation of England was, that Denmark was forced to make new concessions. But they were of no avail, and in the beginning of 1861, the Confederation again threatened an armed intervention. War seemed inevitable; and the government made active preparations for it, supported by popular feeling among the Danish nation, who in various ways evinced their sympathy: an address to the King was drawn up by the Rigsdag and signed by the people in great numbers; in which they stated, that they did not intend to dictate laws for Holstein and Lauenburg, nor would they allow the Germanic Confederation to meddle in the internal affairs of the Danish kingdom. In March 1861 the government made a last attempt to smooth over difficulties, by laying before the representative council of Holstein new plans for a general and a special Constitution; but this effort proved as futile as the former, and it would certainly have been more advantageous, if everything had been settled in the spring of 1861, while Frederik VII was still alive, for the result would undoubtedly have been far better than was the case three years later. The enthusiasm of the people had been aroused, and the great powers would perhaps have taken a more favorable attitude than they did afterwards.

War, however, did not break out. After fresh and very considerable concessions on the part of Denmark, the result of renewed attempts of mediation on the part of England, the Diet expressed itself willing to defer military intervention; and negociations were again opened with Prussia and Austria. But they only led to the self-same wrangling; the German powers once more interfered in the internal affairs of Slesvig, and the Danish government again protested. In February 1862, Prussia and Austria renewed their demands with regard to Slesvig and a month later the Diet endorsed them.

Now recommenced the same interminable interchange of diplomatic notes. But in the kingdom the feeling was becoming more and more general, that the idea of the Union must be given up, the important question to be solved now being what the future connection between Denmark and Slesvig was to be. Whilst a more moderate party wanted to maintain the Joint Constitution of 1855, the more extreme members of the party on the side of the yeomen ("Bondevennerne") wished to have it done away with, in favor of the Ground-law of 1849 extending to the Eider. And of what use were all the concessions, appeals to European powers, and protests against Germany's interference in the affairs of Slesvig? In August 1862 Austria and Prussia came forward with their strange demands, that the Joint Constitution of 1855 should be set aside; that all parts of the kingdom should have Legislative Assemblies, enjoying equal rights, with an equal number of members irrespective of the amount of their several populations; that the question of language should be regulated as before 1848, etc. The Minister of Foreign Affairs in England, Lord John Russell, decidedly took the part of Germany, although public opinion in England was in favor of Denmark. Added to this, when the Holstein representative Council met early in 1863, they refused to discuss the proposal of the Danish government. Things of course could not continue to go on in this way. Something more decided must be done, particularly as the conflict was unavoidable. At numerous meetings, and especially at one held at the Casino in Copenhagen, the necessity was urged of breaking off all connection with Holstein, and of uniting Slesvig to Denmark by the same constitutional tie; and on the 30th of March 1863 the government published a Manifesto, by which it was settled that Holstein and Lauenburg should be separated from the kingdom in many matters formerly common to both; notably they were to have a military organization of their own, as a contingent of the German Confederation. Although by this Manifesto great liberty was granted to Holstein — so great that it caused misgivings in the minds of many Danes — a cry of indignation was raised against it in the duchies and throughout Germany; what they wanted, was naturally the old to Denmark most unfortunate union between Holstein and Slesvig. Prussia and Austria protested against it; the Confederation in July 1863 declared it invalid, and called upon the kingdom within six weeks to draw up a new common Constitution in which Holstein and Lauenburg should be placed on the same footing as Slesvig, in relation to the rest of the monarchy. Again diplomatic notes crossed and recrossed each other. England strove to induce France to join with her in averting military intervention from the side of Germany, but as England refused to take the responsibility of such a step, France also drew back; while on the other hand Russia had been gained over to the cause of the Slesvig-Holsteiners by the position Prussia had taken up in the Polish question.

There was nothing left for the Danish government to do, but to continue in the course it had once begun. It was quite evident to everybody that it was impossible to go on governing with the Constitution then in force; especially as the German members of the Slesvig representative Council in the summer of 1863 resigned their seats. They thus broke up the Assembly and rendered impossible the elections for the Rigsraad, which were to have taken place before the new year. At the Rigsraad, which assembled in September, the government brought forward the draft of a Fundamental Law for the joint affairs of the kingdom of Denmark and the duchy of Slesvig, which after violent debates was passed on the November 13th. This was the much-talked of, important and yet so short lived November Constitution. It was based on the principle of 1848 — Denmark as far as the Eider — and thus was an abandonment of the union project. Slesvig, however, was not to be incorporated with the kingdom, for the Slesvig representative Council was not restricted in its powers to internal affairs; but the real advantage was that Slesvig was drawn closer to Denmark. The new Rigsraad was to be constituted on much the same principle as the Danish Rigsdag, and at the same time to enjoy far greater constitutional rights.

A decisive step had been taken, and a peaceable understanding was no longer possible. About the same time that the draft was laid before the Rigsraad, the Confederation had declared its intention of carrying out its threat of a military intervention, if within three weeks the Danish government did not rescind the Manifesto of March 30th. The answer given was, that the government would be willing to permit a discussion, as far as regarded details, but would not swerve from it in its integrity. War was thus at the gates, always supposing that is was a serious threat on the part of the Confederation. Besides her own strength (which was but small in comparison to that of the great German powers), Denmark had some reason to count upon assistance from Norway and Sweden, as also moral support from France. On the 15th of November 1863, two days after the November constitution had been approved by the Rigsdag, Frederik VII died at the castle of Glücksburg in Slesvig; — the wish for the continued union with Denmark of this duchy had caused this stubborn struggle throughout his reign. With him the Oldenburg line of kings, which had occupied the throne for over 400 years, became extinct. But before we proceed to sketch the results of this momentous event, we will in a few words sum up all that had been done for the internal bettering of the country under Denmark's first Constitutional King.

Although development had been repeatedly checked by the ever recurring quarrel with Germany, this period had nevertheless been one of progress and improvement, and many of the pledges given in the Fundamental Law had been redeemed. Thus liberty of the press was established; then freedom in religious matters by the enactment of several laws — such as the complete emancipation of the Jews, the institution of Civil Marriages for persons of different persuasions; immunity from parochial restrictions ("Sognebaand"), everybody being thus free to choose a spiritual teacher from among the state clergy, the abolition of compulsory Baptism etc. etc. Education was advanced, and the National School system extended; great reforms in the administration of justice were introduced, the Maritime and Commercial Court in Copenhagen was established, and a new Criminal Code framed. This last does not bear the name of Frederik VII, as it was not thoroughly worked out in detail until some months after the accession of Christian IX, and did not come into force until February 10th 1866. Several laws were passed for the introduction of general equality among the citizens, the farmers being put on the same footing as their fellow subjects, and the principle of general conscription enforced. Much was done for the material advantage of the country, hindrances to trade were removed, and railways and telegraph lines greatly developed. The Rigsdag especially directed its attention to agriculture, as the most important source of revenue; thus socage was almost done away with, and the change of leasehold farms into freehold property facilitated. The Sound dues fell away by treaties with the Maritime nations, which gave Denmark an indemnification once for all; and a palpable testimony to the increasing well-being at this period was the reduction of the National Debt; after the war it had risen to over 260 millions, while in 1863 it had been reduced to 208 millions of Kroner.

With the exception of the unfortunate Slesvig question, Frederik the Seventh's reign was on the whole regarded by the Danish people as one of prosperity. The King himself contributed not a little to the general contentment, being beloved on account of his homely Danish temperament, and the conscientiousness with which he maintained the constitutional system, which had been legally accorded to the land through the Ground-law. His motto was with truth: "The people's love, my strength". There was real sorrow at his death, and it was augmented by the stormy clouds which were gathering over the country.

On the death of Frederik VII Prince Christian of Glücksburg, in accordance with the terms of the treaty of London, ascended the Danish throne under the title of Christian IX. From the very next day the state of affairs was patent; the right of succession was at once made over to Prince Frederik of Augustenborg by his father, though the latter had previously most solemnly renounced all claims. This Prince now came forward as the Pretender to the sovereignty of the duchies, under the name of Frederik VIII. In the duchies the flame of revolt was immediately kindled, and the excitement all over Germany became intense; it was everywhere supported by the reigning princes; that German brethren must be freed from the Danish tyranny, was the cry. The Confederation, which had never acknowledged the order of succession established by the treaty of London, ranged itself at once on the side of the Pretender; but this neither Prussia nor Austria would do: they had both affixed their signatures to the said treaty, and they had reasons for maintaining it; what they wanted, was only a pretext to interfere in the internal affairs of Denmark, and they succeeded in making the Diet determine on carrying out the military intervention, while the question of the order of succession was left open. The result of this adhesion on the part of the Confederation was, that Russia, England and France called upon the Danish government to withdraw the Constitution signed by Christian IX on the 18th of November — a measure which could only have protracted matters, without solving the question at issue —; but the pressure exercised by these powers resulted in the evacuation of Holstein by the Danish troops, upon which the Confederates crossed the frontier on December 23rd. Wherever they went, the Pretender was proclaimed Duke; and on the 30th of December he took up his quarters in Kiel.

In the meanwhile the intervention of England and Russia had brought about the fall of the Hall Cabinet. On the last day of the year it was succeeded by another with Monrad at its head, and on the 1st of January 1864 the new Constitution came into effect. Events now crowded upon each other in rapid succession. On the 11th of January, Prussia and Austria proposed to the Diet to demand from Denmark the abrogation of the November Constitution; in case of refusal, Prussian and Austrian troops were to occupy Slesvig, and although the Diet protested against this, the two powers, on the 16th of January, sent the Danish government an ultimatum, with a respite of 24 hours to consider it. The Ministry offered to yield to the demand, if the time necessary for consideration were allowed — a new Rigsraad would in any case have to be summoned — but all was unavailing. War was inevitable. And in this struggle against two great powers, little Denmark would have to stand alone! No help could be expected from the arbitrating powers; the only hope now lay in Sweden and Norway, but this also failed when the decisive moment arrived. The two kingdoms all through the diplomatic negociations had stood on Denmark's side, but they had required the separation of Holstein; and when by the Manifesto of 30th March 1863 a great step had been taken towards complying with this demand, King Karl XV, Frederik the Seventh's personal friend, proposed a defensive alliance, which was on the point of being concluded when Frederik died, and the Swedish-Norwegian government drew back.

On the 21st of January 1864 the Prussian and Austrian troops under Field-Marschal Wrangel, well-known from the war of 1848, marched into Holstein. The Danish army, numbering a little over 35,000 men, under the command of Lieut. General De Meza, had taken up its position at the Danevirke, whose fortifications had been slightly strengthened during the preceeding years, and so in the eyes of many was looked upon as impregnable, if only it were occupied by the number of troops necessary to defend it — the ancient rampart boundary of the Danish kingdom. On the 31st of January the Danish army was called upon to evacuate Slesvig, and on receiving a plain refusal the enemy crossed the Eider on the 1st of February. Thus began the Second Slesvig war.

After the Prussians had made an ineffectual attempt at Mysunde to break through the left wing of the Danish garrison, led by Lieut. General Gerlach; and after the Austrians the next day, February 3rd, had been more successful in their attack on the centre at Jagel and Övreselk, to the south of the old Kovirke, the general assault was expected every day — when suddenly the Danevirke position was evacuated on the 5th of February. This determination had been decided on in one of the Councils of War called by de Meza, and was instantly carried out without the Danish government having been apprized of it. In the darkness of a winter night, aggravated by a sudden frost, under hardships and privations and with sorrow-laden hearts, the army retired northwards. When this was known, the grief and exasperation of the Danish people became intense, and cries of treachery were raised; but after-events showed de Meza had acted rightly, for the fastness was untenable with the small Danish force he had at his command; and besides, the submerged country towards the west had been frozen over by the severe frost, which thus considerably extended the line which had to be defended and made any attempt at so doing sure to end in utter defeat. But the disappointment was profound, and all enthusiasm was at an end. De Meza was dismissed, and his successor Lieut. General Lüttichau, the only one in the Council of War who had opposed the evacuation of the Danevirke, in his turn soon yielded his place as Commander in Chief to General Gerlach.

The troops retired towards the north, pursued by the enemy; but the Danes had so considerably the start of them, that only the rear-guard under Max Müller fought with the Austrian vanguard at Oversö and Sankelmark, an honorable and very bloody battle. The main strength of the Danes took up a strong position behind the Dybbel redoubts, in the peninsula of Sundeved opposite the island of Als, whilst a smaller force under Hegerman-Lindencrone retreated to North Jutland. Slesvig was soon overrun by the pursuing foe; they dismantled the Danevirke stronghold, dismissed the Danish functionaries from their posts, established the German language everywhere, mutilated the Isted Lion in Flensborg and afterwards carried it off to Berlin — in short, endeavored to efface everything that could call Danish rule to mind. Whilst the Austrians marched into North Jutland, and after an obstinate fight near Vejle drove Hegermann-Lindencrone's corps further northwards, the Prussian main army invested the Dybbel redoubts — the centre round which Denmark's last desperate and hopeless effort should be made. It was however a month after the commencement of the siege, before Prussia brought up a sufficient amount of heavy artillery; whereupon in the middle of March the bombardment began in earnest, and drew nearer and nearer by means of trenches. On the 2nd of April and the following days, the little defenceless town of Sönderborg on the island of Als was bombarded and for the most part destroyed, which Lord Shaftesbury described as "one of the most shameful and cruel deeds that has ever been done, not only in civilized, but even in uncivilized warfare". Although the Danes fought heroically, or rather to speak correctly continued to guard their ramparts under constant showers of projectiles, they had so small a force and their artillery was so inferior to that of the enemy, that there could be no doubt as to the final issue of the unequal contest. As soon as the redoubts had been reduced to heaps of ruins a general assault was made on the 18th of April, and after 12 hours desperate fighting the Danes retreated in good order to Als. Their losses were 5000 men, killed, wounded or taken prisoners, while the enemy's amounted to about 2000; the Danish losses at Dybbel from first to last were about 8000 men. The immediate result of the fall of Dybbel was the surrender of Fredericia, which had been besieged by the Austrians; whereupon they occupied North Jutland as far as the Limfjord, Hegermann-Lindencrone cautiously retiring further north thereof.

A few days before the fall of Dybbel England had finally succeeded in arranging the preliminaries for a Conference, which however was not opened until the 25th of April, the German delegates refusing to meet until after the fall of Dybbel. The first result of this Conference was a suspension of hostilities for a month from the 9th of May (it was afterwards extended a fortnight longer), during which time Denmark was to raise the blockade of the German ports, the Danes were to keep Als, and the Germans that part of North Jutland occupied by them. That same day fell the only gleam of light that cheered the Danes throughout the whole of this miserable war; namely the engagement at Helgoland, where two Danish frigates and a corvette under Captain Suenson defeated two Austrian frigates and a corvette under Tegethoff, together with some Prussian gunboats. But this truce was all that resulted from the negociations at the Conference. For Prussia and Austria demanded the entire independence of Holstein and Slesvig under a joint constitution, as also material guarantees for the same; whilst the Confederation asked the independence of the duchies under Frederik VIII of Augustenborg as regent. As it was impossible for the Danes to agree to these terms, England, supported by France and Russia, proposed that Denmark should cede Holstein and Lauenburg, as also the southern part of Slesvig; but this did not lead to anything, on account of disagreements respecting the boundary line; for England proposed the line Slie-Danevirke, while the great German powers insisted on the line Aabenraa-Tönder. After several other proposals and attempts at arbitration, the Conference was broken up, on the same day that the truce expired, June 15th; beyond the boundary line Slie-Danevirke, Denmark would not go in her concessions, both the government and the people being determined on this point.

Hostilities, therefore, recommenced. The Danish forces were stationed in Als under Major General Steinmann, whilst the ironclad "Rolf Krake" lay in Alssund, to prevent the enemy crossing over to the island. Yet the Danes allowed themselves to be completely taken by surprise; on the eve of the 29th of June the enemy crossed over Alssund, the "Rolf Krake" looking on without making any attempts to prevent them doing so, fearing to run aground. After some bloody fighting, Als was taken in the course of the day, and the Danish army retreated over to Funen, with a loss of 3200 men killed, wounded or taken prisoners. After this luckless battle Hegermann-Lindencrone also evacuated Vendsyssel; only the Frisian islands on the west coast of Slesvig still held out, and when Captain Hammer on the 19th of July was also obliged to abandon them, a new truce was concluded.

The hopeless struggle was over. The Monrad ministry was obliged to resign — it would have resisted to the last — and a few days later the Bluhme ministry replaced it. None of the great powers would interfere, and after a short truce preliminaries of peace were arranged in Vienna on the 1st of August; the final act however was not concluded until October 30th, after some opposition in the Rigsdag; which nevertheless in the beginning of November was obliged to confirm it. By the terms agreed on, Denmark was forced to cede Lauenburg, Holstein and Slesvig as far as the Kongeaa to Prussia and Austria; only Ærö and the district round about Ribe remained to the kingdom; at the same time Denmark was obliged to promise to confirm the resolutions come to by the two powers relative to the duchies. The Prince of Augustenborg was never mentioned.

For, Prussia and Austria had no intention of allowing the duchies to slip through their fingers; and the rival victors, as is well known, soon began to quarrel over their booty. Prussia in a short time repudiated the Slesvig-Holstein party, to which it had only attached itself out of dissimulation; and declared the claims of the Pretender invalid, according to the treaty of London, a step which caused intense indignation in the duchies and indeed over the whole of Germany; whilst Austria as a rival of Prussia placed itself on the side of the Confederation supporting the Prince of Augustenborg. Both powers continued to occupy the duchies, and it was only a question of time, when the decisive conflict between the rivals would break out. For a while it was warded off by the Convention of Gastein in August 1865, in which it was decided that the two states should enjoy equal rights with regard to the duchies — Prussia should rule in Slesvig and Austria in Holstein. But this did not last long; for while the Prussian government, under General Manteuffel, pursued a most violent policy — both against the Slesvig Holsteiners and the Danish party — the Austrians in Holstein under Gablenz employed far milder measures, and it was just this of which Prussia made a pretext for re-commencing the conflict. As is well known, this led to war in July 1866, in which Austria got the worst of it. Of the terms of the treaty of Prague, the only one of interest to Denmark is Article V, which is as follows: "The Emperor of Austria cedes to the King of Prussia all rights acquired by him at the treaty of Vienna to the duchies of Holstein and Slesvig, with however this reservation, that the northern districts of Slesvig shall be ceded to Denmark, if the population by free vote express their desire to be united to that country." It was the Emperor Napoleon III — who always advocated the right of the people to decide for themselves — to whom these words owe their origin. But as years went on, the hope which was thus dawning for the Danish North Slesvig population of being once more united to their fatherland, grew fainter and fainter; for the negociations set on foot by Denmark never led to anything. Prussia wished to keep Flensborg, Als and Dybbel, as also to have guarantees for the protection of the German population in North Slesvig, in short it was evident that she would not willingly give up one inch of ground, and finally in October 1878 she persuaded Austria to agree to the erasure of Article V in the treaty of Prague. The loyal North Slesvigers, however, still keep up the struggle, a struggle so well-known from Polish Lands, as also from Alsace and Lorraine; but unfortunately Prussian rule possesses too many effective weapons with which to combat and banish the national language of the weaker party.

But to return to Denmark's internal affairs during the years subsequent to 1864. A serious blow had been dealt to the national pride of the country; mutilated and smaller than ever, it had emerged from the contest; everything now depended on being able to reap the benefit of the lesson taught by the past misfortune, and to work on, uniting with might and main for moral and material development. In the first place a revision of the Constitution was necessary; there was no reason to have both a special and a joint constitution, now that Slesvig no longer formed a part of the kingdom. When the Rigsdag met in October 1864, there was a strong party, notably of the so-called "Friends of the Farmers" ("Bondevenner") who were of opinion, that the Joint Constitution of November 1863 should be pronounced null and void, and the full legislative authority vested in the Rigsdag — in fact that the Ground-law of 1849 should again come into force. But the government wished to have a fusion of the Fundamental law and the November constitution, and it maintained that the latter had not been rendered null and void by the loss of Slesvig; also, that both the Rigsraad and the Rigsdag ought to be consulted about the new Constitution. At the end of the year the Bluhme ministry laid before the Rigsraad the draft of a new Constitution, which by including several clauses of the November arrangement deviated a good deal from the Ground-law. This plan met with great opposition in the Rigsraad's Folketing, which after a dissolution in May 1865 came in again as strong as ever. It was only after long debates, principally on the mode of constituting the Landsting, and after the fall of the Bluhme ministry (occasioned by a coalition between the large and the small farmers in the Folketing), that the Rigsraad accepted the new plan in November 1865, under the Frijs ministry. All that was necessary now to legalize it was, that the Bill should be passed in three successive meetings by the Rigsdag. And after violent opposition, especially on the part of Tscherning, this was done; on the 28th of July 1866 the King's signature was affixed to "the Revised Ground-law of the kingdom of Denmark, of June 5th 1849". This law is essentially identical with that of 1849; only in one very important point does it differ, viz. in the mode employed to constitute the Landsting. The intermediate election is retained, but the alteration consists in twelve of the sixty six members being elected by the King for life, and the rest being chosen by a very complicated mode of election, the amount of the electors, income having a decisive influence on the matter.

In material respects the country recovered itself quickly, business was soon brisk, and strenuous efforts were made to encourage trade. Much was also done for agriculture, the heaths in Jutland began to be planted and cultivated; in short prosperous days commenced, and the people looked forward to the future with confidence and courage. The controversy over the Fundamental law seemed at an end, and legislative work, which had been laid aside during the war and the Parliamentary debates, could now be resumed. But, unfortunately, it was soon apparent that the conflict regarding the Constitution was not at an end, but rather just about to begin in earnest; what had gone before was but of slight importance compared with what was to follow. It was now proved that those men, especially Tscherning, who in strong language had denounced the alterations made in the Ground-law of 1866, and who had foreseen the impending discord, had been right in their theories. A good deal certainly was done during the first few years; several trade-laws were passed, Commercial and Postal conventions were concluded with foreign countries, and Military and Naval affairs were temporarily regulated by the laws of 1867 and 1868, as also by a new conscription law in 1869. But matters at the Rigsdag began to assume a more and more threatening aspect. The national-liberal party, which previous to the war had been almost absolute, had now lost its prestige, and the opposition, which consisted almost entirely of the party favorable to the yeomen, increased in force. From a steadily rising minority it grew stronger and stronger, until in the autumn of 1872 it had attained the majority. The great point in the contest was, whether the majority in the Folketing as elected by the people, should have any voice in constituting the government. That is, whether the Parliamentary system, as the opposition assumed, was contemplated in the Fundamental law, which the government party just as positively denied, supporting their arguments by referring to the constitution of the Landsting — in which they had the majority — and which, contrary to the custom in other countries, was also partly chosen by the people. But an essential reason for the outbreak of the controversy was the difference of opinion as to how the defence of the country was to be organized, the opposition being unwilling to agree to greater expense for the Army and Navy, and especially opposing the plans proposed by the government for the construction of a system of fortifications round Copenhagen. In the opinion of the opposition the country could not afford this outlay, and they thought it out of keeping with the modest position Denmark occupied among the states of Europe; and besides, such fortifications round Copenhagen they said would be no defence, but rather place the other parts of the country, especially Jutland, at the mercy of the enemy. But this plan of fortifying Copenhagen, brought forward for the first time in a complete form in 1872, the Cabinet considered of paramount importance; their party maintained that it was necessary as a point of vantage for the army and navy, to preserve Denmark's neutrality and prevent her falling a victim at the first attack of a foe. Besides this important question, the Finance-bill was another constant source of dispute; the Folketing struggled to get the ascendency in the debates regarding this matter. They said, the Ground-law had in paragraph 48 provided for its enjoying this prerogative by enjoining, that the Budget should first be laid before this Chamber, a decision which was kept constantly in the foreground to tranquilize the minds of those who were uneasy at the change made in the Fundamental law in 1866. But the government was just as zealous in combating these demands on the part of the Folketing; they resisted more particularly every effort made by the Chamber to introduce questions of administration into the debates on the Budget.

The Holstein ministry, which in May 1870 succeeded the Frijs ministry, could not emerge from the difficulty. It was under their regime that the opposition for the first time formed themselves into one party, under the name of the "United Left"; as above mentioned the elections of September 1872 gave them a decided majority, and after repeated addresses of want of confidence in the government, the Left in the autumn of 1873 refused the Budget a second reading. Upon this the Folketing was dissolved. This however was of no avail, and in the summer of 1874 the Ministry was obliged to cede its place to the more moderate Fonnesbech ministry. When at the end of ten months of brief existence this Cabinet was also forced to resign, after the Budget had been accepted owing to an arrangement between the moderate party of the Folketing and a part of the Left, it was followed by the Estrup ministry in June 1875. This was a Cabinet of landed proprietors and members of the Landsting, selected from the extreme Right of that Chamber. It is this Ministry which still holds the reins of government; in the course of years many changes have certainly taken place within it, but it is still the same Chief who is at its head. And from that moment the constitutional struggle has been going on, between the Government and the Landsting on the one side and the Folketing on the other, a struggle in which the work of legislation has been hindered, indeed sometimes even brought to a stand-still, and in which both sides have allowed themselves to drift further than they ever dreamt of doing, while into it almost the whole population has been drawn. In fact it has gone so far that there has been a straining of the Constitution, at all events of its spirit, as is admitted on all sides. It is a task reserved for future historians, when once the parliamentary contest is at an end and political feeling has cooled down, to write the history of these years. It will certainly not be one of the least interesting among the records of constitutional states in their infancy. In the contest, up to this date, the chief events only are mentioned here.

After the government, at the beginning of the autumn of 1875, had opened the campaign by laying before the Folketing an extraordinary law for the defence of the country, and after the Chamber had been dissolved in March 1876, on account of the offensive position which it had taken up, the new Folketing, in which the opposition had become so strong as to command over three fourths of the votes, still adhered to its former point of view with regard to the fortifications. They were willing to grant a sum of about 30 million Kroner for the defences, provided it could be raised by an Income and Property tax, and the fortification of Copenhagen was abandoned, whilst special weight was laid on the coast defence of Sealand, and a strong point of defence in Jutland. These conditions the Ministry would on no account agree to, such a tax in its opinion being utterly superfluous, when the surplus in the Treasury was taken into account, coast defences moreover they considered unnecessary. It was however only in the following session that the conflict led to a serious collision, occasioned by the Budget proposed for 1877—78, in which the government had to some extent included its plan for the defences. The Folketing erased these items, and the Landsting re-inserted them; moreover, several other questions which had been introduced by the Folketing into the Budget, and which the government considered utterly irrelevant to the subject, gave rise to disputes; recourse was had to a joint committee, but this did not lead to unanimity, and as therefore the Financial year had run out and the Rigsdag was prorogued, the government on the 12th of April 1877 issued a Provisional Budget, for which step a warrant was said to be found in the Fundamental law paragraph 25, which is as follows: "The king in urgent cases, when the Rigsdag is not sitting, can issue Provisional laws, which however must not be opposed in principle to the Ground-law, and which must be laid before the Rigsdag in the following session". The government, however, in this Provisional law had only included those grants which had been already under debate, and which had been agreed to by both Houses. The principal argument brought forward against this measure by the opposition was, that in the first place it was doubtful whether this paragraph could refer to the Budget, and in the second place the issuing of such Provisional laws was only permissible in emergencies, which could not be said to exist then; for the Ministry, if it could not succeed in establishing unanimity between the two Houses, had the expedient of resorting to the constitutional means at its disposal, either to try a dissolution of the Rigsdag, or to send in their own resignation. But however this may be, this method of cutting the Gordian knot, from the government's point of view, seemed the right tactics to follow; the opposition, within whose circle men of various shades of opinion had hitherto combined for the purpose of contending against their common enemy, the government, was now split up into parties, the result of a disagreement, as to how such a step should be met. The Folketing, as a matter of course, rejected the Provisional budget in the winter of 1877—78, but at the same time gave the Ministry a kind of vindication, for they voted a Budget which essentially agreed with the Provisional law, and next spring the ordinary Budget was also voted for

1878—79. The Ministry, however, had this time withdrawn the plan of the defences. As the split in the opposition continued, the government took the opportunity afforded by a matter of but little moment, to dissolve the Folketing in December 1878, and the Right really made some progress, so that the excitement began somewhat to cool down in the Rigsdag, and the business of the House began again to be carried on, two very important laws for the Army and Navy being passed in 1880.

This lull was but of short duration, for in 1881 the controversy broke out afresh and with renewed vehemence, owing to a bill relating to official salaries introduced into the Budget by the Cabinet. Two successive dissolutions of the Folketing in May and July only served to bring in the Opposition in greater force, and re-established unity among them; whereupon the Ministry gave up the attempt to gain a majority in the Folketing and returned to its former station — exclusively to look to the majority in the Landsting for the necessary support. In spite of continual and repeated debates in both Houses, the Budget was not voted, and the government went through the Finance year of 1881—82 on a so-called Temporary ("midlertidig") budget, not even trying to lay the ordinary budget before the Rigsdag when it met in November 1881. In the following years, the Budget was certainly voted, but the question of fortifying the Capital, which had been again raised in the year 1882, met with decided opposition from the Folketing. At the Folketing elections in June 1884 the opposition gained a greater victory than they had ever had before — about four fifths of the votes being theirs — and when even Copenhagen, which had hitherto been stanch to the government, deserted with half its votes, the Folketing to ensure the resignation of the Ministry resolved to reject all bills proposed by the government, so as to carry out a policy of protest, or as it was called from an expression made use of by one of the opposition, Withering-Policy ("Visnepolitik"), which the Chamber had occasionally employed at an earlier period, and which the

Landsting had also to a certain degree adopted with regard to the bills brought forward through the initiative of the Folketing.

The government however was not at a loss. It subjoined to the Finance bill new and still more considerable grants for the Army and Navy, and when the Folketing on the strength of its majority refused to agree to them — the Landsting meanwhile supporting the government with equal zeal — a provisional Budget was again issued on the 1st April 1885. This included matters of far greater importance than that of 1877, the government not only including those measures agreed to by both Chambers, but also those voted by the Landsting, but refused by the Folketing, notably the military subsidies and preliminary steps for fortifying Copenhagen on the land side. Nor did it stop here. In the autumn, when the Folketing protested in the most violent terms against this so-called infraction of the Fundamental law, and at the same time the people's exasperation rose to so alarming an extent that an attempt was actually made on the life of the Prime-Minister, an act however in which the Opposition had no share, the government found in this crime an ostensible reason for dissolving the Rigsdag and issuing other Provisional laws; among them laws respecting the Police and Gendarmes, a law providing against offences committed by the Press, as also a so-called Rifle Law — forbidding the importation of rifles — a step which proved how seriously the government looked upon the situation. It also took several other steps, and one of them may be described as having a phenomenal character in that the president of the Folketing, M. Berg, was sentenced to six months imprisonment, for having countenanced contumacious conduct against the authorities at a public meeting. Things went so far, that when the Folketing in the beginning of 1886, by rejecting the Provisional budget, sought to cut away the ground under the feet of the Ministry, and it not being possible immediately to fill up the gap by a new Provisional law, as the Rigsdag was still sitting, the Ministry by a Royal order of 26th January 1886 was empowered to defray the current expenses.

Since that time there has been no regular budget, and the government has endeavored to carry out the plan for the land fortifications of Copenhagen, by means of the Provisional budgets of 1886—87, 1887—88, 1888—89, and 1889—90, under continual protest from the Folketing, but on the other hand energetically supported by a large party firmly convinced of the necessity of fortifying the Capital. As was to be expected, the Right gained ground for a time, the result partly of the attempted assassination of the Prime-Minister in the autumn of 1885, which of course caused great consternation, and partly of a judgment given by the Supreme Court on the 15th of October 1886, to the effect that Provisional laws could not be regarded as null and void, though they were rejected after having been brought forward by private initiative, or because they had not been passed in that particular session of the Rigsdag, in which they had been proposed. The government had, in fact, laid the ordinary Provisional laws first before the Landsting, which had hitherto referred them to a Committee without allowing them to go to the Folketing, while this Chamber had rejected them after they had been privately proposed by one of the Members of the opposition. This success of the government party was confirmed by the new Folketing elections in January 1887, in which nearly the whole of the Capital was re-conquered — which of course afforded a strong moral support to the government — though the advantage gained was for the moment without much practical significance, with regard to their position in the Rigsdag, as the Opposition still commands a large majority in the Folketing and has now again, at the elections in January 1890, regained half the Copenhagen seats; and even if the Left have given up their policy of protest (which must be looked upon as having been useless), and have begun to carry on the ordinary legislative work, no profitable result can be attained, the Provisional laws being a stumbling block between the parties, and neither of them being willing to yield. — Such is the situation; matters for the present being at a standstill.

The new House which ascended the throne of Denmark with Christian IX in 1863, is nearly related to the Oldenborg dynasty. The present King's Mother, Louise Caroline, who was married to Wilhelm, Duke of Slesvig-Holstein-Sönderborg-Glücksborg, was a grand-daughter of Frederik V of Denmark, while the Queen, Christian IX's consort, is a grand-daughter of the Hereditary Prince Frederik, a son of the same Frederik V.

Rooted as is the House of Glücksborg in the past, it will doubtless also grow far into the future. It will share fates not only with Denmark, but with most of the Royal families in Europe. A large circle of descendants already surround the no longer youthful sovereigns. The eldest of their six children, Crown-prince Frederik is united to Princess Louise of Sweden and Norway; of their offspring the eldest son, Christian, is the destined heir of Denmark. Princess Alexandra, the next in order, became Princess of Wales. How her aimable qualities have endeared her to her adopted country is well known; — "The Sea-king's daughter from over the sea" — will one day be Queen of England, and Empress over the realm on which the sun never sets. Then follow Georgios I, King of the Hellenes, who seems to have founded a firm throne in that historic land; Princess Dagmar, now Maria Feodorovna Empress of Russia, whose life has been so full of vicissitudes, and whose only moments of thorough repose are spent in her home-land, where the Danes think of her as the bright Princess Dagmar of old; Princess Thyra, married to the Duke of Cumberland, and sharing with him the troubles of his position in honorary exile; and Prince Valdemar, who lately gained the hand of Princess Marie of Orleans, the Duke de Chartres' daughter. Well known is the loving affection which binds this large family together; and the peaceful summer gatherings at the modest Fredensborg Palace with its idyllic surroundings on the shores of Esrom lake in North Sealand have gained nearly European fame. It was under trying circumstances that King Christian IX mounted the throne, and the difficulties and anxieties have scarcely lessened as years have gone. But of one thing the Danes are sure: when the King and Queen retire to meet their summer guests at Fredensborg, and are surrounded by bairns and children-in-law, and the merry flock of youngsters (now 32 in all) rush and romp about them — then they feel happy. Denmark is grateful to them; the example set to the world at large, by the beautiful family life witnessed at the Court, brings many feelings of sympathy and good wishes to the little far off country.

March 1890. **H. Weitemeyer.**

Of sources of Danish history we may name: *Scriptores rerum Danicarum medii ævi*, Copenhagen 1772—1878, 9 vol., edit. by Langebek, Suhm etc. *Monumenta historiæ Danicæ, Historiske Kildeskrifter og Bearbejdelser af dansk Historie, især fra det 16d. Aarhundrede* (Historical sources and essays on Danish history, particularly from the 16th century), Copenhagen 1873—88, edit. by Holger Rördam, 4 vol. *Diplomatarium Arna-Magnæanum*, Copenhagen 1786, 2 vol., edit. by Thorkelin. *Répertoire historique et chronologique des traités conclus par la couronne de Danemark depuis Canut le Grand jusqu'à 1800*, Göttingen 1826, edit. by Reedtz. *Danske Traktater efter 1800* (Danish Treaties after 1800), Copenhagen 1874—86, 4 vol. *Regesta diplomatica historiæ Danicæ*, Copenhagen 1847. *Udvalg af hidtil utrykte danske Diplomer og Breve fra det 14de, 15de og 16de Aarhundrede* (Selection of hitherto unprinted diplomas and letters from the 14th, 15th and 16th century), Copenhagen 1858, edit. by C. Molbech et N. M. Petersen.

Of the numerous Collections and Periodicals, can be specially mentioned: *Suhm, Samlinger til den danske Historie* (Collections for Danish history), Copenhagen 1771—76, 2 vol., and *Nye Samlinger til den danske Historie* (New collections), Copenhagen 1792—95, 4 vol. *Dänische Bibliothek*, Copenhagen and Leipzig 1738—47, 9 sheets, edit. by Harboe, Langebek and Möller. *Sagabibliothek* (Cyclus of Sagas), Copenhagen 1817—20, 3 vol., edit by P. E. Müller. *Danske Samlinger for Historie, Topographie, Personal- og Literaturhistorie* (Danish collections for history, topography, Personal and Literary hist.), Copenhagen 1866—79, 12 vol. *Aarsberetninger fra det kongelige Geheimearchiv, indeholdende Bidrag til dansk Historie af utrykte Kilder* (Yearly Accounts from the Royal Privy Archives, containing contributions to Danish history from unprinted sources), Copenhagen 1852—83, 7 vol. *Danske Magazin* (Danish Magazine), Copenhagen 1745—. *Historisk Tidsskrift* (Historical Review), Copenhagen

1840—. *Kirkehistoriske Samlinger* (Collections for the history of the Church), Copenhagen 1849—, etc.

Of treatises on the entire history of Denmark or large parts of it: *Saxonis Grammatici historiæ Danicæ libri XVI*, edit. par P. E. Müller et Velschow, Copenhagen 1839—58, 3 vol. (in Danish by Anders Sörensen Vedel 1575, and by N. F. S. Grundtvig 1818—22). *Adami Bremensis historia ecclesiastica* (in Danish by Christensen, Copenhagen 1862). *Arild Hvitfeldt*, Danmarks Riges Krönike tilligemed Bispekröniken (Chronicle of the kingdom of Denmark together with the Chronicle of the Bishops), Copenhagen 1595—1604, 10 vol. 4°, et 1652, 2 vol. Fol. *J. Meursius*, Historia Danica, Florence 1746. *Ludvig Holberg*, Danmarks Riges Historie (History of the kingdom of Denmark), Copenhagen 1732—35, 3 vol. *Gebhardi*, Geschichte der Königreiche Dänemark und Norwegen, Halle 1770, 2 vol. *Mallet*, Histoire de Danemark, Copenhagen 1758—77, 3 vol. *Suhm*, Historie af Danmark fra de ældste Tider til Aar 1400 (History of Denmark from the oldest times to the year 1400), Copenhagen 1782—1828, 14 vol. (in German, Leipzig 1830, 2 vol.). *Baden*, Danmarks Riges Historie (History of the kingdom of Denmark), Copenhagen 1829—32, 5 vol. *Anderson*, Norse Mythology or the Religion of our forefathers, 4 edit., Chicago 1888 (also in French). *N. M. Petersen*, Danmarks Historie i Hedenold (History of Denmark in the times of Paganism), 2 edit., Copenhagen 1854—55, 3 vol. *L. C. Müller*, Danmarks Historie (History of Denmark), Copenhagen 1836—40, 3 vol. (goes to the reign of Christian II). *Dahlmann*, Geschichte von Dänemark, Hamburg 1840—43, 3 vol. (goes to the year 1523). *Chr. Molbech*, Fortællinger og Skildringer af den danske Historie (Narrations and pictures from the history of Denmark), Copenhagen 1837—38, 2 vol. (goes to the year 1200). *C. F. Allen*, Haandbog i Fædrelandets Historie (Manual of the history of Denmark), 8. edit., Copenhagen 1881 (into French, Copenhagen 1878; into German, Kiel 1842, but neither conformed to the Danish edition, nor accepted by the author). *Jahn*, Danmarks politisk-militære Historie under Unions-kongerne, fra Kong Oluf og Dronning Margrethe indtil Kong Hanses Död (Political-military history of Denmark under the kings of the Union, from king Oluf and queen Margrethe to the death of king Hans), Copenhagen 1835. *C. F. Allen*, De tre nordiske Rigers Historie under Hans, Christian II, Frederik I, Gustav Vasa og Grevefejden (History of the three Scandinavian kingdoms under Hans, Christian II, Frederik I, Gustav Vasa and the Count's War), Copenhagen 1864—72, 5 vol. (the work, which only goes to the year 1526, was interrupted by the death of the author). *C. Paludan-Müller*, De förste Konger af den oldenborgske Slægt (the first kings of the Oldenborg dynasty), Copenhagen 1874. *N. Bache*, Nordens Historie (History of the Scandinavian kingdoms), Copenhagen, 2. edit., 1879—87, 5 vol. *Thorsöe*, Den danske Stats politiske Historie fra 1800 til 1848 (Political history of the Danish

State from 1800 until 1848), Copenhagen 1872—78, 2 vol. *C. F. Allen*, Det danske Sprogs Historie i Slesvig (History of the Danish language in Slesvig), Copenhagen 1857—58, 2 vol. (in German, Slesvig 1857—58 . *Troels Lund*, Danmarks og Norges Historie i Slutningen af det 16de Aarhundrede (History of Denmark and Norway to the end of the 16th century), Copenhagen 1879—; 8 vol. are to be published (2 and 3 in German: Das tägliche Leben in Skandinavien während des 16ten Jahrh., Copenhagen 1882). *E. Holm*, Danmark-Norges indre Historie under Enevælden fra 1660—1720 (The interior history of Denmark-Norway under Absolutism), Copenhagen 1885—86, 2 vol. *Worsaae*, Minder om de Danske og Nordmændene i England, Skotland og Irland (The Danes and Northmen in England, Scotland and Ireland), Copenhagen 1851 (in English, London 1852, in German, Leipzig 1852). *J. C. H. R. Steenstrup*, Normannerne (The Northmen), Copenhagen 1876—82, 4 vol. (1 in French: Etudes préliminaires à l'histoire des Normands et de leur invasion, 1880). *A. D. Jørgensen*, Bidrag til Nordens Historie i Middelalderen (Contributions to the history of the North during the middle-ages), Copenhagen 1871. *A. D. Jørgensen*, Den nordiske Kirkes Grundlæggelse og første Udvikling (Foundation and first development of the Church in the North), Copenhagen 1874—78, 2 vol. *E. Holm*, Danmark-Norges udenrigske Historie under den franske Revolution og Napoleons Krige fra 1790—1807 (History of the foreign policy of Denmark-Norway during the French Revolution and the Napoleon Wars), Copenhagen 1875, 2 vol. *Vaupell*, Den danske Hærs Historie indtil Nutiden, og den norske Hærs Historie indtil 1814 (History of the Danish army till our own time, and hist. of the Norwegian army till 1814), Copenhagen 1872—79, 2 vol. *Garde*, Den dansk-norske Sømagts Historie (History of the Danish-Norwegian maritime power), Copenhagen 1852—61, 2 vol. *Stemann*, Den danske Retshistorie indtil Christian V's Lov (History of the Danish law until the law of Christian V), Copenhagen 1870. *Holger Rørdam*, Kjøbenhavns Universitets Historie, 1537—1621 (History of the University of Copenhagen), Copenhagen 1868—77, 4 vol.

Respecting the comprehensive historical literature, which treats of shorter periods or individual history, we refer to the detailed bibliography subjoined to "*Allen*, Haandbog i Fædrelandets Historie" (enlarged in the French edition), and to the yearly historical literary reviews, which are to be found in the "Historisk Tidsskrift" (commencing with the year 1875).

COUNTRY AND PEOPLE

Aa in Danish is pronounced as o, æ as ay in Day, ö nearly o in Word, y as the Romance and Old-Greek u, sj as sy, often however the j is silent, as in Kjöbenhavn: d is often soft like the English th, sometimes partly silent as at the end of Sjælland.

---

1 Meter = 3,281 English feet (a Danish foot = 1,030 English); 1 kilometer = 0.621 English miles (a Geographical mile = 4,611 English, a Danish mile = 4,681 English). A square mile = 2,8503 sq: kilom: (a Geographical sq: mile = 55,0628 sq: kilom:).

Denmark, since the peace of Vienna in 1864, consists of the northern half of Jylland (Jutland)[1] or as it has often been called the Cimbrian Chersonesus, stretching northwards from central Europe, and some 150 large and small islands between Jylland and the southern shores of the Scandinavian peninsula, from the Kattegat to the Baltic ("Östersöen"). These isles form, as it were, a natural bridge between the two more northerly folk-groups, kinsmen of the Danes, and their southern neighbor Germany. In the Prehistoric age, the Ice-period, they were probably landfast with upper Scandinavia and with central Europe, until the upheaval of the Scandian coasts and the excavation of the Sounds by the ocean, sundered this connection and changed the Östersö from a lake to an inland sea. The time when Denmark was exclusive Mistress of this water-way is long past. It is more than 200 years since she was forced to share with Sweden the Sound between Sjælland (Sealand) and Scania (Skåne), and in 1864 one side of the Little Belt was ceded to Germany. Now only the middle passage, the Great Belt, is owned by Denmark.

In length and breadth the country is very inconsiderable. From the South boundary line of North Jylland — which runs nearly parallel with the stream Kongeaaen — to the uttermost North point of Skagen (the Skaw) is only about 280 kilometers. The island of Falster with its tongue of land Gjedserodde, is however still further

[1] The geographical names will, in this chapter, as far as possible be retained in Danish.

South than Kongeaaen; the distance hence to the Skagen is about 360 kilom:. Gjedserodde lies under $54^0 34'$ N. Lat:, Skagen under $57^0 45'$ N. Lat:. The most westerly point on the North-sea, Blaavandshuk, lies under $8^0 5'$ E. Long: from Greenwich; while the most easterly, Bornholm, is under $15^0 10'$ E. Long:. Saltholm in Öresund (the Sound) which is the most easterly of the Danish islands proper, reaches only $12^0 47'$ E. Long:, and from Saltholm to Blaavandshuk is about 300 kilom.

Denmark is one of the smallest European kingdoms, 8 times less than Britain, 13 or 14 smaller than France or Germany, and about 20 times less than Sweden-Norway. Its area is 38,300 square kilom: (about 696 square geographical miles). Of these North Jylland comprises about two thirds or 25,200 square kilom: 13,150 sq: kilom: falling to the Islands.

I

The Sea and the Coasts

Before describing the natural features of this country, we must dwell a little on its surrounding waters, which have always had great significance for both the land and the people, and have largely helped to give them their special character.

With the exception of the long reach of land (about 90 kilom:) which connects North Jylland with Slesvig, Denmark has sea on all sides. The West coast of Jylland is exposed to the North-sea, or "Vesterhavet" (the West-sea) as it is called by the Danes; herefrom the Skagerak between Jylland and Norway runs into the Kattegat, between the East of Jylland to the South of Sweden. From the Kattegat the three Belts lead again to the Östersö; whose billows wash the southern shores of the Danish isles. Denmark has thus a great stretch of coast, the more as so large a part consists of islands, and the outline is computed at about 4,000 kilom:. But this coast-length is greatly increased by the numerous and comparatively broad and large inlets or "fjords" (creeks, bays, coves) which the action of the waves has formed in the loose soil. Thus there is almost "a Danish mile of sea-board to every square mile of land." The coast formation is so far favorable; on the other hand, the shores are frequently low and sandy and good harbors scarce, tho in some measure this is counter-balanced by the Fjords which run great distances inland. Another difficulty is the shallowness of the water near land, and the shelves and sandbanks, which form lines beyond the projecting promontories and jut far out into the sea. The navigation is rendered dangerous also by the numerous narrow channels between the islands, and by the strong and changeful currents. In many places a pilot must be employed. About one hundred Lighthouses and Lightships testify sufficiently to these difficulties.

To the above named extreme variety of shore the West coast of Jylland however forms an exception. The so-called "Jernkyst" (Iron coast) runs in one immense line, about 375 kilom: long, bending only in large curves, from the south western extremity (the projecting Blaavandshuk) outside which stretches the dangerous Horns Rev (Horn reef) 40 kilom: into the sea; to the most northerly point or the Skagen which ends in the sharp projection "Grenen" (the Branch). The strong current surging along sweeps or smoothes away the loose sandy or clayey strata of which the soil consists, and steadily eats out the land. To protect the most exposed points there have been constructed of late "Höfder" (breakwaters), stake lines filled in with sea-weed, concrete etc, and running as much as 90 meters into the sea. Only when the soil-strata are somewhat firm, can they resist the ocean; and we thus get such projecting capes as Blaavandshuk and further North Hanstholmen with Roshage, Bolbjerg with the isolated seagirt chalk cliff Skarreklit, and lastly the promontory of Hirshals, or the Ness. It is a singularly inhospitable coast, reminding one of "Les Landes" in the S. W. of France. No harbors are to be found, and the efforts hitherto made to supply this want have come to nothing; probably the natural difficulties cannot be surmounted. Inside the coast line, where the sand accumulates in Downs, or as they are called in those districts "Klitter", the sea forms coast-lakes, some of which are connected with the sea by narrow Sounds, which divide the sand-klitter, without however affording any shelter for ships; the coast is too dangerous for them to approach, the inlets are too shallow and the strand-lakes too full of shoals. Ringkjöbing Fjord with the inlet Nymindegab is the most important of these lakes, Nissumfjord with the entrance at Thorsminde is very insignificant. Finally somewhat farther northwards there is the narrow Aggertange, which separates the Limfjord from the Western ocean; early in this century the tongue of land was broken thro by the sea, forming the Aggerkanal which again silted up, but a new opening took the place, the Thyborönkanal. Thus the Limfjord was formerly really a Fjord, but is now a Sound, 160 kilom: in length, stretching across Jylland, cutting through the North of the peninsula, and making it an island for itself. The Limfjord is however not adapted for navigation, being very irregular in its course, either narrowing into small channels or suddenly widening into the so-called "Bredninger" (basins) and often obstructed by sandbanks and shallows. The whole of this coast is dreaded, more than most others, by mariners; for parallel with the land are two (from Skagen to Hanstholmen) or three (from Hanstholmen to Blaavandshuk) sandbanks, where there is little water (on the outer bank 6, on the inner 2 to 4 meters), while between and outside is a much greater depth. Storm, current or fog often drive vessels onto these reefs, and then there is but little chance of escape. The ship strikes on the bank and is broken by the tremendous force of the billows, while the crew frequently perish, or are only saved by daring and venturesome helpers from the shore. Since the introduction of Life-boats and Rocket-apparatus etc, destruction is much less, and many a man, in silence and unknown, has there done noble deeds equal to the grandest exploits in history. Vigsöbugt and Jammerbugt

(Bay of Calamity) between the before-mentioned Roshage and Hirshals, are sadly known as the scenes of terrible shipwrecks.

After passing thro the Skagerak — which is clear of rocks and somewhat protected from storms by the high cliffs of Norway — and having doubled the Skagen point, we are in the Kattegat (Sinus Codanus). Not even here is navigation without its perils, owing to the strong and irregular currents, and the many reefs and shoals. Towards the centre especially, from North to South, runs a line of islands, Læsö, Anholt and Hesselö, with no deep water between them. They divide the Kattegat into two sea-ways, of which the western nearest Jylland is most used, as being most free from banks and shallows, but also because ships are more protected from the frequent westerly storms. In addition, the East coast of Jylland has several harbors, tho only Frederikshavn and Aarhus are of any great importance. On the whole, the East side has not the monotonous character of the West. Both have the same loose soil, but the East has not the steady wearing current, and can boast many more spots with solid ground and rocky ledges, able to resist the waves. Especially is the sameness broken by the peninsula Djursland midway on the eastern coast, with its South side deeply indented by the sea. This district has also many fjords and a pleasant aspect, with green banks, partly wooded, sloping to the water's edge. The northerly section, however, as far as the Limfjord, is partly a belt of drifting sand, like the western side. North of Djursland, besides the eastern entrance to the Limfjord, are Mariager and Randers Fjords, and to the South of Djursland Aarhus bay and Horsensfjord.

The northern coasts of the two large islands Fyn (Funen) and Sjælland have a somewhat similar character. On the former Odense Fjord cuts deeply in, bounded on the East by the peninsula Hindsholm; while in Sjælland the Isefjord stretches far inland with its many branches, of which the longest is Roskildefjord. West of the Isefjord, the long narrow neck of land Sjællandsodde, with its dangerous Sjællandsrev, stretches into the sea.

Of the three water-ways between the Kattegat and the Östersö, Lille Belt (between Jylland and Fyn) is the most westerly. Its breadth varies much. Northwards, between Snoghöi and Middelfart, it is barely 80 meters but it widens southwards to 30 kilom: or more. The scenery along the Belt, with its verdant and often wooded hillocks and numerous islets is very beautiful. The traffic is small, vessels avoiding its violent currents and many shoals. The most important of the many inlets are Vejle, Haderslev and Aabenraa fjords on the Jylland side, and Gamborgfjord in Fyn.

Store Belt (the Great Belt) between Fyn and Sjælland, is far from being so irregular as Lille Belt; its breadth varies only from 18 to 30 kilom:. The Steam-ferry plies where it is narrowest, from Nyborg to Korsör. There are many inlets here also, Kjærteminde and Nyborgfjord in Fyn and Kalundborgfjord in Sjælland being the chief. Small islands abound. The tiny Sprogö, midway between Nyborg and Korsör, is familiar to all travellers on this route. It is best known as being the Station for Ice-transports. In severe winters, when the Belt is partly frozen, the crossing is often most difficult, and can only be attempted in open boats pushed along with oars in the water, or dragged by main force when the ice will bear. Towards the South however the islets form a more numerous group, the long narrow Langeland making as it were two channels. That towards the East expands to a large Bay between "Smaalandsbugten" (the Bay between the small lands). Store Belt (a little deeper than the Lille Belt) is the deepest of the three Sounds, being over 60 meters in some places. Even the largest men-of-war can go through it, but like Lille Belt it is so obstructed by shoals that it is but seldom used.

The real practical route into the Östersö is the wellknown "Öresund" or as it is generally called "Sundet" (the Sound), which divides Sjælland from the Swedish province of Scania. From 30,000 to 40,000 vessels pass thro it yearly. It commences at Gildbjerghoved in Sjælland and at the celebrated cliff "Kullen" in Scania, whence it reaches funnel-shaped to the narrowest part between the Danish

Helsingör (Elsinore) and the Swedish Helsingborg. Here it is scarcely 4,000 meters broad, and it is properly only this ribbon of water which is called Öresund. It expands widely at this spot and onwards to the South point of Amager, where it is reckoned to end, so that between Kjöbenhavn (Copenhagen) and Malmö it is over 30 kilom:. Thus it is the shortest of the three water-ways, only about 75 kilom:. Ships generally sail to the West of the little island of Hveen (famous in connection with Tycho Brahe the Astronomer), which has been Swedish since the peace of Roskilde in 1658; then thro Hollænderdybet and Drogden, the course between Amager and Saltholm. Drogden is in one place only somewhat over 7 meters in depth, and ships drawing more water cannot enter that way. Flinterenden, a channel between Saltholm and Scania is somewhat broader and quite as deep as Drogden, but owing to the shoals and strong westerly gales, is seldom navigated. To the North of Drogden the deep Kongedybet, which is separated from Hollænderdyb by the Middelgrund runs to Kjöbenhavn. The narrow and shallow Kallebodstrand, between Sjælland and Amager, flows into Kjögebugt. A sail along the Danish coast from Helsingör to Kjöbenhavn is most delightful, the leaf-garlanded dots of forest slopings, fields and gardens, picturesque fishing hamlets and attractive villas, offering a varied panorama.

When Denmark levied a tax on all vessels passing the Sounds, as they mostly went thro Öresund past Kjöbenhavn, it was called Öresundstolden (the Sound Dues). In olden times this was one of the most lucrative sources of revenue to the country, and has even been called Denmark's "Golden Vein"; latterly however it decreased more and more, and in 1857 this superannuated shackle on commerce was abolished by a Convention of the Maritime Powers.

The south-western side of the Östersö, which washes the southern shores of the Danish islands, is a bay branching in all directions, forming among others Kjöge and Faxebugt on the S. E. of Sjælland; and winding in and out among the islets in narrow straits. The principal of these are Ulfsund between Sjælland and Möen, Grönsund between Möen and Falster and Guldborgsund between Falster and Laaland. All these shores are mostly low, especially Laaland, and are exposed to inundations at periods of high water. The spring-tide in November 1872 committed great devastations. Protecting dykes are therefore in course of construction. The enormous mass of water conveyed by the rivers into the Östersö is the cause of the inconsiderable saline properties contained in this inland sea, and at the same time produces the northerly current prevailing through the Belts, particularly the Sund.

II

The Country

With the exception of Bornholm Denmark is a continuation of the central European plain, and therefore a complete lowland; no portion rises above 200 meters and more than half the land is under 30. The islands, especially, lie so low, that were a depression of 30 meters to occur the greater number would disappear. Yet Denmark cannot be called a level country; only occasionally, as in western Jylland, are large level plains found. On the islands they are so rare, that in common parlance they are distinctly known as the "Heath" or the Common. As a general rule the surface of the country is uneven and undulating; the banks, never of any great height, are separated by small dales which hinder anything like a continuous range. On the islands these hilly tracts occur most irregularly; in Jylland the outlook is easier, as the elevations keep to the eastern and central part. The old theory of a continuous chain running thro the peninsula from North to South, must be abandoned after the careful measurements lately made by the Danish General Staff. But of this later.

The surface of this kingdom has therefore no special interest, and the same holds good generally of its geognostic characteristics. The country has not been exposed, like many others, to violent upheavals or depressions, and as a rule the layers are regular and horizontal lying just as the water formed them. Of course we except Bornholm, the southerly spur of the Scandinavian peninsula's granite mass. Here as in the Middle-European plains the substratum is composed of firmer layers, belonging to the Chalk and Tertiary or Lignite formation; they are however covered by looser strata of diluvial origin, mostly clay and sand, mixed with large and small stones. It is this surface stratum which is called the Drift, chiefly a Moraine produced in the Ice period; Chalk and Lignite being deposited in the sea and gradually raised. Only in a few places along the coasts, or in the deeper channels worn by hill-streams, is the substratum laid bare. The well-known Geologist Forchhammer has pointed out that this upheaval of Denmark out of the sea is still going on, North of a line drawn from Nissumfjord towards the S. E. over Nyborg. Tho this uplifting is slight, yet from the lowness of the coasts it has exercised no small influence on the geographical conditions of the country.

Eastwards, Chalk, the oldest formation, lies nearest the surface. Brown-coal, the younger layer, is found in the West. More correctly, they are in a line from N. W. to S. E., thus the further from this line S. W. the more distinct is the younger stratum. The Chalk formation, which consists of various kinds of chalk and flint (Faxechalk, Limestone, Saltholmchalk) is chiefly found in a zone from S. E. to N. W. in Möen, Falster and the eastern parts of Laaland, in the S. and E. of Sjælland, in Jylland on the Djursland near Grenaa; but also in a broad band from Randers to Bolbjerg and around the Limfjord. In many places the chalk is close to the surface, or even exposed in the cliffs, thus on Möens Klint, where the layer is broken and thrown about helter skelter, Stevnsklint on the S. E. of Sjælland and Bredstrupklint near Grenaa. Lignite (micaceous clay and sand combined with wood-coal, amber and a kind of slate called "Moler") forms the substratum in the S. and W. of Jylland, but is also met with in patches elsewhere, as in the W. of Sjælland and near Middelfart in Fyn. In the Drift a distinction must be made between boulder-clay (glacial clay) and bouldersand (glacial sand) and Heath-sand. The boulder-clay consists of a grey or yellow-brown clay mixed with stones of every size, the greater part not larger than a grain of sand, others of considerable dimensions; the biggest is the Hesselagersten in Fyn, about 45 meters in circumference. Boulder-clay is especially met with on the islands and on the East coasts of Jylland from Mariager to the South, but is also seen in spots in other parts of the peninsula both North and West of Limfjorden. It is not in layers and has mostly a wavy exterior, is very fertile and especially adapted for the beech. Boulder-sand is mixed with a more or less ferruginous yellow or reddish-yellow clay and pebbles, and is found partly on the islands; for instance in North Sjælland and the peninsula of Hornsherred, the North of Fyn between Middelfart and Assens, in the South in the big hills called the "Fyn Alps", but its chief home is Jylland. There it crops up in nearly the whole of Vendsyssel, stretching in a wide belt to the West of the boulder-clay from the Limfjord southwards to the central parts and onwards still westwards in large sections. The boulder-sand lies in very clearly defined layers and generally forms a very uneven surface especially in the middle of Jylland, the so-called Hill-Heaths. It is not so rich as the boulder-clay, but can be cultivated; of late years successful trials have been made to transform the ling-covered banks into arable land. These Moors have formerly been forest land, tho the trees have disappeared from neglect and carelessness; in many parts copses of stunted oak still remain. To the West of the ling-clad hills is the Heath-sand, the least productive part of the country. The complete sterility of these tracts is increased by a later (alluvial) formation, the "Al" — the "Alios" of the French Landes. It is produced under the Heath-sand by the action of the ferruginous sand on the decayed vegetation (ling-mould). All this becomes so compact a mass, that the roots of trees cannot force themselves through it. The commonest kind is the Sand-al, but there is also the Sten-al and the Jern-al (Iron-al) or Myremalm (bog-ore). This last is the most injurious but the scarcest, as it is only found in patches, mostly in the hollows. The Mosses and Downs (or Dunes) are also of a later date. The former are Forest, Fen or Heather-bogs and chiefly occur in Jylland. They are of considerable importance on account of the Peat, which is largely used for fuel. The Forest-bogs are the lowest, and as the quality of the turf increases with the depth, these Mosses furnish the best peat. Along the West coast of Jylland, the Down formation goes on from the sand cast up by the sea, which the wind drives into mounds. Contrary to what happens elsewhere, these never reach a greater height than 30 meters, and steadily push inland. These Dunes are also exceptionally found elsewhere, as on Læsö, Anholt and the South of Bornholm, also in North Sjælland at Tidsvilde. Endeavors are made in Jylland, as on the French Dunes, to stop this flight of sand by planting. But whilst they use Fir, we employ sea-reed, lyme-grass and creeping willow. The Downs occupy an area of about 600 sq: kilom:; the Moors with the elevations between them, the so-called Hill-isles (Bakkeöer), take up ten times this space.

The land being so small and the elevations so trivial, Denmark has no large running waters. They therefore bear the modest name "Aa" (rivulet). The longest is only about 160 kilom:, and even this (Gudenaa) is considerable compared with the others. They have no importance as to communication. There are many lakes, most of them in Jylland; but they are small, the largest 40 sq: kilom:. The small streamlets winding between the hillocks, and the tiny lakes nestling in the fo est shades contribute greatly towards the peculiar charm and grace of the Danish landscape.

We must now enter more fully into details regarding the surface formation of the different parts of the country.

The islands are divided into two clusters by the comparatively broad and deep Store Belt: the Sjælland group comprises Sjælland, Möen, Falster, Laaland and the surrounding smaller islands; the

Fyn group consists of Fyn, Langeland, Taasinge, Ærö and some islets. The sea-way separating the two groups is so shallow, that a lowering of the sea a few meters would transform them into two large islands.

Of the **Sjælland** cluster the main island is, on the whole, the highest; the most elevated points are found it is true on the East coast of Möen, but the rest of the little isle lies very low.

Sjælland contains about 6,900 sq: kilom:, and the highest point, Gyldenlöves Höj, rises to 126 meters about midway between Roskilde and Ringsted, and from this central position four water-sheds can be followed, which, without forming any consecutive chain, stretch towards the coast with great curves and imperceptible elevations. Thus a series of heights run West or N. W. to the peninsula of Refsnæs, forming the boundary of Kalundborg Fjord to the North; and in the same way another lesser range goes S. W. to Skjelskör. The N. E. water-shed can be followed over Maglehöj (69 meters) near Roskilde and further northwards thro North Sjælland (the peninsula between the Sund and Isefjord) to the neighborhood of Frederiksborg, where at Skansebakke it rises to 77 meters. Thence it continues N. E. as far as Kronborg point. The fourth water-shed meanders southwards East of Ringsted, along low hills until East of Næstved it changes bluffly. Here Kobanke, the second height in Sjælland, reaches 123 meters. Near by are Globanke and Overdrevsbakken, about 116 meters. The flow runs on South to the East of Vordingborg. These sections divide the island into four parts, which drop gradually, issuing at the four points of the compass. The eastern slope along the Öresund from Helsingör to Kjöbenhavn is very narrow; the hills extend nearly to the shore, and form lovely forest or corn clad declivities. The streams between the hillocks are very small; Möllena, one of the largest, is the outlet for several of the tiny but beautiful North Sjælland lakes, such as Fure and Farumsö. South of Kjöbenhavn the higher grounds draw back, and make room for a considerable plain between Kjöbenhavn, Roskilde and Kjöge. A part S. E. of Roskilde, called "Heden" (the Heath) is fruitful and nearly level, very sparingly wooded, with an area of about 650 sq: kilom:. Stevnsherred, between the bays Kjöge and Faxe, is likewise tolerably even, rising a little near the sea, where we meet the naked chalky steep of Stevnsklint, whose highest point is only 41 meters. The northerly gradient by the Kattegat is most irregular, owing to the deeply penetrating Isefjord with its many branches. The North of North Sjælland shows undulations and high banks along the coast, and the watercourses generally collect into lakes, such as Gurre and Esromsö at Fredensborg; but the largest lake Arresö (about 40 kilom:) must be regarded as belonging to the Isefjord basin. Southward from here, along the Roskildefjord, is lowland with marches and small streams, while South of the Fjord and in the narrow and irregular peninsulas of Hornsherred and Odsherred the ground is more broken; on the borders of the latter Vejrshöj reaches 121 meters. The neighborhood of Holbæk and to the South of the now drained Lammefjord, is low and full of bogs and wet meadows. The western slope along Store Belt is more regular in width; the largest stream is Hallebyaa, which from the central heights of Sjælland runs thro the considerable Aamose and Tissö. The southern declivity towards Smaalandsbugt, has its chief channel in Suseaa, the largest of the island rivers, with a length of somewhat over 80 kilom:; it receives the waters of several small lakes, among them Tjustrup and Bavelse, and passes Næstved.

The flattest islands in the Sjælland group are Falster (470 sq: kilom:) and Laaland (about 1150 sq: kilom:); the last especially scarcely anywhere rises above 30 meters, whilst the West Laaland plain is nearly level to the westward. The western side of little Möen (200 sq: kilom:) is also low and level, while the eastern half (Höje Möen, High Möen) has in Kongsbjerg (142 meters) and Aborrebjerg (141) the highest points in the Sjælland cluster. Müensklint with its steep chalk cliffs is not quite so high, tho Hylledalsfjeld measures 129 meters; the range is split by a good many wooded clefts called "Fald", fantastical and picturesque in shape, as is witnessed by such names as Dronningestolen (The Queen's Chair) and Sommerspiret (The Summer Peak). The white chalk, the green beeches and the blue waves make an unusual and lovely color-picture.

In the **Fyn** group, usually loftier than the Sjælland, the main island (above 3,000 sq: kilom:) again predominates in height. Here also is a fall to the four points; but not from the centre as in Sjælland, rather near the South coast, the inclines being greatest in the North and West. The southern fall, between Faaborg and Svendborg is very narrow and hilly, especially about Svendborg, where the scenery is famous for its beauty. West of these hillocks on the South, where Lerbjerg near Faaborg rises to 126 meters, stretches N. W. a range of heights called in jest "the Alps of Fyn" — of these Trebjerg attains 128 meters, — and over lower districts this can be traced across to Frö-bjerg Bavnehöj (130 meters), the highest point on the island. It continues in low banks to Strib on the Lille Belt, where the Fyn line of railway ends and the Steam ferry crosses to Fredericia. Its water-shed may thus be said to follow these hills from Faaborg to Strib N. W., while that to the N. E., from the southern heights stretches North to the peninsula Hindsholm East of Odense Fjord, but with evener knolls. The eastern slope following Store Belt southerly to Nyborg is loftier and more broken. The streamlets wind about and cut deep channels among the hills. North of Nyborg the strand districts flatten. The western incline along Lille Belt, is divided by several ranges into basins, each with its own little main current. The northern slope is the largest; to the South it is tolerably hilly, but sinks by degrees till at Odense Fjord we have "Sletten", a perfect plain. West of that Fjord the steeps approach the North coast without quite reaching it. The largest water of the northern bend is Odenseaa (50 kilom: in length), starting from Areskovsö and running North past Odense into the Fjord. — Among the smaller islands of the Fyn group, Langeland (275 sq: kilom:) is level throughout, Ærö (85 sq: kilom:) is extremely hilly and the North of Taasinge (70 sq: kilom:) has a bank rising 74 meters on whose summit, if we climb Bregninge Church Tower, we get a wide and picturesque view of the array of islands.

An examination of the surface conditions in **Jylland** must, as already stated, prove the complete fallacy of the older theory of a chain of hills, in continuation of the low central European plateau along the Östersö, the so-called Ural-Baltic range. This was said to traverse the peninsula close to the East coast, and North of the Limfjord to Skagen, dividing Jylland into a minor eastern and a larger western portion. Recent surveys show that eastern and middle Jylland are highest, the western and lower section shelving gradually to the North-sea. Even tho we admit a partial water-shed line in the great bends from South to North, it does not run parallel to the hill line, which is rather from S. W. to N. E., between Aarhus and Randers in a series of formless clayey low plateaus, often separated by comparatively considerable depressions. Some of these were formerly Sounds, large or small insulated portions of land; afterwards dried by the upheaval of the country. To prove the theory of the hill-range, the water-courses which move transversly, have been appealed to; but there is no lack of streams going longitudinally. Gudenaa, the most considerable of our rivers, is of the latter class; and little rills radiate from most of the banks in all directions.

South of East Jylland the mounds are slight, only a few points reaching 80 meters; the highest is Skamlingsbanke (113 meters) South of Kolding close to the coast. Not till North of Vejleaa and Vejlefjord do we meet the highest part of Jylland, S. W. to N. E., between the towns of Skanderborg and Silkeborg. Immediately North of Vejleaa Möllebjerg reaches 137 meters, and the neighborhood of Vejle, with the deep valley of Greisdal, is considered one of the finest parts in Denmark. But the culminating height is North of Horsens and South of Skanderborg, the Ejer Bavnehöj (172 meters), the greatest elevation in the country, and Himmelbjerget S. E. of Silkeborg. The last is slightly lower (165 and 157 meters), but the more celebrated, as from the top is a charming view over the hills and dales, the many little lakes between large forests, heather clad slopes, cornfields and pretty villages. To the eyes of a dweller in the plains this becomes a mountainous region. As has been said, the hills continue in a N. E. direction as far as Randers with elevations of 100 to 150 meters. Offshoots stretch far East, in many places touching the strand, whence they form steep acclivities, as all along the pretty country about Aarhus. Elsewhere they make room for level coast plains, for instance near Horsensfjord. Most of the peninsula Djursland is however quite low, only in the small irregular deltas branching out southwards are eminencies of 100 meters and over (Agribjerge is 126 meters). Also in the North of East Jylland from Randersfjord to Limfjord, some hills exceed 100 meters between Randers and Mariager Fjords, as also in Himmerland between the latter and Limfjord. Here however the heights are more central with predominating plateaus, whilst small rivulets run E. to the Kattegat, N. and W. to the Limfjord. The upland continues in low ridges to the West as far as Limfjord, but to the East the knolls fall off quickly, giving place to a broadish flat country. Here, South of the entrance to the Limfjord is an impenetrable swamp, the little Vildmose (50 sq: kilom:).

As we have said, some hill-tops are, as in East Jylland, separated by glens once probably sounds, now traversed by rivulets. Such deep beds are Nörreaa between Viborg and Randersfjord (at Viborg only 4 meters above the sea); and Skalsaa from Limfjord eastwards to Mariagerfjord, the southern boundary of Himmerland. But the largest valley in Denmark is formed by the depression of the Gudenaa, at Silkeborg just over 18 and at Randers only 1 meter above sea level. The Gudenaa runs thro it having a length of 158 kilom:, the largest and boldest watercourse in Denmark, its upland being about 2800 sq: kilom:. It starts N. W. of Vejle and winding northwards (lengthways, "Længdeaa") thro the lakelets spoken of at Himmelbjerg and Silkeborg which altogether make only 50 sq: kilom:; after emerging from the lakes at Silkeborg, Gudenaa begins its downward course along the valley to Randersfjord, receiving several brooks, among others Nörreaa. Its last section is 45 to 60 meters broad and reaches a depth of 6 meters. From Silkeborg it is utilized by small boats and barges for the transport of wood from the forests around.

South and middle Jylland as far as Limfjord contains the "Flader" (flats) of the western subsidences of the heights we have described; but the transition is so abrupt, that it naturally gave rise to the idea of a connected ridge. The flats, the well-known chiefly ling-clad Jutlandish heaths, are by no means so level as they seem at first. They are often interrupted by large or small banks, the so-called "Bakke-öer" (hill-isles) whence there is a wide view over the even plains; the most considerable are between Skjern and Storaa, in which last district some mounds exceed 100 meters. The watercourses of these Flats have scarcely any fall and a slower current than the small streams meandering among the hills to the eastward coast. Most of them run transversly and receive tributaries from the bank-islets. Among these rivulets the Kongeaa (above 65 kilom:) is the southern boundary of the kingdom for nearly 30 kilom:; the Vardeaa, (nearly 100 kilom:) falls into the Hjertingbugt; and the Skjernaa (90 kilom: long) has its springs close to that of Gudenaa, with the next largest tributary territory (about 2400 sq: kilom:) of any Danish river. At its mouth in the Ringkjöbingfjord it forms a delta, as also does the Storaa (over 100 kilom:) which runs North into Nissumfjord. North of the basin of the Storaa, the country slopes chiefly to the North as far as Limfjord. Here several tiny rills flow straight on, the most considerable being the 80 kilom: long Skiveaa or Karupaa.

We have still to describe the North Jylland isle, the country North of Limfjord. It may be said to have the same aspect as the rest of Jylland. The irregular hills here are also divided by hollows, and the country is supposed originally to have been islands, Vendsyssel the eastern, Thyland the western, and so Mors — which is still a holm — all enclosed by the arms of the Limfjord.

The real Höjvendsyssel begins a little North of Limfjord, reaching to a line between Frederikshavn and Hirshals. It is highest eastwards, where S. E. of Sæby it culminates in Allerupbakker or "Jydske Aas" (the Jutland ridge) as they are called. Outside this,

Vendsyssel is somewhat low, with several mosses, fens and downs; northwards they reach Skagen, but S. and W. are some isolated hillocks. In its southern lowland is the great Vildmose (about 65 sq: kilom:) N. of Limfjord; and its most considerable stream, Rye Aa, runs from Jydske Aas in a curve past the Vildmose into the Limfjord. Uggerbyaa, which also starts from Jydske Aas flows North thro the downs to the North-sea. The Hanherreds, which connect Vendsyssel and Thyland, consist like Vendsyssel itself of a high middle part with low land on both sides. The Dunes along the coast are here and there interrupted by Chalk hills. The same is the case with the coast of Thyland, whose northern reach is a plateau of limestone, while southward it is more undulating. The island of Mors has nearly the same character, tho slightly higher generally and with considerable steeps along the strand.

We have remarked that **Bornholm** (nearly 600 sq: kilom:) forms an exception to the rest of Denmark. It is distinctly the southern spur of the Scandinavian peninsula. Hammervandet, the water which divides it from the S. E. point of Scania, is scarcely 40 kilom: broad and 50 meters deep, the average depth of the Östersö being 72 meters. The island, a tolerably regular parallelogram 20 to 25 kilom: in length on both sides, is in its larger N. E. part (about 380 sq: kilom:) a plateau of Gneis-Granite. A line S. E. from Hasle on the West coast, to the East between Nexö and Svaneke, is about the boundary. The granite crops up in many places, and at the coast forms small crags and skerries; we have thus a reproduction in miniature of the sea-rocks in Norway. The cliff-groups most favored by tourists are Randkleveskaaret and Helligdomsklipperne; Hammeren on its extreme North point (85 meters), with the large Lighthouse and the ruins of the historical Hammershus Castle; and Ringebakkerne (90 meters) with Jons Kapel on the West. But the granite is often hidden by clay and sand; especially outside the N. E. coast, where there is a rich layer of boulder-clay, while the central "Höjlyngen" — a heather-covered plain — shows nothing but bouldersand and is poor. Höjlyngen rises on the average 100 meters; near the centre is the highest point Rytterknægten (162 meters), from whence there is a magnificent view over the whole island. The southern and lesser part of Bornholm, where the substratum is Silurian (sandstone, schist and limestone) is a little lower and slopes gently to the coast. The subsoil is also here covered by clay and sand, the most fertile is the layer of slate with a dressing of boulder-clay. A third kind is the Jura formation, from the West coast at Hasle southwards; it contains sandstone and coal, the latter however of so little value that the pits have not been worked of late years. Lastly we have Chalk in patches, along the coast; in several places along the shores, as S. E., we also meet drift-sand. Thus Bornholm presents geognostically a great variety of formation. To omit nothing, the small low granite islands N. E. of Bornholm, Ærteholmene may be mentioned. They are generally known as Christiansö, from the largest, and are always looked upon as belonging to Bornholm. —

Owing to the equalizing influence of the sea, the climate of Denmark is mild, far softer than its northern latitude would lead one to expect. The prevailing winds are West and S. W., but the effect of continental gales from the East is often felt, as they bring strong contrasts and sudden veerings, with severe cold in winter and dry heat in summer. In April and May East winds are as prevalent as West. Actual storms are felt along the coasts of the Northern ocean, where the vegetation is dwarfed or entirely blighted by the constant blast. The few trees look stunted and bend to the East. The dry sharp Northwester called "Skaj" which blows in the spring, is especially pernicious; but equally trying to plants, animals and men, is the dense summer mist known as "Havgusen" (sea-fog), which broods over these coasts. With regard to temperature, there is of course no great variation between the North and the South. The difference is mostly between the coast and the inland region; this is especially perceptible in Jylland, where on the Heath is well-nigh a continental climate. The mean annual temperature varies between 6,8 and 8,5° C., that of Kjöbenhavn is 7,4°. The coasts of Fyn and the southern islands are the warmest, the highest parts of Middle and North Jylland the coldest; in general the coasts of the peninsula have 1°, those of Fyn and Sjælland 0,5°, greater mean warmth than the interior. The mean temperature of winter is 0°, of summer 16°, of spring 5,5° and of autumn 8°; the mildest winters are in West Jylland, the southern islets and the West of Fyn; North and central Jylland with Sjælland have the coldest. Summer is warmest in the southerly isles and Sjælland, coldest in central and North Jylland. As a rule the climate must be called very changeable; during some winters navigation in all the Belts is stopped for many months by frost and ice, during others ice-transport is not needed for a single day. The average yearly rain-fall is computed at 550 m. meters (21 inches), the number of rainy days at about 150, of which 34 are days of snow-fall. As the S. W. and W. winds bring most rain, the rain generally decreases from W. to E., altho considerable deviations occur. Between the western, northern and southern Jylland shores and the East coast as far as Aarhus, the rain-fall varies from 700 to 650 m. meters, also to the South in Fyn and Sjælland it is over the mean; but in N. E. Fyn, western and N. E. Sjælland it is under. The rain-fall in Kjøbenhavn is about 560 m. meters. It is least in spring, greatest in autumn, especially in the regions bordering on the North-sea; along the Øresund, however, the maximum fall is in summer.

The Flora and Fauna of Denmark are about the same as in the central European plains and in South Sweden. The variations in the vegetable world depend on the soil, not on the country bending from South to North, which makes too slight a difference to be of consequence. In the fertile regions humidity produces a luxuriant growth of grass, and the area of meadow and pasture land is steadily increasing by the draining of lakes and fjorda rms. On the other hand the land has little wood, compared to what it once had, when immense tracts were entirely covered by continuous forests. Even West Jylland was formerly well wooded; only the Flats, the real "Jydske Heder" (heaths), have never borne trees. The area of forest is computed at about 5 per-c; thus Denmark belongs to the least wooded countries in Europe. The islands are most favored, with their 9 per-c., tho Jylland only reaches $2^1/_2$ per-c. and is "as naked as the steppes of South Russia". This violent destruction of the forests, which is more due to the ravages of man than to the climate, has been in progress from the earliest period, but strange enough the greatest share of the criminality must be given to the last 100 or 150 years. But owing to the energetic efforts of the Government and of private individuals, the area of forest is now increasing year by year especially in Jylland and on Bornholm. The tree most met with all over the land is the Beech, the nature of the soil being most favorable to its growth. It has nearly superseded the Oak. which throve formerly in the boulder-sand. In the earliest time however our forests were chiefly of Fir, which is now being brought back to us and seems to have a great future before it; it is chiefly used in the new plantations. — It is long long ago since Denmark had the great Mammals, such animals as Elk, Reindeer, Bison, the Beaver, Wild-boar, Bear and Wolf. They are gone. The wide and solitary districts which favored their existence, have disappeared.

Of wild quadrupeds the only ones now found are the Red Deer, the Roebuck and the imported Fallow Deer, and these only in fenced deer-parks. The largest beasts of prey are the Fox, the Badger and the Otter. As in other Northern latitudes the Birds are chiefly represented by wild water fowl. The only poisonous snake Denmark possesses is the little viper ("Hugorm"), which is principally seen in the Jylland Heaths and Bornholm.

III

The State and People

The kingdom of Denmark is small compared to what it was. Its periods of greatness — under Canute the Great it ruled over

England; under the Valdemars it held all the Baltic provinces from Holstein to Estonia; and during the Union-epoch Queen Margareth's sceptre glittered over all Scandinavia — passed away with the Middle Age. In later times Denmark still ruled a part of South Sweden, the provinces of Scania, Halland and Blekinge, all ceded to Sweden in 1658 at the Peace of Roskilde. With the loss of Norway in 1814, vanished the last remnant of the former power. Denmark had now not much more to lose, and yet, by the unfortunate complications with Germany, she was doomed to be stripped not only of the German duchies Holstein and Lauenburg, but also of the ever Danish folkland Sönderjylland (South Jutland, Slesvig). The peace of Vienna legalized this in 1864.

The Kingdom of Denmark includes: Denmark proper, 38,300 sq: kilom: (about 696 sq: miles), and the distant Færöes, a little over 1300 sq: kilom:, together 39,600 sq: kilom: (720 sq: miles). To these must be added Iceland, 3 West Indian Islands and the Greenland colonies. We here confine ourselves to Denmark proper, the dependencies and the colonies will be mentioned in conclusion.

The kingdom proper contains a population nearly entirely Danish, belonging to the Scandinavian branch of the Gothic race. Danish (or Dano-Norwegian) like Swedish and Icelandic, are later local dialects pointing back to the Scandinavian of olden times. Of this "Dansk tunge" or "Nörrönasproget" (Danish tongue or the Norrana language) there are many varying dialects; for instance in Denmark, those of Sjælland, Fyn, Jylland. The Danes are generally fair, of middle height, well and strongly built; foreign authors describe them as courageous, industrious, persevering and patient, but rather slow in forming a resolution. Judicious and practical in the general affairs of life, they are in science solid and sober thinkers. A calm and phlegmatic exterior (slightly akin to that of the Dutch) often hides an unusual vivacity and poetic susceptibility (says Reclus) which at times approaches the visionary. An occasional touch of melancholy may be partly owing to climate and mode of life. The celebrated geographer Malte-Brun, a Dane by birth, who spent the last half of his life in Paris (died 1826), characterized the people correctly enough in general, tho here and there somewhat severely, as follows: — "It may be that the humidity of the air and the quantity of flesh and fish they consume, has contributed to make this nation heavy, patient and difficult to move. In former times insatiable conquerors, they are now brave but peaceable; little enterprising but plodding and persevering; modest and proud, hospitable but not over assiduous. They are cheerful and frank among compatriots, but somewhat cool and ceremonious towards foreigners; loving ease before luxury; rather sparing than industrious. Imitators of other nations, we also find them discriminating observers; deep but a little slow and minute thinkers; endowed with more energy than fertility of imagination. Constant, romantic and careful of their cherished aims, they are capable of a rush of enthusiasm, but rarely of flashes of inspiration, that suppleness of thought which commands success or admiration. Bound are they by strong ties to their native soil and to the interests of the fatherland, but not jealous enough of the national glory, and tho accustomed to the calm of a monarchy, enemies of servitude and despotism. This is the portrait of the Danes."

There are few foreign elements in the population. The inhabitants of Amager descend in part from some Dutchmen, who were brought in under Christian II to improve the cultivation of vegetables. Their quaint costume, which has continued to our day, is now dying out, only a few of the women still retain it. In some of their words also the original Holland home may still be traced. The German element is insignificant now that Sönderjylland is lost; but on the Alhede South of Viborg are yet found the descendants of German colonists, introduced in the last century to cultivate the heaths. Then there are the Nomads of the Jylland heaths, the so-called "Tatere" or "Kjæltringer" (from kjæltre, to beg), gipsies, vagabonds, also termed Natmændsfolk, who roam about, supporting themselves by tinkering and begging. They have been called Danish gipsies and may well be a mixture of the nomads of Europe with other low rabble. They speak a slang of their own, called "Rotvælsk", a hodge-podge of

Danish with peculiar final syllables and German. In the genial Steen Steensen Blicher they had an able exponent.

The population of the country in 1890 was 2,172,200, something above 56 to every sq: kilom: (about 3100 to every sq: mile); relatively therefore the land is well filled. Of course the density is very different in various parts of the country. Whilst the islands are far above the average, the western parts of Jylland are far below.[1] Nearly all the denizens belong to the Danish Lutheran State Church; altho there is religious toleration, not 1 per cent is outside the Established Church. Of this small percentage 3000 are Roman Catholics, and about 4000 Jews. Over one third of the dissenters are found in Kjöbenhavn. Fredericia in Jylland enjoyed religious freedom, before it was established by the Ground-Law, hence, comparatively, the greatest number of sectarians dwell there.

Denmark ranks among the best instructed nations in Europe, as nearly every one is said to be able to read and write. Elementary education is given in Parish Schools, both paid and free; every child is bound to have tuition, this being made compulsory in 1814. For the further advance of the country youth, there are Evening Schools and a great many (over 70) private so-called "Folkehöjskoler", chiefly for oral teaching, many of which receive State grants. Elementary-school teachers are trained in some private and four Royal Seminaries. Higher instruction is given in many private commercial and learned Colleges ("Latinskoler", Grammar-schools), and besides this there are Royal learned Schools in the chief towns all over the country. The University in Kjöbenhavn, founded 1479, has over 40 Professors and between 1200 and 1300 students (since 1875 women are also allowed to pass), distributed in 5 Faculties. The University Library has 260,000 volumes and 5000 manuscripts. The University also possesses rich collections and endowments, among others "Communitetet" and "Regensen" for lodging and supporting poor students. Besides all this Kjöbenhavn, as the centre of Denmark's intellectual life, has also higher

---

[1] For further details see the Essay on Statistics.

training establishments, such as the Royal Academy of Fine Arts, a Theological Seminary, a Chirurgical College, the Polytechnical School, a Veterinary and Agricultural College, and many rich museums and collections, among which the Great Royal Library (Nationalbibliotheket) deserves special mention. This numbers over $\frac{1}{2}$ million volumes and about 20,000 manuscripts. Add hereto the Old Northern, the Ethnographic and the Zoological Museums, a Royal Picture Gallery, where of course Danish art is best represented, Thorvaldsen's world renowned Museum of Sculpture, and the Glyptothec, which has been presented by a private gentleman (C. Jacobsen) to the State; it contains fine specimens of antique and modern art. Among learned societies the Royal Danish Society of Science, the Royal Society of Northern Antiquaries, the Society for the study of Denmark's Language and History, the Royal Geographical Society etc, are the most worthy of mention.

The most important source of production is agriculture, which employs one half of the population and furnishes the principal articles of export. Denmark is very fertile, only about 20 per cent being uncultivated; most of which falls to Jylland, to the islands little more than 7 per cent. By the unceasing efforts of the inhabitants the uncultivated area stadily diminishes. The endeavors made to stop the sand-drifts by constructing Höfder (breakwaters) and making dikes, with the spread of agricultural information, is of great assistance. But special stress must be laid on the reclaiming and planting of the heaths, for which the "Hedeselskab" founded in 1866 deserves immense credit. It is especially in Bornholm, and W. and North Jylland, where the greatest stretches have been brought under the plough. A little over half thus reclaimed is used for pasturage; on the islands the corn-land predominates. Ordinary cereals are preferred, and the yearly production is placed at 28 to 30 million hectoliters, or over four times as much as at the beginning of the century. The commonest grain is oats, then barley and rye, wheat last of all, mostly on the islands. This great supply exceeds the consumption, hence there is a considerable export, but not of rye, the home-market requiring most of it. Buckwheat, peas and other pulse are also suscessfully cultivated, with large quantities of potatoes, and some rape, sugar-beets, flax, hemp, hops and tobacco. Hand in hand with farming goes cattle breeding, an important industry in the less favored Jylland districts; the export of beasts and dairy produce is therefore on the increase, whilst that of corn decreases. Such articles of export as butter, provisions and live stock go principally to England. According to its area Denmark possesses the greatest herds of horned cattle in Europe. The Jylland breed is celebrated for its excellence; Danish horses also have high fame, and are much sought abroad as draft animals for military purposes, while sheep and pigs are exported in considerable numbers. Landed property is mostly owned in farms of a moderate size (from 1 to 12 acres Hartkorn, standard of landtax) and small cottages with a little land attached. The "Gaardmænd" (farmers) are commonly freeholders, whilst as a rule the "Husmænd" (cottars) rent their lots. The parcelling out of larger estates ("Proprietærgaarde", "Herregaarde", Country-seats, Manors) goes on rapidly; but still the nobility and gentry hold over one seventh of the soil after its value. Most of this belongs to about 80 "Gods-Fideikommiser", (entailed estates), Grevskaber, Baronier and Stamhuse (Countships, Baronies, Entailed family estates), which generally descend to the firstborn. They all date prior to 1849, as according to the Ground-Law almost all privileges formerly belonging to the nobility are now abolished. No fief or entail can therefore now be granted.

Forestry and fishery are minor sources of income. The woods, as explained, are trifling; and not till the Forest-act of 1805 could they be said to be managed at all. There is therefore no great yield, timber and wood for fuel being largely imported. The mass, 500 sq: kilom:, are State forests. Fish is of course a more important article, and yet, considering the extent of coast, it is far from what might be expected. Herring, cod, flat fish (plaice, turbot etc.) are of most consequence; then come eels, mackerel, garfish, salmon and trout, obtained in quantities round Bornholm and in the rivers and fjords of East Jylland. Besides fish proper, porpoises (Delphinus phocæna) are caught, mostly near Middelfart, but also in the Isefjord, and yield train oil. Along the coasts of the North-sea lobsters are caught, and oysters come from Limfjord, Frederikshavn and Ribe. The artificial oyster-beds attempted, especially in the Great Belt, have not succeeded, the water not being salt enough. The export of fish is far below the import.

Mining operations are naturally out of the question, tho at one time bog-ore from the Jylland heaths was used for smelting iron, and as the necessary fuel was taken from the forests, this largely shared in their destruction; but the profits being too small, this industry has ceased. The minerals are limited to a little chalk, lime, clay (porcelain clay) and cement, amber along the west coast of Jylland and the stone-quarries on Bornholm, whose coal-fields are now no longer worked. Thus Denmark is not in a condition to become a real industrial country; and even tho one fourth of the population may be said to be so employed, its industry is subordinate to agriculture and on a great scale scarcely exists. Those branches which depend on agriculture are of most importance, such as mills, breweries and distilleries. Large manufactories are found in only a few places, besides Kjöbenhavn, where there are factories for machinery, iron foundries (as also in the little North-Sjælland town Frederiksværk) and some works of Porcelain, Faience and Cloth factories. Gloves are made in Randers, Horsens and Odense, and paper at Strandmöllen North of Kjöbenhavn; besides these there are tobacco-factories, manufactories of sugar (beet), bricks etc. Danish manual trades stand high, especially in Kjöbenhavn. Domestic industry ("Husflid"), successfully assisted by a Society founded in 1873, takes a respectable position, and we may draw attention to handknitted woollen goods produced on the Jylland heaths, to the wooden shoes (sabots), made especially in the Jylland woodland (Silkeborg), and to wood carving and pottery (Jydepotter), with some lace making near Ribe.

Owing to the large surplus of farm-produce, Commerce is an important source of income, as about one tenth of the people live by trade and shipping. Business with foreigners is on the increase, having quadrupled within the last 30 or 40 years. England and Germany are the chief markets, especially to the former is the export very considerable, while from the latter Denmark have the largest import. We have previously mentioned the export. The imports are chiefly colonial goods, raw-produce and manufactures, of which the import far exceeds the export. The shipping-trade is of course the largest, and the merchant-fleet is considerable in proportion to the size of the country, tho not comparable to that of Norway, Holland or Greece. One third of the tonnage belongs to Kjöbenhavn, and next ranks the little town of Svendborg in South Fyn. As most of the towns are on the sea-board or in the Fjords, inland business is generally by water, tho there are excellent means of communication in all directions. The high-ways are as a rule in capital condition; and the railroad system, chiefly State property, considering the area and population, is large. Most of the towns are accessible by rail. Of the two large islands, Sjælland has the greatest line of rail; Kjöbenhavn, or more correctly Roskilde, is the junction. Jylland has trunk-lines along the whole of the East and West coast, with several connecting and cross branches, Fredericia and Aarhus being the chief junctions. Canals are few and have only local importance. Telegraphic communication in Denmark is also upon a large scale. "The Great Northern Telegraph Company" deserves mention here, as having brought the National name honor and renown far and wide. It works with a capital of 27 million kroner and exclusively employs sub-marine cables (18 in number), running nearly 6,200 sea miles. The "Forenede Dampskibsselskab" (the United Steamship Company) with a capital of 16 million kroner and nearly 100 steamers, is also highly important. These two Companies, founded by the great merchant and financier C. F. Tietgen, have been the means of making a name for the country in the European mercantile world.[1]

According to the Ground-Law of June 5th 1849, revised July 28th 1866, Denmark is an Hereditary Constitutional Monarchy. On this

[1] For further details on the sources of production, see the article Statistics.

point we refer to what is said in the Historical chapter and to the Ground-Law itself. The department of Justice, according to the Fundamental-Law, is |to be separated from the Executive, and the judges are not to be dismissed except after judicial sentence, unless they are over 65 years of age; nor are they to be removed unless there be a re-organization of the Courts. This separation of Justice and the Executive has not yet been carried out; thus the judges in the First Instance or the Lower Court (in the country called "Herredsfogder" and "Birkedommere", or District Judges and Country Magistrates, and in the towns "Byfogder", Town Judges or Magistrates) being at the same time Administrators of Police or Mayors, can as such be removed. Appeal lies from the Lower Court to that of Second Instance, the Superior Court in Viborg (one Chief Justice and eight Puisne Judges), and in Kjöbenhavn (one Chief Justice and sixteen Puisne Judges). In Kjöbenhavn the organization is however somewhat different, as the Upper and Second Courts are incorporated with the Civil Tribunal, known as "Hof og Stadsret" (Inferior Court of Justice). The Criminal and Police Court, and the Maritime and Commercial Court are also under the Highest Tribunal in the country, "Höjesteret" (Final Court of Appeal), which consists of one Chief Justice, twelve Puisne Judges and eleven Special Judges, making the Third and last Instance. According to the Ground-Law, the administration of Justice must as far as possible be public and oral, and in criminal and political cases a jury is to be called. But these regulations have not yet been carried out.

The economical position of the country may be called very good, its resources are adequate. The soil is mostly divided among small proprietors, not is there, to any great degree, the unequal distribution of means so usual in the large industrial states such as England, where enormous wealth is in the hands of the few, while the masses are steeped in deepest poverty. Of late this prosperity, which increased steadily from the middle of the century, is on the decrease; neither the farming nor the industrial classes are as safe as before. The national property was in 1884 estimated at from 6 to 7 milliards of kroner. The rate of taxation is about 20 kroner per head, of which the direct taxes are only one third to one fourth; if the local burdens are added, the sum is 30 kroner per head. The State Budget, about 55 million kroner, generally shows a surplus. The National Debt is over 200 million kroner. But on this we refer to "Statistics" under the chapter "Public Revenue".

The present Army-organization is based on Laws of July 6th 1867 and July 25th 1880. It is recruited by conscription, which begins at the age of 22, and continues for 16 years, eight being passed in the Regular army and eight in the Militia. The term of instruction varies; in the Infantry it is six months, in the Cavalry nine. Those trained as under-officers and for garrison duties must remain longer, but no one over twelve months. Afterwards the men are called in twice during four years for a short drill. In Kjöbenhavn the Militia forms a separate detachment (called "Kjöbenhavns Væbning", the Copenhagen Reserve), and the same is the case with Bornholm. The troops in time of peace are under two Brigade Commanders, one East, the other West of the Great Belt. First there is the Infantry consisting of 10 regiments, each counting 3 Line-battalions and 1 of Militia, four companies in every battalion; the Guards consist of 1 battalion (on occasions of mobilization increased to two). Second, the Cavalry, 5 regiments, each of three squadrons and a School. Third, the Artillery, the Field Artillery organized in 2 regiments, each in two divisions, in their turn each consisting of 3 Line and 1 Reserve battery; the Train has one division in two companies; the Fortification Artillery has two battalions, the one numbering four Line-companies and two of Reserve, the other, two of the Line and 1 Reserve. Fourth, an additional technical section, the Corps of Engineers, five Line and three Reserve companies; the General Staff, the Auditors, Medical Staff and Commissariat etc. When mobilized every Line-regiment shall be 1,000 strong and every squadron 120, a Field-battery 163, and every company of the Fortification Artillery 400 men. The Officers of the Army are instructed at the Military College in Frederiksberg Palace close to Kjöbenhavn. There is also a Training School for Non-commissioned Officers of the Artillery and Engineers.

The Royal Navy possesses a Fleet (in January 1890) of 5 Iron-clads carrying 89 guns (37 being rifled); 3 Iron-clad batteries with 28 guns of which 12 are rifled; 9 cruisers carrying 104 guns (40 rifled); 8 Iron-gun-boats with 34 guns, 14 rifled; 9 Torpedo boats of the 1st class with 13 rifled cannons; and 10 of the 2d with 6 rifled. Besides there are 4 Mine-boats, 1 steamer for the use of the King, 6 School-ships, Surveying vessels, Transports, Exercise-boats and Tenders, etc.; in all, 336 guns of which 140 are rifled, and about 46,000 horse power. The rolls of the Navy show above 6000 men regulars, and as many reserve. Kjöbenhavn is the Military port and Arsenal, besides being the only fortified place of any consequence. Hitherto it has only been fortified sea-wards, but latterly, as already explained in the Historical section, exertions have been made to fortify it on the land side also. The other fortresses, such as Kronborg and Fredericia, are of no account.

Administration. Denmark is divided into 18 "Amter" or counties (with the Færöes 19) each under an "Amtmand" (Governor, Lord-lieutenant). As the islands and Jylland, nearly double in size, have the same number of counties, the isle-counties are naturally smaller than Jylland's; the former are tolerably equal in size, with the exception of Bornholm whose limits nature has fixed, the latter are very unequal. The counties are again subdivided into 126 "Herreder" (hundreds), which as a rule are more nearly equal in size, the islands having 44 and Jylland 82; every Hundred has a "Herredsfoged" or "Birkedommer" (Justice of the Peace). In the market-towns the subordinate authorities are the Magistracy (a Mayor nominated by the Government and in some places supplemented by Aldermen). The Hundreds are again separated into Parishes (about 1068, the number varies). Kjöbenhavn is outside the county division and forms a district for itself; here the Magistracy includes both a Superior and Inferior section. The former consists of an President appointed by the

King, with four Burgomasters and four Aldermen, all chosen by the Municipal Council; this Chamber of 36 members is elected by the Citizens in much the same way as the Folketing, but with a slight census. The Magistrates and the Municipal Council both agreeing have absolute power, the State supervising thro the President.

The following table gives in round numbers the population in the different counties, according to the census taken February 1890.

		sq: kilom:	Inhabitants
Kjöbenhavn Amt (Country)	about	1,250	312,400
Kjöbenhavn By (City)			152,700
Frederiksborg	·	1,350	84,700
Holbæk	·	1,700	94,200
Sorö	·	1,450	89,000
Præstö	·	1,700	100,600
Hornholm	·	600	38,800
Maribo	·	1,700	100,600
Odense	·	1,750	136,100
Svendborg	·	1,650	130,700
The islands together		13,150	1,229,800
Hjörring	·	2,800	110,600
Thisted	·	1,700	69,400
Aalborg	·	2,900	104,800
Viborg	·	3,050	100,800
Randers	·	2,450	110,500
Aarhus	·	2,500	157,200
Vejle	·	2,350	111,900
Ringkjöbing	·	4,500	98,600
Ribe	·	2,900	78,600
Jylland		24,150	942,400
Denmark proper		38,300	2,172,200

The Ecclesiastical division into 7 Dioceses or Bishoprics, is equally employed in daily life. The diocesan authorities are the Bishop, and the Civil Governor resident in the Cathedral town; but the latter has no secular power outside his own County, and in rank is not above the other Amtmænd (Governors). The Bishop of Sjælland resides in Kjöbenhavn and is considered the Primate. The Dioceses are subdivided into 72 Deaneries and these again into Livings. Kjöbenhavn has two Deaneries and eleven Livings. The County in general is a part of the Diocese, but they are not always quite the same, as sometimes a small portion of a County belongs to another Diocese than that to which the principal part belongs. The 7 Bishoprics are:

Sjælland's, which embraces Sjælland, Amager, Möen and some minor isles, with Bornholm; and the Counties Kjöbenhavn, Frederiksborg, Holbæk (Samsö belongs to the See of Aarhus), Sorö, Præstö and Bornholm.

Laaland-Falster, which holds Laaland, Falster and some small islands; with only one County, Maribo.

Fyn, made up of Fyn, Taasinge, Langeland, Ærö and some islets, with the Counties of Odense and Svendborg.

Aalborg: the North Jylland isle, Mors and some small eyots in the Limfjord, a stretch of land South of Limfjord round Aalborg, and Læsö in the Kattegat; its Counties are Hjörring, Thisted and a part of Aalborg.

Viborg, South of Limfjord, bounded on the South by Mariagerfjord, in Middle Jylland stretching to the town of Viborg; it comprises the greater part of Aalborg and Viborg Amts.

Aarhus: East Jylland from Mariager to Vejlefjord with the islands of Anholt and Samsö, the Counties are Randers, Aarhus and fractions of Viborg, Vejle and Holbæk (Samsö).

Ribe: the largest and most sparely peopled, embraces West and South Jylland with eastern Jylland S. of Vejlefjord; the Amts are Ringkjöbing and Ribe with most of Vejle.

Over one fourth of the inhabitants dwell in the towns, 75 in all; of these 69 are Market-towns and 6 Trading-stations, the first having a few privileges more than the latter. The towns are throughout small, most of them petty. Only one, the Capital, can be called a City; it has about half the entire population of all the towns, and between $1/7$th and $1/6$th of the souls in Denmark, and is thus comparatively one of the largest capitals in the world. Of the other towns, eight only (according to the last census) had over 10,000 souls, thirteen over 5,000, 26 did not reach 2,000. The islands have nearly double the number of towns in Jylland, but on the other hand those in Jylland are larger. The greatest part are situated on the sea-board, on the Sounds or up the Fjords. The town houses are of red or yellow bricks and tile roofed. The earlier mode of building, with timber or frame-work, is now forbidden; it caused endless fires. In market-towns the houses are generally low, of one or two stories; in Kjöbenhavn, as in most large cities, they are four to five, even six stories high. In the country the houses and farms are mostly near together forming villages, and these are sometimes larger than the small towns; but in West Jylland and Bornholm, the farms are wide apart. A Danish farmhouse is as a rule built as a square, one side being the dwelling house, the other sides the farm-buildings, stabling etc. Generally speaking these buildings are of brick, of stones or cement, some old-fashioned houses are of frame-work, the roofs thatched with straw, but on the heaths with ling.

IV

Topography

1. Kjöbenhavn (Latin Hafnia, Copenhagen, Cheapinghaven, Copenhague, Kopenhagen), the Capital of Denmark, is the Residence of the Sovereign, the Seat of Government and of Parliament, the only Fortress in the kingdom, and its Arsenal and Naval Station. It is also Denmark's principal mercantile emporium as well as its

intellectual centre, for it holds the University and many valuable museums, and everything belonging to science, literature and art. Very pleasant and favorable is its position on the Sound in Sjælland, Amager and some holms, rising 13 meters over the sea level, 55^0 41' N. Lat. and 12^0 35' E. Long. (Greenwich).

The history of Kjöbenhavn goes far back. It is thought there was a fishing hamlet here as early as the 9th century; we know that this was in fact in 1043, when it was called Hæfn ("Havn", Haven, harbor), later Köpmænnehæfn, Köbmanhafn, Kopinghafn (the harbor of chapmen, merchants), Saxo's Portus Mercatorum. This has by degrees become Kjöbenhavn; the names used by foreigners are only distortions.

The place became of importance when the famous Bishop Absalon raised a Castle on Tyvsholm, part of the Slotsholm of our time, for the defence of the harbor against Wendish pirates; this stronghold was called like the town, Hafn. Axelhus and Steileborg are names of later date. King Valdemar the Great is supposed to have given the town and neighborhood, a little before this, to Bishop Absalon, who is always spoken of as the founder of Kjöbenhavn. In his turn he gave it to the See of Roskilde. But it received its first chartered Rights in 1254 from the powerful Archbishop of Lund Jacob Erlandsen, long continuing a possession of the Roskilde Bishopric. Valdemar Atterdag became its owner, but after his death it reverted to the Prelates, until in 1416 they were forced to give it up to Erik of Pomerania, when it became the Capital and grew apace. From very early times it was fortified, as indeed its site and daily events made a necessity. In 1248 it was taken and burnt by the Lübeckers, in 1259 fell it into the hands of Jaromar Prince of Rügen, in 1368 the same fate overtook it, while Valdemar Atterdag was fighting the Hanseatic League, and again in 1428 it had to defend itself against the same enemy. The old fortifications were repaired and improved in the middle of the 15th century, by adding a new rampart of earth, which withstood the two sieges 1523—24, when the town held out for seven months against Frederik I, and

1535-36, when it resisted Christian III a whole year. On both these occasions it sided with the idol of the populace, Christian II. At the end of the 16th century, the fortifications were again improved. It was in the 17th century, under Christian IV and his successors, that the town began to increase perceptibly. The population can first be computed, with any certainty, in the year 1635, when it numbered about 25,000 persons, in 1685 it was over 50,000, a growth which can be compared with that of our own time. We must recollect however, that the city's eventful year (1660) was in this period. Christian IV improved and enlarged it considerably; he not only took in the extensive new quarters Christianshavn and Nyboder, but also planned most important additions to be carried out during the next age, especially the district round Amalienborg Palace. Frederik III in 1661 gave his capital special privileges, as a reward for its heroic defence at the siege by Carl Gustav 1658-59; both King Frederik and Christian V built considerably. The Citadel to protect the town from the sea-side was constructed in 1663, and the new fortifications on the land-side, the ramparts and moats, were completed. These are now disappearing, making room for the broad boulevards between the inner and the outer city, which owed its protection to these ramparts when bombarded by the combined English, Dutch and Swedish fleets in 1700. In the 18th century the sea-defence was extended by the battery Trekoner (1713); the new Amalienborg quarter, Frederiksstad, was settled under Frederik V. In the last century however the numbers increased but slowly; in 1735 there were not 80,000 souls, the plague, which harried Kjöbenhavn and other large towns, having carried off above 22,000 persons in 1711. The census in 1785 gave the numbers at 90,000. In our own period, and chiefly since 1852 the increase has been immense, especially after a rage for building began outside the demarcation lines, and then (the ramparts gone) all along the fortification territory and the harbor area between Nyhavn and Slotsholm, the so-called Gammelholm, and in Nyboder. In 1835 the population was 120,000; in 1850, 130,000; 1880, 235,000 and in

1890, 312,000; thus it has more than doubled during 25 years. Including those parts not belonging to the "City" proper but yet really grown together with it, as Frederiksberg westerwards, Utterslev to the N. W. and Sundbyerne in Amager, there were in 1890 375,000 inhabitants. Kjöbenhavn "City" covers an area of about 23 sq: kilom:; divided into 19 quarters, it has over 400 streets, more than 20 markets and squares, 20 churches (with chapels etc. 30), 4 large theaters and nearly 9,000 houses. It is therefore densely built, with about 40 persons to each building, the "Kasernesystem" (Barrack system) being much used. London is not to be compared, the circumstances there being exceptional, with only 10 persons to a dwelling, while Paris has 35. Kjöbenhavn however does not come up to Berlin or Vienna, which number respectively 58 and 60.

In spite of its age the town has no antique appearance and most of the older buildings of note date only from Christian IV's time. The reason is the frequent and disastrous fires, especially those of 1728 — when 1640 buildings, and of 1795 — when 940 buildings were laid in ashes; at the bombardment in 1807 by the English over 300 were destroyed.

The capital now comprises, 1st the "City" within the ramparts, or within the line of the boulevards which have succeeded them. 2d, the old fortification ground or the rampart quarter between the boulevard and the longish narrow lakes of Sortedam, Peblinge and St. Jörgen, which lie in a line N. E. to S. W. Last, the suburbs, the so-called "Broer" (bridges). The City proper includes a large western section in Sjælland, marked off by the narrow estuary of Kallebodstrand between Sjælland and Amager, and a minor eastern quarter, Christianshavn, on the N. W. point of Amager.

The southern half inside the ramparts is the oldest. Northwards it is bounded by Gothersgade, a long street running from E. to W. This is the most irregular part of the City, the streets being crooked and narrow in this really "Gammel (old) Kjöbenhavn", as the stranger soon sees after passing the principal artery from Kongens Nytorv along Östergade, Amagertorv, Vimmelskaftet, Nygade, Nytorv and

Frederiksberggade to Halmtorvet. The most prominent feature in this district is "Kongens Nytorv" (the King's new Market), the largest open square in the town, adorned by the Royal Theater finished in 1874, with statues of the poets Oehlenschläger and Holberg placed outside, and Charlottenborg Palace, now used for the Royal Academy of Arts in connection with the new edifice behind, for the Exhibition of Paintings, Sculpture etc.; in addition to these, the fashionable Hôtel d'Angleterre takes up one side. The centre is unluckily occupied by a poor leaden effigy of Christian V on horseback, in summer mostly hidden by trees, shrubs and flowers. The people never speak of it otherwise than as "Hesten" (the horse). Another striking quarter surrounds "Frue Kirke" (Our Lady's Church), the oldest we have, and already mentioned as the principal ecclesiastical edifice in the 12th century. It has often been rebuilt after great conflagrations. Destroyed in 1728, the new pile with its spire 120 meters high became the prey of the bombardment in 1807. The present church, with a tower 65 meters in height, has its chief decoration within, the statues of Christ and the twelve Apostles, Thorvaldsen's masterpieces. Opposite is the University-quadrangle, consisting of the University (rebuilt after the bombardment), the handsome University-Library and the Zoological Museum (with a famous collection of Whale-skeletons). Close by is the German "St. Petrikirke" (Church of St. Peter), rebuilt after the fire in 1728; it also suffered at the bombardment. The double squares Gammeltorv and Nytorv are near, with the large Town Hall. Not far off are also "Trinitatis Kirke" and "Rundetaarn" (Trinity Church and the Round Tower), both erected by Christian IV. The Round Tower is very curious and original, 35 meters high, with a characteristic view of the city from the top. In Vimmelskaftet is "Helligaandskirken" (Church of the Holy Ghost), built in the 15th century. Of the considerable and handsome "Nicolaikirke" burnt in 1795, all that is left is the tower (now used as a Fire-brigade-station), unhappily hidden by butchers' shops.

"Slotsholmen" (Castle-holm) which is surrounded by canals, the remains of former sounds, spanned by seven bridges, is a characteristic part of the old town. Here are the mighty ruins of "Christiansborg Slot" (Palace), erected first by Christian VI on the spot where had stood the old "Kjöbenhavn's Slot". When this was destroyed by fire in 1794, was built a new edifice, which was burnt in 1884, when many treasures perished. The paintings in the National Gallery, however, were saved, and are at present deposited in Charlottenborg. On Slotsholmen there is besides the Palace Church, saved in 1884, also Thorvaldsen's Museum, an original Etruscan mausoleum. It contains all the great Master's works, and in the central court he himself lies buried. The Arsenal, the National Library, the Record Office and the Treasury Offices are near by. Opposite stands the "Börs" (Exchange) in Gothic Renaissance style, also the work of Christian IV; the tower is very remarkable, four copper dragons twining their tails into a spire. On the Place in front of the ruins of the palace is an equestrian Statue of Frederik VII by Bissen. Behind the ruins on the opposite side of the canal is "Prinsens Palais" with the Old Northern and Ethnographic Museums. Crossing one of the bridges in front we come to "Holmens Kirke", with the tombs of the Naval heroes Niels Juel and Tordenskjold.

Christianshavn also belongs to the older portion of the city; it is built on the northwestern point of Amager and on the eastern side of the port; its foundations were laid 1618; the straight streets crossing each other at right angles testify to the fact that an order from Christian IV originated the plan; in 1674 it was incorporated with the town. Christianshavn communicates with Slotsholmen by two bridges, Langebro and Knippelsbro; the last leads direct to the street thro which runs the general traffic to the town. Christianshavn is divided from the rest of the town by a canal; its most remarkable building is "Frelsers Kirke" (Our Saviour's Church) erected at the end of the 17th century, with a very quaint tower and steeple 91 meters high (the loftiest in Denmark) outside of which runs a winding-stair. To the north are several small isles, Frederiksholm, Nyholm and others, forming the eastern side of the inner harbor, at this point 7 meters deep. Here are the arsenal, store-houses, Royal dockyard etc.

To the more modern parts within the ramparts belong "Gammelholm", and the quarter round Amalienborg, also called "Frederiksstaden", North of Slotsholm and along the western side of the harbor. They are chiefly separated by the canal Nyhavn, reaching to Kongens Nytorv from the quay. The first houses on Gammelholm, formerly a part of the dockyard, date from 1861. It is now one of the best sections, with straight, broad streets. The finest edifice is the National Bank, with a statue of Niels Juel a little higher up. The Navigation School, the Royal Mint and several hotels are also in this quarter. The quay along Havnegade, from "Holmens Kirke" to Nyhavn, is one of the liveliest, busiest thoroughfares in the City. Round Amalienborg is Kjöbenhavns "West-end" or most aristocratic quarter. Bredgade and Amaliegade, its two straight and broad streets, are north of the large open tree-planted avenue "St. Anna Plads", and extend to the plantation below the Citadel. Here are the Amalienborg Palaces, enclosing the octagonal "Frederiksplads", the equestrian statue of Frederik V in the centre; built by Noblemen under Frederik V, afterwards transferred to the Crown, they contain the King's and Crown-prince's residences and the Foreign Office. In Bredgade are the Russian Church, the Roman Catholic Chapel and the Marble Church. Begun under Frederik V, the materials of this last were bought by a private gentleman (Tietgen), who is building a magnificent rotunda or dome-shaped church. In this same Bredgade are the provisional apartments of the High Court and the Parliament, which lost their homes at the burning of the Christiansborg Palace; higher up is Frederik's Hospital. West of Amalienborg near the rampart line, and north of Gothersgade lies the only Park of the City, "Kongens Have", in which is the small Rosenborg Castle, like the Exchange built by Christian IV, in his usual Gothic-renaissance style. Rosenborg contains the chronological collections of the Danish monarchs, chiefly arranged by the archæologist Worsaae. In the pretty park, — a paradise for children — there is a statue of Hans Christian Andersen, famous for his fairy-tales.

"Nyboder", with its straight streets and low dwellings a townlet in itself, is north of Rosenborg and is the abode of the men regularly employed in the Royal Navy. Lately however some of the small rows have given way to more modern houses. The St. Paul's Church and Freemasons Hall are here. — The Citadel "Frederikshavn" is the most northerly point of the inner town. With moats, ramparts and drawbridges, it is quite a self-contained borough; below it along the outer harbor is the fashionable promenade "Langelinie" (the Long-line); raised slightly above the sea, and ornamented with trees and shrubs, with seats here and there, it affords a most pleasant walk of about 1 English mile, with a lovely view across the Sound. The Citadel formerly served to protect the town from attacks by sea; its fortifications are now antiquated, and the outer haven is defended by sea-forts, such as Trekroner, Lynetten and Prövestenen. Just outside the entrance to "Langelinie" stands the slender and graceful St. Alban's Church amid the trees, and reflecting its beauty in the Citadel moat. Inside also, with its stained glass windows and other decorations, it fittingly harmonizes with the noble English liturgy. The English colony in Kjöbenhavn owes it, chiefly, to the kind exertions and interest of their Royal Highnesses the Prince and Princess of Wales.

As explained, the ramparts between the inner town and the lakes have given place to the broad boulevards, with their avenues of trees, modern buildings and ornamental grounds like "Östre Anlæg" (the eastern plantation) in which a part of the rampart and moat is preserved, and where at present the new National Gallery is building. In the beautiful little "Örstedspark" is a statue of the great naturalist of that name; and many casts, chiefly from antique sculptures. The new Botanical garden and the Observatory with a statue of Tycho Brahe are opposite Rosenborg on the rampart side. West of the Botanical garden is the "Communehospital", the largest in Kjöbenhavn; close by is an entirely new building occupied as a Polytechnical Institute. To the south, beyond Orsteds-park, we come to the Dagmar Theater and Vesterbropassage, near the railway stations, one of the busiest and most animated districts in Kjöbenhavn. At the passage are the space railed off for the new Town-Hall, the Industrial-palace, standing since the Exhibition of 1872, and the well-known pleasure garden "Tivoli" of well-nigh European renown.

Beyond the lakes (Sortedams-, Peblinge-, St. Jörgenssö) stretch the suburbs; Österbro, North of the Citadel keeping to the coast line; Nörrebro, reached by the fine new bridge "Dronning Louise's Bro"; and Vesterbro, thro the "Vesterbropassage", just mentioned. Of late years these suburbs have grown enormously, and closed in upon the villages beyond not belonging to the town. Thus Nörrebro is now joined to Utterslev, Vesterbro to Frederiksberg. The new churches in these parts (St. Jacobs at Österbro, St. Johannes at Nörrebro and St. Matthæus at Vesterbro) have been built chiefly by voluntary contributions. Frederiksberg is only a trading-station without any privileges, and is yet the second largest town in the kingdom, having in 1890, 47,000 inhabitants. Its name is taken from the palace raised by Frederik IV, now used as a military college and surrounded by the charming, much frequented parks "Frederiksbergs-have" and "Söndermarken". In Frederiksberg is also the Veterinary and Agricultural College. The fourth suburb Amagerbro is situated outside Christianshavn and is joined with the artisans' villages Sundbyöster and Sundbyvester outside the town.

The environs of Kjöbenhavn with their diversity of sea and forest, lakes and fertile fields, hamlets and picturesque country-seats have justly gained a name for rural beauty. The "Strandvej" (coast road) along the Öresund northwards, is best known. All along, the eye feasts on pretty scenes, straggling fishing-hamlets, fashionable bathing-places with hotels and villas in every direction, among gardens glowing with color, waving cornfields and beautiful forest trees — a continuous town of villas. The greater part of the well-to-do "Kjöbenhavners" have their summer residences along this route; the best known bathing-establishments are Klampenborg and Skodsborg. North of Kjöbenhavn are the Royal Summer Palaces Bernstorff and Charlottenlund, where the King and Crown-prince reside each year. The last lies in the Charlottenlund pleasure park, the easiest of access for the townsfolk, and always thronged in spring and summer. "Dyrehaven" the grand deer-park with its shooting box "Eremitagen", the work of Christian VI, lies still further northwards. Slightly inland, near the large village of Lyngby, is "Sorgenfri Slot" (Sans-souci). It is in these northern outskirts of Kjöbenhavn that forts have of late years been erected, for the defence of the capital on the land-side.

2. Of other towns in Sjælland may be mentioned: Helsingör (Elsinore) 5 or 6 Danish miles N. of Kjöbenhavn, at the narrowest point of the Öresund; an old town which from its position has been of considerable consequence. It was here that the Sound dues were exacted, for which reason a keep was erected in early times. Kronborg, the present stronghold, was built by Frederik II and replaced the older forts Flynderborg and Örekrog. Kronborg Castle on a narrow outshooting tongue of land, domineers the Sund with its many towers; the highest of these, a lighthouse, throws bright rays far into the Kattegat. Useless as a fortress, the pile is now barracks; the chapel and some of the rooms are shown to visitors. The fine old myth of Olger Danske (Holger the Dane) is attached to Kronborg. He sits sleeping in the vaults below, till called to the rescue by his Fatherland. The tradition of Hamlet too, made immortal by Shakespear, is associated with Kronborg and Helsingör; and a grave-heap has been raised and is pointed out as Hamlet's, in Marienlyst Park. Helsingör has only 11,000 inhabitants. The abolition of the Sound dues has injured it; still its capital position and good roadstead render it the most important town in North Sjælland. The trade with passing vessels is not inconsiderable.

To the south-west is the loveliest part of North Sjælland; along the shores of Esrom lake nestles the little town of Fredensborg with a palace constructed by Frederik IV, which has become renowned far and near during the last few years, by reason of the visits of the Russian Czar, the Prince of Wales, the King of Greece and other notabilities, as guests of the Royal House of Denmark. The Park is famous for its beauty and also for the collection of statuary, most of it by Wiedevelt. Slightly more to the south-west and like Fredensborg on the line of rail from Kjöbenhavn to Helsingör, is Hillerød, which owes its existence to Frederiksborg Castle. Settled first by Frederik II, it was reconstructed by his son Christian IV in the well-known Rosenborg style. The destruction of this interesting pile by fire in 1859, was a great calamity. By private initiative and State assistance, however, this National monument now lifts its characteristic red brick towers and spires once more above the waters of the little lake out of which it seems to rise. But the many valuable works of art lost in the flames, can never be replaced. The galleries and halls are now a National Museum, which bears favorable comparison with collections of the kind abroad. The Chapel and Knight's Hall are especially resplendent in coloring. The other North Sjælland towns are not worth mention. Frederiksværk, prettily placed at the northern side of Roskildefjord and close to Arresö, may be named because of its ironfoundries and the government gunpowder mills. In Hornsherred is Jægerspris, a palace which owes its fame to the Hereditary Prince Frederik; who last century caused monuments to be erected in the park to the memory of a great many celebrated Danes and Norwegians. Now it is transformed into an educational establishment for poor girls. — The old capital of Denmark, the Cathedral town of Roskilde, "Kildernes By" (the town of many springs), the old seat of Sjælland's bishops and which in the Middle Ages held most of the power of the land, lies at the innermost extremity of Roskildefjord. When the seat of government was removed to Kjöbenhavn it began to decline, and at the Reformation, when it also lost the Bishop's see, it sunk still more; at present it has only 7,000 inhabitants. Still, it remains one of the most interesting towns, thanks to the Cathedral which, with its two spires, commands the surrounding plain. This cathedral dates from the 13th century, and is assuredly the finest Denmark possesses. None other is so rich in historical associations, for here are the tombs of Queen Margrethe and most of the Kings of the Oldenburg race. Besides which Saxo Grammaticus and many other great men rest beneath its aisles. Of the many other churches which stood here during the Middle Ages, only one remains. Near Roskilde is the "St. Hans Hospital" (Bistrup), the Lunatic Asylum belonging to the Kjöbenhavn municipality. Not far off is the little village of Leire, a name often found in Denmark's legendary history. It was the seat of Kings earlier than Roskilde. Along the western railway route to Korsör, we come to Ringsted, Sorö and Slagelse, all old towns connected with the tales of our forefathers. In the Convent Church at Ringsted more rulers of the Valdemar line are buried. But Sorö is the most famous. Beautifully situated between woods and water, it grew around the monastery founded by Bishop Absalon; which later was remodelled into a college for noblemen. Its honor was doubled by Ludvig Holberg, when he left it his large fortune, and here the great Comedy-writer reposes in the attractive little cloister-church, near the remains of Bishop Absalon. This is the sole vestige of the past. When Denmark became a free State, the college became a Royal grammar school and educational establishment; the names of several Danish authors (Ingemann, Wilster etc) are associated with its walls and with the friendly surroundings of lake and park. Korsör on the Store Belt has special significance as the terminus of the West Sjælland railway, and as the Station for steam communication with Nyborg in Fyn and Kiel in Holstein. Kalundborg, more to the North, is also the terminus of a line from Roskilde and has steamers direct to Aarhus in Jylland. It is remarkable for its church with five towers, dating from 12th century. Lastly, there are the two venerable townlets Næstved and Vordingborg; the first on the banks of Suseaa, is known by its grammar school Herlufsholm; close to the last, on the coast and facing the island of Falster, stands the solitary keep

"Gaasetaarn", the small remnant of the Castle raised by Valdemar I, and later on the favorite resort of Valdemar Atterdag. The name "Gaasetaarn" (Goose Tower) was derived from the Golden Goose placed by Valdemar Atterdag on the top of the tower to jeer the Hansetowns, which he called a flock of screaming geese. The petty East Sjælland towns, Kjöge, on the bay of that name, and Storeheddinge in Stevnsherred, are of no moment, as is the case with Skjelskör on the Store Belt and Holbæk and Nykjöbing northwards on the western side of the Isefjord.

Bornholm has no less than seven market-towns, all very inconsiderable; Sandvig, on the northerly point near the ruins of Hammershus, has only 400 inhabitants and is the smallest in Denmark. Rönne with 8000 is on the west coast and is famed for its clocks and terracotta ware. All the towns but one are situated upon the shore. The island has four wonderful old "Rundkirker" (Round Churches) of granite, used by the people in olden times also as places of refuge and defence against sea-rovers. In the rest of Denmark are there only three such temples.

From Vordingborg where the South Sjælland railway ends, is the steam-ferry to Falster. Here the line runs by way of Nykjöbing to the southermost station Gjedserodde, whence steamers ply to Warnemünde-Rostock en route to Berlin. — Of the five townlets in Laaland only two need be mentioned. Maribo sprang up round the mediæval Convent of St. Birgitta, of which nothing now remains but the pretty little church, where Eleonora Christina Ulfeldt lies buried. Nakskov, the largest (nearly 7000 inhab:), was at one time a fortress and defended itself bravely against the Swedes under Carl Gustav in 1659; it has some trade with the surrounding islets.

All the towns in Fyn, save Odense the largest, lie on the coast. Apparently situated in the heart of the island it is in reality about 5 kilom: from the far-inland running Odensefjord, with which it is connected by a canal, suitable only for small craft. Odenseaa which runs thro the town, is not navigable. Odense is one of the chief towns (30,000 souls), and is a lively trading place. It is of great antiquity, reaching even heathen times, as its name shows, compounded of "Odin" (the god Woden) and "Ve" (sanctuary, temple). It has always been of consequence, especially in the Middle Ages. King Knud (Canute) the Saint, after his murder during a revolt in 1086, was canonized and his relics enshrined here in the Stone Church he had founded, now the handsomest edifice in the town; his shrine stands in the crypt, and hither crowds of pious pilgrims wandered during the Romanist period. The remains of King Hans and Christian II are also here. Odense is rising quickly, and is the centre of much industry and trade. The Fyn railway goes thro the country over Odense from Nyborg on the E. by the Great Belt, which played a part in Danish history and once was a fortress. It has a garrison; which, with the steam-traffic carried on with Korsör and its good harbor, give it no little life. The main line ends westward at Strib on the Little Belt, whence the steam-ferry crosses to Fredericia. Here, at the narrowest part of the Little Belt is the ancient Middelfart, often mentioned in Middle Ages history. The beautiful environs make it more and more a much sought bathing place. Its chief attraction is its southern environs round the old Manor of Hindsgavl, where there was once a Royal castle. From Odense a branch line in South Fyn reaches Svendborg, the second place in size (nearly 9000 inhab:). This old town is charmingly situated at Svendborgsund, which separates it from Taasinge. It is partly built on the sloping heights of the coast, so that several streets are steep, giving it quite a different appearance to most other Danish towns. Considering its moderate extent, it is a bustling spot, with shipbuilding-yards and some commerce, especially with the island group to the South; while its mercantile fleet is second only to that of Kjöbenhavn. — It is impossible to travel much in Denmark without being struck by the fine and characteristic gentlemen's seats, many of them from the time when the nobility were really nobles, during the reigns of Frederik II and Christian IV. These monarchs had themselves a passion for building grandly, as we know. The S. E. corner of Fyn, between

Svendborg and Nyborg is especially rich in these chateaus, as Örbæklunde, Rygaard and Hesselagergaard. The rest of the Fyn towns, Bogense on the Kattegat, Kjærteminde on the Great Belt, in early times the port of Odense, with Faaborg and Assens on the Little Belt, need no comment. — On Langeland is its one market-town Rudkjöbing, on the western shore. The fertile and well populated Ærö has two townlets, Æröskjöbing and Marstal; the last is a sailor's town; comparatively speaking it has a considerable merchant fleet.

3. After what has already been said, it follows that the eastern side of the Jylland peninsula is best populated, most productive and hospitable with its coast indented by many fjords and good harbors. All the greater towns are here, and as a rule they are larger than the island towns, tho not so close together; in the interior they are few and smaller, which is still more the case along the harsh and inaccessible West coast.

The first place reached on the eastern side after leaving the Kongeaa is Kolding, on the fjord of the same name. It existed as early as the 10th century and with market privileges at the beginning of the 14th, and has suffered much during the various rebellions and wars of old until now, as for instance during the struggle between the brothers Erik Plovpenning and Abel, and from the battle in its streets in April 1849. To the North, on a hill outside, we reach the ruins of Koldinghus Castle, burnt in 1808 whilst Bernadotte and the Spanish troops were quartered there. S. E. is Skamlingsbanken, so well known for the extensive view from its top, and for the granite pillar raised in memory of the gallant stand made by the Slesvigers for their mother-tongue. North of Kolding on the Little Belt, opposite the ferry of Strib, is Fredericia, a fortress built by Frederik III. The streets are very regular and straight, but it has never had any importance as a fortification, nor expanded as was expected. Large plots of ground in the middle of the town are used for gardens. No Danish town but Kjöbenhavn occupies so large an area, tho it has only 10,000 inhab:. A great part was destroyed at the bombardment in 1849; it suffered too in the battle on the 6th of July of the same year. In memory of these honorable days Bissen's statue "Den tapre Landsoldat" (the brave foot soldier) was raised; and in one giant mound rest the fallen warriors. To induce people to settle there, several privileges were at one time given, amongst others religious freedom, and in consequence Fredericia has a Romanist and a Reformed chapel and a Synagogue. As a junction for several railways, it boasts considerable railway traffic. N. W. of Fredericia and close to the inner side of Vejlefjord, nestles Vejle in a lovely region; the wooded declivities along the fjord and Greisdalen, which winds between high hills, are always admired. N. W. of Vejle is the village Jellinge, on the site of the old King's seat. The church lies between the two celebrated Kæmpehöje (barrows) over Gorm den Gamle (the old) and Thyra Danebod. The East coast railway, connecting the above mentioned towns, continues North by way of Horsens on the fjord of the same name, once a considerable place; in the Middle Ages it dwindled seriously, but has now revived and is one of Jylland's larger towns, (18,000 souls). Its special trade is in cattle and agricultural produce.

The railway extends thence to Aarhus, the largest city in Jylland (about 33,000 inhabitants); it is a lively commercial place, thanks to its harbor, the best on the whole of the East coast. Here also several railways meet, and it has direct steam communication with Kjöbenhavn. During this century it has advanced immensely, for in 1800 it had only 4000 inhabitants. Aarhus is an ancient spot, and had in the 10th century its Bishop; still there are but few quaint houses, the frequent fires, here as elsewhere, having destroyed everything. The most interesting building is the Cathedral, dating from the 13th century, the longest church in the country (93 meters); the steeple, 89 meters high, was erected at the late restoration, the former one having fallen in a hurricane a century and a half since. The town is prettily situated, having to the south the woods round Marselisborg and northward Risskov, with the Lunatic Asylum for North Jylland. Further to the North, close upon Mols, the southermost part of Djursland, are the ruins of Kalö Castle, inside the little Kalobay. This old place, pulled down a hundred years ago, was most remarkable for having been the prison of Gustavus Vasa, before he became King of Sweden. N. W. of Aarhus, inland, is Frijsenborg, the Residence in the county of the same name, the largest estate in the land (about 200 sq: kilom:). Besides the townlets Æbeltoft and Grenaa on the Djursland, are three market-towns in the East, S. of Limfjord, Randers on the Gudenaa, close to its outlet into Randersfjord, Hobro and Mariager on the Mariagerfjord. These last are small, Mariager indeed is next to the smallest market-town (700 inhab.), Randers being one of the larger (nearly 17,000 inhab.) with commerce and shipping and some trade. This old place is chiefly known in history from the exploit of Niels Ebbesen in 1340, when he killed Count Gert; it is ornamented by a statue of the knight.

In this part inland, S. of Limfjord, there are only three towns Skanderborg, Silkeborg and Viborg. The first is on the main line between Horsens and Aarhus; it is prettily situated, with a church, the only existing vestige of its former striking castle. Silkeborg to the N. W. is the youngest town in the kingdom, having risen after the establishment of the Paper Mills in 1845; of late it has become a much visited watering-place, from its beautiful environs, the ling and forest clad undulating banks among the little lakes. Viborg, almost in the middle of Jylland to the S. of Limfjord, is the old capital of the province; it traces its history to heathen times. From the days of Svend Estridsen it has been an Episcopal See. In the Middle Ages and very much later, when it was the meeting-place of the Jylland nobility, and until the introduction of Absolutism, it enjoyed a high reputation and is often mentioned in history. Especially is it bound up with the Reformation, for here Hans Tausen first preached. It has now only about 8,000 inhabitants. Next to Kjöbenhavn and Fredericia it has the greatest extent on a low hill and is very irregularly built. Viborg, Vebjerg, is "det hellige Bjerg" (the holy mountain). High above the houses towers the imposing Cathedral, which in its original form dates from the 11th century, but in the course of time it has undergone much ill usage and alteration, and has only recently again been rebuilt and restored. The granite pile as it now stands, in Romanesque basilica style, is one of the handsomest sanctuaries in the country; the crypt is the best preserved bit of the old structure. The Patron Saint of Viborg, St. Kjeld, and the Kings Svend Grade and Erik Glipping, who both perished in the vicinity of the town, are buried here.

On the South shores of the Limfjord are several towns, Lemvig, Skive, Lögstör and Nibe, and the large Aalborg (about 20,000 inhab:), which has a considerable shipping trade on the Limfjord. Aalborg is mentioned as early as the 11th century; in contrast with the other towns in the country, it has kept its old-fashioned air in its crooked, narrow streets and cross-beamed houses with gable ends towards the streets or outside galleries and bow-windows; but they are quickly disappearing. From Aalborg the East Jylland railway extends across the Limfjord into Vendsyssel; the solid bridge on very firmly bedded brick pillars, to withstand the current and icedrift in the Fjord, is the most considerable triumph of engineering skill in Denmark.

In the bleak poor regions of West Jylland, the towns are insignificant and far apart. Holstebro on the Aa (stream) of that name has its quay at Struer on the Limfjord. Ringkjöbing, also on the fjord of that name, is chiefly a fishing-station; Varde is likewise on its own stream. Ribe on Ribeaa is the chief place on the coast, about 3 kilom: from the sea, but has only 4000 inhab. Ribe was of great consequence as early as the 9th century; when the second church in the land was built there, it was renowned as a flourishing commercial city. Later on the Kings often resided at Riberhus Castle in the neighborhood, of which now nothing is to be seen but the rampart site. As a proof of its former grandeur we may add, that it has had 5 monasteries and 14 churches. After the Reformation it declined, and it has also suffered much from fire and flood. Of the churches two only remain; the Cathedral, dating from the 11th century, is Romanesque in its architecture. Between Varde and Ribe on the Hjertingbugt is the important port of Esbjerg, the only harbor on the west coast. It was constructed in 1868—74 especially for the export trade to England, after Denmark by the Treaty of Vienna had lost her West coast harbors. All these towns communicate by a coast-railway, which again joins several branch-lines and thus connects with the Eastern lines.

From Aalborg the highway to Vendsyssel is by rail, over Limfjord inland to Hjörring, the oldest place in the North Jylland isle, which we should not suspect, so much has it suffered from conflagrations. Leaving Hjörring, the railway turns eastwards to Frederikshavn on the Kattegat. This is a rising place with a good harbor, frequented by ships seeking to double the Skagen point; the transit-trade with Sweden, led this way by railroads, is also noteworthy. South of Frederikshavn on the Kattegat is pretty little Sæby, and at the entrance to the Limfjord the trading-station Hals. On the East-coast we still have Skagen, the most northerly and in many ways most remarkable town, evidently founded in the 14th century. Lying right out on the cape of Jylland, it touches both Skagerak and Kattegat. The low dwellings built of cross-beams and surrounded by black tarred plank palings, do not form regular streets, as the houses have to be raised separately under cover of the "Klitter" (dunes) to protect them from the drifting sand. This hides everything, rendering pavement impossible; it has been necessary to erect a new church, as the old one was too exposed; the tower alone now reaches above the surrounding sea of sand. The population (2,000) subsists mainly by fishing and the salvage from the frequent wrecks. The western coast of the North Jylland isle from Skagen to Limfjord has no towns; but here and there a small fishing hamlet peeps between the dunes, as Lönstrup, Lökken, which may be looked upon as the loading-place of Hjörring, and Blokhusene. Of late the splendid bathing has tempted people to spend their summer holidays there. On the whole these strands present a desolate expanse of sandy waste; and the fragments of wrecks, cast about in all directions, tell a sad tale of suffering and death. The town on the western side of the North Jylland isle, the so-called Thyland, is Thisted on the northern side of Limfjord; on the isle of Mors is tiny Nykjöbing.

V

Dependencies and Colonies

1. The Færöes lie in Nordhavet (the North sea) Lat. 62° N., and 7° W. Long:, about 380 kilom: N. of Scotland's most northerly point, nearly 700 kilom: from the western shores of Norway and over 1000 kilom. from the nearest Danish coast. The cluster consists of 17 inhabited islands, of which the largest (Strömö) contains scarcely 400 sq: kilom:, and of several small holms and crags, together about 1300 sq: kilom: (24 sq: miles). All are composed of volcanic rocks, trap and basalt, and have rugged coasts with steep cliffs descending to the ocean. The solid trap-porphyry is mixed with a softer stratum, which decays and falls, forming terraces, the "Hamre" (cliff-walls). The sides of the fjords have an amphitheatrical look, one terrace rising above the other. Farther inland on the contrary the cliffs form plateaus, over which isolated blocks rise to 800 or 900 meters. In the lower districts the rocks are covered by a thin layer of soil, which produces a rich crop of grass; cattle breeding is therefore the principal means of subsistance for the population. The mild insular climate, due to warm currents from the Atlantic, is especially favorable to this pursuit. The mean temperature is above 6° C. and the winters are far milder than in Denmark, thus the cattle can live out all the year round. The principal domestic animal is the sheep, whose wool is prepared by the people themselves, and made into articles of clothing (vests, gloves and stockings). The thin subsoil is however not sufficient for trees or for agriculture, tho a little barley is raised, but generally only potatoes and turnips. Fishing and birdhunting are important occupations, as is also the catching of the "Grindehval" (Ca'ing whale, Delphinus globiceps) which seeks the bays and creeks in great numbers.

In the Middle Ages the Færöes belonged to Norway; it was at the close of the 9th century under King Harald Haarfager (Fairhair), that they were colonized; when Norway was separated from Denmark in 1814, they remained with the latter country. The limited population (about 11,000) speak a peculiar dialect of the old Norse tongue, but the language of Church and School is Danish. The islands belong to the kingdom, and form a county for themselves; ecclesiastically they are under the diocese of Sjælland. There are no towns, only houses grouped together, or trading-stations on the larger isles. The most considerable mercantile center is Thorshavn on Strömö, and this is the most like a town.

2. Iceland (Island) is about 560 kilom: (75 miles) N. W. of the Færöes, between 63^0 23' and 66^0 33' N. Lat., and 13^0 30' and 24^0 30' W. Long:. It is a roundish island about 350 kilom: from N. to S. and 500 kilom: from W. to E., the whole area 105,000 sq: kilom: (1900 sq: miles). It is a high mountainous country with broken rocky shores, especially to the N. and W., whence three considerable peninsulas project, divided by the Breidi and Faxafjord. The soil consists entirely of volcanic masses, such as tufa (compact volcanic ashes), trap and basalt. Only in a few places along the coast and in the river valleys are there low parts, the interior (which is but little known) is with these exceptions one vast continuous plateau with an average height of somewhat over 600 meters. It shows generally large bare sweeps, where the rocks stand naked or covered with lava-gravel and sand. A good many rise above the average level, and as the snow-line is between 850 and 950 meters, there are great glacier districts (about 14,000 sq: kilom:), also called "Jökler"; the biggest is Vatna or Klofajökul to the N. E., with the neighboring Jökler the largest ice field in Europe. In this part of the island are the highest points, Oræfajökul 1960, Snæfell 1824 and Eyafjallajökul 1706 meters. The mountains of the northern part of the land are not so lofty, and the glacier formation is not so extensive. Right across from S. W. to N. E. stretches a volcanic belt with over 20 active volcanoes (to the S. W. is Hekla 1538 meters), the one most celebrated for its frequent and terrible eruptions, whose rain of ashes often destroys the surrounding grassfields. Of other volcanoes in the chain, may be mentioned the Dyngufjæld, with the lavafield Odadahraun 3000 sq: kilom:

(Hraun, signifies lavafield) and Lejrhnuk to the N. E. at the lake Myvatn. Due to volcanic agency are also the boiling springs, the best known being Geyser to the N. of Hekla, which once in the 24 hours sends up a column of boiling water 2 or 3 meters in diameter and 30 meters in height; this name has become synonymous for all such springs. From the great "Jökler" (glaciers) as also from many lakes, of which, besides Myvatn, Tingvallavatn to the S. W. may be mentioned, there flow in all directions streams of no great length (the longest 150 to 200 kilom:), transporting large quantities of milky-white or yellow-brown water which create imposing cataracts. The largest run northwards, as Lagaflod, the two Jökulsaaer and Skjalfandaflod. There is a great difference between the climate of the north and south; as the South coast comes in contact with the warm Gulf-stream, it has a mild insular climate with much dampness, fog and ice-free harbors. The North coast on the other hand, exposed to the cold Polar current, has a more rigorous climate, so that the harbors are ice-bound up to July. The mean annual temperature at Reykjavik is $5,3^0$ C., in summer $10,3^0$, in winter $1,6^0$, whilst at Akureyri on the North side the mean is $0,6^0$, in summer $7,5^0$, in winter — $6,3^0$.

After what has been said of the character of the country, it follows that it is thinly populated; in 1890 there were a little more than 72,000 souls, or not one person for every sq: kilom:; only 44,000 sq: kilom: are considered as inhabited, and stretch along the coasts, especially to the S. and W., and also the larger river valleys. The people speak a language akin to the old Northern and have kept up a great love for the old Sagas and the history of the past. In fact, as we all know, this is the home of the songs of the Eddas, and the traditions of Snorre Sturlasson, the author of the Chronicle of the Kings of Norway. The education of the Icelanders is universally good, altho it almost entirely owes its existence to domestic influence; it is only quite of late that a few Parish-schools and Higher Educational Establishments have been instituted. As on the Færöes, sheep-farming is the chief employment; the small hardy

Iceland pony too is of great importance, as only by its help can one travel along the difficult roads. The raising of corn is well-nigh out of the question; potatoes and roots are easy of cultivation. Trees there are none, the fuel is turf (peat), and the timber is what drifts to the coast with the warm currents in great quantities. Fishing and fowling here, as on the Færöes, play a great part in the economy of the island.

Island like the Færöes was colonized during the reign of Harald Haarfager; but the island maintained its independance as an aristocratic republic until the 13th century, being governed by the great chieftains. It then fell under the dominion of Norway; in 1814 it also remained Danish. It does not, like the Færöes, belong to the kingdom, but occupies a special position, regulated by the Law of 1871, which says that: "Iceland is an inseparable part of the Danish dominions, but with special national privileges." By the Constitutional Law of 1874 for the Affairs of Iceland, the King rules with a responsible minister for Iceland at his side, sharing the Legislative powers with the Alting; of the 36 members one sixth are appointed by the King; at its meeting the Ting (Assembly) divides into two bodies. The local authority is maintained by a governor, and the judicial rule is vested in the Icelandic Court, but all appeals are referred to the Supreme Court (the Höjesteret) in Kjöbenhavn. The Administration in Iceland is divided into three counties (again separated into "Sysler" and "Repper", answering to the parishes and hundreds of the kingdom); ecclesiastically the island is a diocese of itself.

Iceland has only three small market-towns, Reykjavik to the S.W., Isafjord and Akureyri to the N., besides some trading-stations along the coast; in a few of the valleys are sundry farms. The houses are nearly all of wood. Reykjavik, the capital, is the only town of any consequence, with about 3000 inhabitants. It is the seat of the Governor, the Bishop and the Alting (Parliament). The town has a statue of Thorvaldsen, whose father was the son of an Icelandic priest.

3. The Danish colonies in Grönland (Greenland) all lie on the West coast, and are supposed to extend over about 88,000 sq: kilom: (1600 sq: miles). The western side is known as far as $83°$ N. Lat., but the East has not been explored further than $77°$ N. Lat:; the last is but slightly explored and is very sparingly inhabited. The interior is thought to be one continuous plateau, eternally covered with snow and ice, whilst here and there the dark jagged peaks of the Nunatakker tower above it. On account of the cold currents which surround the sea-board, Grönland belongs to the coldest regions on the globe, altho the southern extremity of Cape Farewell lies under the same latitude as the capital of Norway. Julianehaab, under $60°$ N. Lat:, has an annual mean temperature of a little above $1°$ C., and in winter $-5°$, in Upernivik, under $73°$ N. Lat:, the annual mean is over $-11°$ and that of winter $-24°$. Vegetation is scanty, but the western coast during the short summer has surprisingly luxuriant pasturage. The inhabitants, about 10,000, are nearly all Esqimaux who live by hunting and fishing. Of paramount importance is the seal fishery, which supplies the people with all the necessaries of life. The flesh furnishes food, the oil supplies warmth and light, the skin clothing and covering for their boats and tents. The only domestic animal is the dog, employed to draw the sledges. The Esquimaux are in fact christianized, but in the scale of civilization they stand on a very low point.

Grönland was discovered and colonized from Iceland at the close of the 10th century, but in the Middle Ages all trace of the route to these distant regions was lost, and the colonists with their settlements perished in the struggle against the Esquimaux. During the reign of Christian IV an attempt was made to re-open communication with the lost colony, but it led to no result; not until the beginning of the 18th century, when the Norwegian Hans Egede made his way thither as a missionary, did the Danish colonization of the west coast begin; later on the Moravians also have established missions. Trade is carried on exclusively with the Danish State, and is on the whole lucrative; the exports are: cryolite, from which soda is made, feathers, train-oil, hides and dried fish. The colonies are divided into two inspectorates, South and North. In the first among other places, is Godthaab, the first colony, established 1721, and Julianehaab, the largest of all the settlements; in the northern inspectorate Egedesminde, and Upernivik, the most northerly trading-station in the world.

4. The Danish West-Indian colonies consist of the three small islands St. Jean, St. Thomas and St. Croix; the two first were acquired at the end of the 17th century under Christian V, the last under Christian VI in the 18th. Together they comprise 360 sq: kilom: ($6^1/_2$ sq: miles) with 34,000 souls. They are fruitful, especially the largest, St. Croix; the most important products are sugar and rum; St. Thomas is of most consequence because of its capital harbor, which makes it the chief steam-packet station and a commercial centre. The population consists mostly of Negroes and Mulattos, who speak English. At the head of the colonial government is a Governor appointed by the mother-country.

H. Weitemeyer.

Among the works published on the Geography of Denmark may be mentioned: Bergsöe, Den Danske Stats Statistik (Danish State Statistics), Cop: 1844—53, 4 vol:; Falbe-Hansen and Scharling, Danmarks Statistik (Statistics of Denmark), Cop: 1878 - 85, 5 vol: Trap, Statistisk topographisk Beskrivelse af Danmark (Statistical and topographical description of Denmark), Cop: 2nd: ed. 1872—79, 6 vol: with map. A. Baggesen, Den danske Stat betragtet geographisk og statistisk (The Danish State from a geographical and statistic point of view), Cop: 1840, 2nd ed: 1862. Ed. Erslev, Den danske Stat, en geographisk Skildring for Folket (The Danish State, a popular geographical description) Cop: 1855—57; Ed. Erslev, Jylland, Studier og Skildringer til

Danmarks Geographie (Jutland, Essays and descriptions of the geography of Denmark), Cop: 1886. Statistisk Tabelværk (Statistical Tables) edited from 1835, Maps. Generalstabens topographiske Kort over Danmark (The topographical maps of Denmark by the General Staff), published from 1845, not yet finished. Physisk-geografisk Kort over Danmark, med tilhörende Bilande (Physical and geographical map of Denmark and its dependencies), composed by the topographical section of the General Staff, Cop: 1889.

The above Article: "Country and People" is in part a reproduction of the section "Denmark" in H. Weitemeyer's Geogrnphisk Haandbog (Handbook of Geography), Cop: 1886.

LITERATURE AND ARTS

Language and Literature

The **Danish language** belongs to the great Scando-Gothic group, and with Norwegian (Norse), Swedish and Icelandic forms its northern section. From the commencement of the historical era "Dansk Tunge" (the Danish tongue) was spoken in all Scandinavia, tho of course in many local dialects. This is proved by the Runic memorials, of which a great number remain in the northern lands and in England. About the year 1000, however, more fixed literary forms emerge, and thereafter still later Scandinavian dialects develop, change and decay. The chief of these in Denmark are the Jutlandish, the Sealandish and the Scanian. The last approaches nearest to the oldest known book-Danish.

During the Middle Ages not a few Latinisms crept in, from literary culture and the services of the Roman Church. But, from the middle of the 14th and far into the 15th century, the language is inundated with Low-German, as a natural consequence of the commerce carried on with the Hanseatic towns, and continual intercourse with traders and craftsmen. Of this influence we have still indelible marks.

The Reformation brings with it a refreshing spiritual revival of great importance. The most considerable work of this period is Christian III's Bible (1550), which was chiefly due to the labors of Christiern Pedersen (1480-1554), formerly Canon of Lund Cathedral, and of Peter Palladius, the first Bishop of Sealand after the Reformation. This version is characteristically clear and pure, and at once places the Sealand dialect at the head of the others, as the book-language of the country. At the end of the 16th century appeared a book of great linguistic value, Saxo's Chronicle, translated by the Court Chaplain Anders Sörensen Vedel (1542-1616). At this time the mother-tongue still sounds pure and pithy, but later on it was corrupted by Latin brought in by the Renaissance. Our own language was not worth studying, and became greatly neglected from the moment Latin was made the literary vehicle of the learned and cultured classes. Even when such men as Anders Arrebo, Anders Bording and Thomas Kingo wrote in Danish, no one heeded it. The parson Peder Syv (1631-1702) is about the only one who gives it any attention, altho in his "Danske Sprogkunst" (The Art of Danish) he is obliged to use Latin, "that he may the better be understood". Ludvig Holberg inaugurates a happy period. His great genius not only created a national literature, but "polished the language." Even Holberg was not entirely free from mixing French or Latin words with his Danish; but his contemporaries, Eilschow, the linguist and philosopher, and Jens Sneedorf, counteracted this tendency. At last, in spite of every narrow-minded objection and mistaken idea of refinement, the new Danish literary language broke thro all hindrances with the great poets Wessel (1742-1785), Ewald (1743-1781), Baggesen (1764-1826), and Oehlenschläger (1779-1850). We cannot but wonder at the growth of the language in the poetical works of the last of these.

In our days the purification goes on apace. The successful war of 1848-50 put Danish authors and journalists on their metal, to clear out Germanisms, and the unhappy issue of the last conflict in 1864 has driven the authors still farther in the same direction. This new life has enriched the tongue with many new expressions, and the literature actively continues to bring in words from the Scandinavian brotherlands or to find Old Danish and modern dialect synonyms for foreign terms.

Among older grammatical works, besides that of Peder Syv, there are these of J. Höjsgaard, R. Rask (1787-1831), "A Grammar of the Danish language", and J. Lökke's "Etymology of the Northern tongue." In order to improve orthography, Rask wrote his curious and controversial book "Scientific Danish spelling." During our own time N. M. Petersen, Lyngby and Wimmer (the last has also published an exhaustive volume on Runes) have studied our linguistic history. The Scientific and Literary Society is publishing a great lexiographical work, and Molbech's labors in the same direction must not be forgotten. Professor Svend Grundtvig has added a small "Handbook for the newest Orthography", which cannot be called very complete. A great deal has also been done to throw light on the language, dialects and old literature of Denmark by the "Universitets Jubilæets Danske Samfund." Among other valuable things they are issuing the great dictionary of Danish from 1300 to 1700 by Dr. Kalkar, and a large dictionary of the Jutlandish (Jylland) dialects by Pastor Feilberg.

The dialects have not been neglected, for besides Feilberg, we have Varming's "Popular language in Jutland," Kock's "The Tongue of the people in South Jutland," Hagerup's "Danish in Angel" and Espersen's Dictionary of the Bornholm Dialects (not yet printed); these give ample testimony of solid work. E. v. d. Recke has written a good book on "Danish Metrical Law."

Danish Literature. The Danes may have had a share in the rich and original old Northern literature. In the Middle Ages however, all the culture was in the hands of the religious orders; hence the spoken language had to give way to the Latinism of the Schools. Latin was the only language these men could write. The chief work of this period is a didactic theological poem: "Hexaëmeron" by Archbishop Andreas Sunesen (died 1228), who belonged to the illustrious Hvide family; and the "Danish Chronicle" by the Clerk of Sorö Convent, Saxo Grammaticus (who died early in the 13th century), also said to have been of noble lineage. Saxo wrote his Chronicle by desire of Archbishop Absalon, and in spite of having no literary aids, the composition is in the most correct and elegant Latin. This was an admirable volume, making the greatness of Denmark during the Middle Ages widely known among the learned all over Europe, and has thus deserved its renown.

Side by side with this Latin book-making, we possess a remarkable national treasure from an early period, the popular ballads, which were long kept alive by being recited or sung by the people. The authors of this enormous collection of Romances and narrative verse are unknown; they seem however to have sprung from all classes, especially the higher. The feelings and sentiments of knight and cleric, serf and citizen find expression in the burden, which always accompanies the stanzas and constitutes its lyrical form. The Ballads are classified in five cycles: 1st the Heroic ("Kæmpeviser") which takes its inspiration from the old Northern myths and traditions, changing all however into the garb of the Middle Ages; 2nd the Magical ("Trylleviser") in which the superstition of the times, with belief in goblins, elves and sea monsters, the tremendous power of Runes and such like weird notions, find expression; 3rd Legends ("Legendeviser"), from biblical stories and saintly miracles; 4th Knightly lays ("Ridderviser"), chiefly dwelling on love, and by their minute descriptions of life and manners in the castles, of the costumes of knights and dames, have a high historical value; 5th Historical songs from Danish sources, which, to make up for the primitive want of all true criticism are full of subtle poetry—the Dagmar ballads, the tales of Marsk Stig and his daughters, Niels Ebbesen, etc. These Treasures were copied in the 16th century by many a noble lady and thus escaped oblivion, as the Folksong of the Middle Ages was then dying away. Much has of course lived on until now among the common people, after being neglected by the upper classes. The composer Berggreen, who died a few years ago, has the merit of having collected many of the melodies, worked out often by the musician, whilst the words have been a gold-mine to the poet. The first attempt to collect these Ballads was made by Abrahamson, Nyerup and Rahbek, but Svend Grundtvig's later collection is far more complete.

As we have said, the national literature was for a time crushed by the Latin, but with the Reformation a fresh current of vigorous life came in. As already mentioned, Christiern Pedersen had the chief honor of using the mother-tongue during those dark days. Besides his part in Christian III's Bible, he edited Saxo and published a translation of the old knightly romance "Olger Danske." His "Jærtegnspostil" (Miracle-Homilies) is remarkable for nobility of feeling and language. Bishop Palladius's "Visitatsbog" (Pastoral visitations) is very instructive, giving an insight into this fervent reformer's endeavors to forward evangelical Christian enlightenment, and to change the old ritual according to the spirit of the new doctrine. Povl Helgesen (born about 1480) is a most interesting author; he was wrongly called turncoat ("Vendekaabe") because he wished a reformation within the Church, considering it however to be "the devil's work" to rend the Danish province from the Mother-Church. His style is powerful, but often disfigured by extravagant recklessness.

By the middle of the 16th century, the Reformation had stiffened into distinct dogmas, and the Church service had finally formed itself; all spiritual life is blighted, and we enter the learned period, with Latin dominating all thought, whilst the one idea is defence of pure Lutheranism. Every leaning towards Calvinism is reprehensible and must be punished, be the victim learned and honorable or not. Such was the fate of Niels Hemmingsen (1513-1600), one of Melanchthon's beloved pupils. He is the author of a popular dogmatical work "Livsens Vei" (The way of life). Jesper Brochmand (1585-1652), who became Bishop of Sealand, was an erudite theologian and a strict Lutheran. His best known volume is the still perused "Huspostillen" (Home Sermons), a series for every Holy day throughout the year. The chief historian of this age is Anders Sörensen Vedel, the teacher of Tycho Brahe. He translated Saxo and edited the first collection of Ballads from the Middle Ages. He was invited to undertake the task by King Frederik II's Queen Sophie, when she visited Tycho Brahe on the island of Hveen.

Arild Hvitfeld (1549-1609), Lord of Dragsholm and Chancellor of the Kingdom, wrote "the Chronicle of the Kingdom of Denmark" (Danmarks Riges Krönike), which abounds in historical documents of great importance.

With the 17th century commences a new interest in Northern antiquities. Professor Ole Worm (1588-1654) published a collection of Runic inscriptions "Monumenta Danica;" his readings are however obsolete now. Peder Syv continued Vedel's ballads and made a wonderful collection of Danish proverbs, containing the philosophy of the people during many centuries.

In natural science Tycho Brahe eclipsed everyone, but his self-willed and unamiable temperament made him enemies everywhere; at last his life by reason of this was made so burdensome to him, that he was obliged to leave his beautiful Castle of Uranienborg and Stjærneborg, his observatory on the isle of Hveen, and accept the Emperor Rudolf II's invitation to come to Prague, where he died in 1601. His cleverest successor was Ole Römer (1664-1710).

In medicine Kaspar and Thomas Bartholin (father and son, the latter a celebrated anatomist), and Niels Stensen (Nicolaus Steno, 1638-1686) son of a Copenhagen goldsmith, also made a name in this science; but Stensen is especially known and remembered as the founder of Geology. Unfortunately Stensen became a Romanist in Florence and was afterwards made Apostolic Vicar General of North Germany, and was thus lost to Science.

Altho this scholarly lustrum was far from favorable to poetry, still Anders Arrebo (1587-1637) inaugurated a new era for the Muse in the mother-tongue. Being gay and addicted to the love of women, he was deprived of his bishopric; it was with great difficulty that a small curacy was obtained for him—but his bardship consoled him for every trial. His poem "Hexaëmeron" or the "six days Creation" is rich in fine descriptions of nature, and metrically it denotes a great improvement, as the author builds his verse on the accent of the syllable. Anders Bording (1619-1677) also wrote facile and flowing verse. He is also the first Danish Journalist. By Royal desire he printed once a month the "Danish Mercury", a newspaper in rhyme. Thomas Kingo the Psalmist, who died as bishop of Fyn 1703, was without doubt the reigning Scald during the 17th century. His "Spiritual Choir" (Aandeligt Sjungekor) denotes a depth of feeling and a vigor and loftiness of sentiment, seldom met with in Protestant church poetry.

Birket Smith has published a most remarkable volume from this time, as important for originality of style as for historical authenticity. It is entitled: "Recollections of the sufferings of Eleonora Christina Ulfeldt ("Eleonora Christina Ulfeldts Jammerminde"). The illustrious prisoner gives a touching description of what she endured, during 22 years of captivity in the Blue Tower at Copenhagen.

With Ludvig Holberg Danish letters make a new start. His authorship is so considerable, that he alone may be said to fill the period. The greatness of his genius especially manifests itself in his comedies: "Jeppe paa Bjerget," "Erasmus Montanus," "Ulysses von Ithacia," "Jacob von Thybo," "Den politiske Kandestøber (The political Coppersmith), "Barselstuen" (The Lying-in-Chamber), "Den Stundesløse" (The Busy-body), "Don Ranudo", "Den 11te Juni", etc. The typical figures of the day are made immortal in these pages. Holberg was also no mean historical writer ("History of heroes and heroines", "Church History until the Reformation," "History of Denmark"). Being a clearsighted critic, his compositions are terse and lively; and tho the rationalistic dryness of the 18th century held him under subjection, his books may yet be read with pleasure and profit. Holberg gave new and vigorous ideas to the Dano-Norwegian peoples by his writings, and by his never tiring energy in combating the pedantry of the University and the barren learning of the time. We see this from his very first volume, the satirical heroic poem "Peder Paars." His constant demand was for sound and reasonable patriotism. He gave his large fortune to found a College at Sorö, where political science, history, moral philosophy, the mother-tongue and modern languages should chiefly be taught. Altho he continued his favorite

Comedy-writing up to the last, he nevertheless became by degrees more an observer than an author. Much of what he thus gathered he has laid down for us in his "Epistles" (5 vol:). Holberg died in 1754 as treasurer at the University. He gained his experience and culture chiefly by travelling in England, Holland, France and Italy. His favorite study was old Roman authors (notably Plautus), and the great French masters of Louis the XIV's age. German he did not like, nor was there anything to be learnt from Germany at that moment. On the contrary they were taught by him; Lessing and the Romanticists (especially Tieck) greatly admired him, and Goethe too is said to have known his works.

Nobody was able to replace Holberg, tho some of the Sorö Professors were inspired by him, among others Jens Sneedorf (1724-1764), who edited the "Patriotic Spectator," and the political writer Andreas Schytte. These authors were able, like their master, to give subtle thoughts in clear language. Toward the end of the century, Wivet imitated his dramatic style.

Johannes Ewald (1743-1781) brought a fresh current into the national poetry. The son of a well-known pietistic clergyman, he inherited from his father deep religious sentiments. When a youthful student he fell in love, and believing that he could easily make his way as a military man, he started for Germany, to place himself under the standard of his admired hero Frederik II of Prussia. He returned broken in health and disappointed, having endured great hardships. To add to his trouble, he now found himself jilted by the girl he loved—she married another. At first he sought oblivion in a life of wild orgies, but being of too noble a nature to find any satisfaction in debauchery, he found alleviation from pain and grief in penmanship, and the Muse henceforth soothed his aching heart. Reduced by poverty and helpless from gout, forsaken by his well-to-do mother for a less worthy brother, his mighty spirit rose above all. He created Danish tragedy in "Balder's Death" and its opera in "The Fishermen", national poems of intrinsic worth and perfect form, taking into consideration the epoch in which they saw the light. His Odes ("To the Soul", "Reflexions at the Communion", "To my Mother") show his powers to perfection and still remain unsurpassed in lyrical poetry.

This great poet was only appreciated by a small group of young men, by others he was treated with contempt or indifference. This feeling emanated from the "Norwegian Society", a small coterie of clever young Norwegians who continued the Holberg tradition and in contradiction to the Ewaldians, who worshiped Klopstock and Ewald, chose Greek or French models. To this circle belonged Fasting, a writer of tasteful prose, the brothers Frimann and Rein, lyrical writers of some note, as well as Zetlitz the Ballad writer. The most remarkable was Johan Herman Wessel, a relative of the famous naval hero Tordenskjold. Wessel was a noble mind, whose studies of the best productions had developed and enriched his æsthetic taste. The publication of his satirical tragedy "Kjærlighed uden Strömper" (Stockingless Love) won for him honor and renown, and at once made him widely known. It is a parody of great power, on the hollow pathos of the French tragedy with its affected passion, and will for all time remain a grand protest against what is unnatural and forced in poetry. Wessel also died poor and neglected, four years later than Ewald (1785).

The same year in which Wessel died, Baggesen's "Comical Tales" came out. They were written in the style of Wieland and Wessel, and were very successful. Jens Baggesen (1764-1826), from being a poor student from the small township of Korsör, all of a sudden found himself admired and flattered by the literary world. He was even accepted as a friend and guest by the Minister of State, Ernst Schimmelmann, and by Count Reventlov of Brahetrolleborg. Thro their assistance means were found for a journey. Baggesen travelled thro Germany, Switzerland and France. When in Bern he became engaged to Miss Sophia de Haller, daughter of the Patrician and poet A. de Haller. The fruit of this trip was the first Danish book of travels of any importance, "The Labyrinth", in which the young author, in a style sparkling with flashes of wit and humor, describes his impressions and his visits to several famous men in the countries he traversed. Altho his position at home was a very comfortable one, he was of too restless a nature to settle down. After publishing his "Youthful labors" (in which was the "Chronicle of Kallundborg", a masterly comic tale), he started for the continent with his sickly wife. She died during this absence, and Baggesen returned to Copenhagen to enter upon his post as director of the Royal Theater. His second wife, Fanny Raybaz, a French Swiss, was also unable to stand the Northern climate, and thus Baggesen was once more obliged to travel. At the farewell festival given on this occasion, he "willed away his Danish lyre" to the young man who had written the song for this event. Baggesen was from this time forth only to write in a foreign language. The youth who took up his garment was Adam Oehlenschläger.

Oehlenschläger (1779-1850) became the creator of the Danish Romantic School, but his influence extended also to the whole of Scandinavia. His friends were the best men of his time, Dr: O. H. Mynster, J. P. Mynster the Theologian, H. C. Örsted the Naturalist, the Lawyer A. S. Örsted, etc. Thro these friendships his mind was prepared for the influence of the young philosopher Henrik Steffens (1773-1845), who, on his return from Germany, appeared as the prophet of the gospel of romance. Inspired by him, Oehlenschläger wrote the genuine romantic poem "Guldhornene" (The Golden Horns), and later the dramatical tale "Aladdin", a poem which the German romanticism cannot surpass. Then came a series of beautiful pieces, from "En Langelandsreise" (A trip to Langeland) to the cyclus "The year's Gospel", which in some points reminds one of Novalis. This mighty poetical genius showered his gifts — as if a marvellous spring-tide had fallen over the land. During a journey in which he visited Steffens in Halle, Madame de Staël in Coppet and Baggesen in Paris, he wrote the glorious Northern tragedy "Hakon Jarl", the mythological tragic play "Balder's death", and published these, as well as the lovely epic "Thor's journey to Jotunheim", under the title "Northern Poems", in 1807. In Paris he wrote "Axel and Valborg" and in Italy "Corregio"; both were so admired, that people well-nigh fought over a manuscript copy, before they were printed. On his return, he was made Professor of Æsthetics at the University.

Meanwhile Baggesen had endeavored, with some success, to write German verse. But, during a trip to Copenhagen in 1806, he made the acquaintance of and became deeply attached to Mrs. Sophie Örsted, Oehlenschläger's brilliant sister, and she won him over to the new School of Danish thought. Baggesen sent Oehlenschläger, who was then on the continent, one of his characteristic letters in rhyme (an art in which he excelled). Later on he attacked the votaries of the older Danish art of poetry, chiefly K. L. Rahbek, author of dramas and ballads, and editor of Reviews. These delightful and witty wordy wars appeared in "Gjengangeren" (The Ghost). In Paris, Baggesen and Oehlenschläger had lived on the friendliest footing together, and the great national calamity of 1807 had still further bound them to each other; but, after Baggesen's return to Copenhagen, several years later, the friendly feelings cooled. Oehlenschläger, according to Baggesen — and he was not far wrong — had allowed "stagnation to displace activity"; he therefore criticized him sharply, especially were such poor effusions as "Hugo von Rheinberg", "The Robber's Castle" and "Ludlam's Cave" severely censured. Oehlenschläger's younger admirers however, having grown up to worship him in his first splendid works, were ever ready to take up the cudgels on his behalf, and they now said, that Baggesen was jealous of their hero's honor. This was certainly not the case, as when Oehlenschläger in 1814 brought out his beautiful Northern poem "Helge", and in 1818 the dramatic idyl "The little shepherd boy", both were hailed with enthusiasm by Baggesen. The warmblooded young Academicians forgot this, and when he afterwards made fun of his very inferior "Letters from a Journey", 12 Students ("Tylvten") challenged him in Latin to defend his æsthetic opinions. The whole literary world was in an uproar. Baggesen jeered his foes in witty epigrams and long satirical poems, (such as the excellent piece "Per Vrövlers Kommentar"), and the youngsters, amongst whom were some of the cleverest of the University men, were not afraid of retaliation. Oehlenschläger kept silence; probably he felt that he could not cope with Baggesen in questions of reflection and polemics, of satire and æsthetics. The dispute degenerated into a scandal. Oehlenschläger and his young fiery friend Hjort accused Baggesen of literary theft, the former reservedly in his "Robinson in England", the latter openly in his pamphlet "The history of the Magical Harp". At last Baggesen closed the feud by expatriating himself. He never saw his fatherland again, the country he had sung of so rapturously and to which he belonged more fully perhaps than most others. Baggesen's last strains were in German, a humorous piece of g eat excellence called "Adam and Eve".

The struggle between the Romanticism of the 19th and the Rationalism of the 18th century may now be said to close. Baggesen's young friend J. L. Heiberg (1791—1860), once more opened the question after his death in a more sober and gentle tone, but the elected favorite of romance Adam Oehlenschläger was now considered by all as "King of Northern Poets", and crowned laureate in Lund, by the greatest of Swedish bards Esaias Tegnér, 1829. This was a sublime moment in the history of intellectual life in Scandinavia. In beautiful Swedish hexameters it was said: "That the hour of dissension was now for ever gone".

Baggesen was not the only one who was eclipsed by the genius of Oehlenschläger; the highly cultured poet Schack de Staffeldt shared the same fate. But whilst the former always kept some firm admirers from the old school of thought, Staffeldt stood well-nigh alone all his life. His poetry was too profound and noble to be understood by the masses, only a few philosophically educated could appreciate it. Staffeldt died in solitude and melancholy as Sheriff of Gottorp (1826). In 1809 the young Theologian N. F. S. Grundtvig (1783—1872) threatened to become a rival. In his "Scenes from the close of the Heroic age in the North", the master himself was fain to own: "That this serious pupil has penetrated farther into the national character of our forefathers than I have". Grundtvig did not long continue to give his powerful mind to Northern poetical subjects, but devoted himself to mythology (Nordens Mythologie" 1818), history ("Verdens Krönike", 1812, and 1817 "Middelaldrens Historie"), and theology. He especially influenced Danish poetry thro his psalms ("Sangværk til den Danske Kirke").

B. S. Ingemann, sometime Professor at the Sorö College, where he died in 1862, may in some sense be called Grundtvig's younger spiritual brother. His first efforts were however rather moonlight-romantic and sickly-sentimental ("Procne" and "Varner's wanderings", also a tragedy "Blanca"). J. L. Heiberg satirized his effusions in Aristophanes' style in "Julespög og Nytaarslöjer" (Christmas jests and New year drolleries), on which Grundtvig took his young friend's part. Heiberg was much too agile to be wounded by Grundtvig's hard blows, he kept well out of range, and tho public opinion was against Heiberg, yet he may be said to have come out of the fray victorious. Ingemann however was wearied and upset, and went away to restore and calm his mind. After travelling for some time he returned to an appointment as professor in that famous spot — Sorö — and at once began to write his historical novels: "Valdemar Sejr", "Erik Menved", "Kong Erik og de Fredlöse", and "Prince Otto af Danmark". The historical and literary critic has found much fault with these books both then and later; but, whatever their weak points, they have strengthened nationality and love of the Fatherland very considerably. Ingemann became a most popular poet in his later years; he was so highly thought of, that on his 70th birthday the women of Denmark made a demonstration in his honor, and presented him with a golden horn as a thank offering for his scaldship. Ingemann may be called "Woman's Minnesinger", as Oehlenschläger was man's. The festival given in Copenhagen in 1849 on the occasion af his 70th anniversary, by the most distinguished men of the capital, bears witness to this fact, and is the counterpart of the women's celebration of their hero in Sorö 1859.

At the Oehlenschläger fête J. L. Heiberg said: "this was the Adam from whom all the poets of the present day have sprung". This was a pretty sentence, but unfair even to Heiberg himself, as both he, Henrik Hertz, Paludan-Müller, Mrs. Gyllembourg and Carl Bernhard are as much allied to Baggesen as to Oehlenschläger; his influence is however very distinctly perceived in Hauch, Poul Möller, Christian Winther, H.C. Andersen, Bödtcher and Aarestrup.

Carsten Hauch (1790—1871) was a great admirer of the master; whilst Professor at Sorö, he and his colleagues, P. Hjort and Christian Wilster (the classical translator of Homer and Euripides), entered into a controversy with J.L. Heiberg, because he had dared to censure Oehlenschläger's writings. Hauch and Wilster were decided opponents of Heiberg's vaudevilles, considering them vulgar imitations of realities. In this second Heiberg warfare, the Soröans lost the day; Henrik Hertz (1798—1870), Heiberg's young pupil, came to his assistance and proved a capital ally. Hertz showed great taste and an excellent talent of versification in his "Ghost's letters", 1830. Heiberg, tho he teazed Hauch a good deal, still gave him due meed of praise, when the tragedy "Svend Grathe" appeared in 1841; it was a worthy successor of "Tiberius", which he wrote in his youth. Hauch takes a high place as a tragedy and novel writer ("En polsk Familie", "Robert Fulton" etc:); he is however still greater in the three lyrical volumes he published.

Among the novel-writers of this time, Mrs. Gyllembourg-Ehrensvärd (1773—1856), J. L. Heiberg's mother, made for herself a large circle of readers by her "Every day Histories". Carl Bernhard (1798—1865, his real name being Saint-Aubain), whose writings somewhat resembled hers, shared her popularity.

Steen Steensen Blicher (1782—1848), the solitary genius who stands aloof from any influence of the masters mentioned, but on that very account all the more remarkable in his independence and unbiassed strength, is the one only songster of whom Jutland can boast; the glory of his one name suffices. His novels in the Jutland dialect, full of the characteristic life of country folk and gipsies are still unsurpassed. Such are "The Diary of a Parish-clerk" (En Landsbydegns Dagbog), "Marie", "A Fortnight in Jutland" (Fjorten Dage i Jylland), "E Bindstouw" etc. His powers as a lyrical writer were also of the highest order, as is apparent in "The bird of passage" (Trækfuglene). Poverty and home troubles embittered his days. He died a clergyman in Jutland.

The reason why Blicher's novels were so little recognized during his life, was in great measure owing to his isolation so far from the literary center. That his lyrics were overlooked was due to the fact, that Denmark has a greater wealth of lyrical poetry than any other European country. Lyrical poets of the first rank are Christian Winther ("Wood engravings" (Træsnit); "Anette"; "Legends and songs" (Sagn og Sang); "To one" (Til En); "The Deer's flight" (Hjortens Flugt); "Verner og Malin" etc.); also Emil Aarestrup (two volumes of poetry) and Ludvig Bödtcher. Henrik Hertz is also a fine lyrical versifier, but his chief strength lies in his romantic dramas, "Svend Dyring's House", "King René's daughter", "Ninon", and his excellent comedy "Sparekassen" (The Savings Bank). Fr. Paludan-Müller has left us sundry finely conceived and profound poems, but most significant are the modern epic "Adam Homo" and the tragedy "Kalanus"; in this last he compares the Greek and Indian philosophy in a lucid and beautiful manner. Hans Christian Andersen we may call a lyrical prose writer, when reflecting upon his "Picture-book without Pictures" (Billedbog uden Billeder), and his other sketches replete with poetical fancy. His tales and stories are so well known and have been translated into so many languages, that they need no comment here. We cannot however refrain from saying, that their purely Danish tone cannot be rendered in any other tongue, altho the humor by which they are penetrated may be elucidated.

A great wave of Liberalism swept over the Danish student circles (Academicum) from the July revolution until 1848, and this brought a new style of poetry into fashion. The most famous representatives of this tendency were Carl Ploug, Hostrup and Christian Richardt. Hostrup is however best known by his Comedies "The Neighbors" (Gjenboerne), "Sparrow in Crane's Nest" (Spurv i Tranedans) and many more. Kaalund, who began life as a sculptor, stood aloof as an independent lyrical writer ("Spring" and "Aftermath"), besides which his exquisite "Fables for Children" bring him near to Hans Christian Andersen.

After the death of Oehlenschläger in 1850, a period of comparative stagnation ensued, as political life absorbed every other interest. After the sad troubles of 1864 however, the novels and writings of Meir Goldschmidt began to attract public notice. His novels, "A Jew" and "Homeless", had already created a certain sensation, but the author's peculiar political views placed him at a disadvantage. Now however, as the time was so barren of æsthetic interest, his "Ravnen", "Maser", "Love stories from many lands", etc., brought him into favor. A few men of the old school may yet be spoken of. C. K. F. Molbech first deserves mention both as a lyrical and dramatic poet ("Dante" and "Ambrosius"); he is also noted for his translation of Dante's "Divina Commedia". E. Lembcke is the greatly admired translator of Shakespear's plays. V. Bergsöe's novels (his best known book is "From the Piazza del Popolo") have had a wide circulation.

J. L. Heiberg, P. L. Möller and Georg Brandes are critics of talent and renown. The last (born 1842) is well versed in European literature and is inspired thereby; his first book in 1871 created quite a hubbub, and æsthetic life at home woke to new vigor. With the exception of V. Topsöe ("Jason and the Golden Fleece"), E. v. d. Recke and Rudolf Schmidt, nearly all the younger authors are under his sway. Thus it is with Holger Drachmann, one of the most prominent lyric poets (several volumes of poetry, novels "Young blood", "Sailors tales", etc); S. Schandorph (the tales "Little folks", „The Forester's children", and novels describing peasant and town life in Sealand); J. P. Jacobsen ("Mogens",

"Marie Grubbe" etc); E. Skram ("Gertrude Coldbjörnsen"); Edvard Brandes (the plays "Lægemidler", "Et Besög", "Kjærlighed"); K. Gjellerup ("Spirits and Times", "Brynhilde"); H. Bang (the latter-day novel "Tine"); H. Pontoppidan ("From the Cottages") and many other younger men whom space denies mentioning.

In spite of the small population, Danish poetry holds an exceptional position in the world; not only does it compare favorably with that of other nations, but it is well able to make some amends to the people for their political disappointments.

Danish prose is not so rich during the modern epoch as the sister art; still we are able to cite a few remarkable names. Whilst at an earlier period Gram, Langebek and Suhm, living in the 18th century, by their painstaking and far reaching investigations illumined many doubtful periods, many a difficult point in the history of our country, Guldberg (the celebrated statesman), F. Sneedorf and Engelstoft are remembered as capital exponents of historical facts. C. Thomsen, Worsaae, Japetus Steenstrup come nearer our own time; they have left us a legacy of erudite antiquarian lore. Peter Erasmus Müller and Finn Magnusen have expounded the Old Northern history; and N. M. Petersen (spoken of above) taught Danish literature, whilst C. F. Allen and Caspar Paludan-Müller were critical commentators of history, especially of the period of the Union. N. Höyen by his fine lectures, worked for Art-history and education throughout a long and busy life, especially for developing a Northern school of art. Of late the historians F. Schjern, Birket-Smith, Edvard Holm, A. D. Jörgensen, Johannes Steenstrup, K. Erslev, Fridericia, Chr. Bruun, Troels Lund etc. have given substantial contributions to and descriptions of the History of the Fatherland. Georg Brandes (in respect of style one of the finest penmen) has, in his most important work ("Hovedströmninger i det 19de Aarhundredes Literatur", Head-currents in the literature of the 19th century), given an account of the literary movement in Europe. Julius Lange in his art-histories ("Billed-Kunst", "Sergel and Thorvaldsen") has contributed many brilliant ideas of great benefit to Science. E. Bloch, K. Madsen and E. Hannover are also to be named as writers upon art.

Theological literature is voluminous, as religious life and thought have always played a great part in the development of the Danish people. Already as far back as the Pietistic days of Christian VI, a whole series of devotional and edifying tracts and larger works saw the light. And later, during the Rationalistic and Freethinking latter half of the 18th century, many controversial books were printed. The defender of the Faith was the persevering Bishop Balle, and the talented representative of pure Reason was Bastholm. The Voltairian Horrebov, who edited a weekly paper, "Jesus and Reason", was the standard-bearer of the more moderate Freethinkers. Rationalism for a long time preponderated in the Church, but at last its power was undermined by J. P. Mynster (he died as Bishop of Sealand), who had especial authority with the cultured classes, whilst N. F. S. Grundtvig spoke more to the hearts of the common people, and especially to the country folk and peasantry. Side by side with his religious teaching, went always the strength of his love of nationality. The last University rationalist, H. N. Clausen, was a great scholar with whom Grundtvig had an encounter which obliged him to resign his position in the Church (1825). This was however a moral victory, as from that moment Grundtvig's power grew, and his partisans became a large congregation. The so-called Grundtvigianism consists in the assertion of the Apostles Creed, "the words uttered by our Lord", being the foundation of Christianity; the Bible, on the other hand, "the written word", being only secondary. Sören Kierkegaard was a highly gifted apologist for the Christianity which renounces the world, when he maintained that "Belief is a paradox", and that between it and science there was an impassable gulf. With these asseverations he faced the old orthodoxy as well as the Hegelism of H. L. Martensen, who declared faith and knowledge as one to the philosopher. Kierkegaard's weapons were several essays entitled: "Either-Or", "Stages on the road of life", "Unscientific postscriptum", "Christian Apprenticeship", and yet others, all bearing witness to the author's dialectic mastery, æsthetic taste and psychological penetration. He succumbed from overwork in 1855. His disciple R. Nielsen, who held the chair of philosophy at the University, carried on the contest, but found worthy antagonists in the philosopher H. Bröchner and in Georg Brandes. This contest is now at an end; the struggle at present raging on the intellectual arena is between modern Orthodoxy and Positivism. A. C. Larsen, the eloquent representative of New-rationalism, has not gained many adherents.

Whilst most of these men of letters have enriched the National literature by their labors, Denmark also possesses several distinguished savants who, by their work in different branches, have given new impulse to discovery. These men belong not merely to the literature of their own country, but to the great world of science, tho they write in Danish. There are many names deserving notice. Among the philosophers Sibbern, Höffding ("Psychology") and Kroman ("Natural knowledge"). Exponents of Theology and Church history are Rudelbach ("Christian Biography", "Psalmody,") and Hermansen; while Helveg has given us the "History of the Danish Church before and after the Reformation". In addition to these are Holger Rördam and F. Nielsen ("The Roman Catholic Church in the 19th century"). In Jurisprudence: the founder of Danish Law, A. S. Örsted (died 1860) and the law-historians: J. E. Larsen, Stemann and H. Matzen; Bornemann and Goos in criminal law. In classical philology: I. L. Ussing and Madvig (died 1886); the latter an eminent critic of texts, who terminated his brilliant career with an erudite description of "The Constitution and Administration of the Romans". Oriental philology boasts: the late Westergaard (Zend-Avesta), Fausböll (learned in Pali and other dialects) and Vald. Schmidt; also E. Brandes (The Hymns of Ushas, and a version of the "Car of clay"), while M. Hammerich has translated "Sakuntala". Rasmus Rask, G. Stephens, Thor Sundby, K. Nyrop and Wilhelm Thomsen have distinguished themselves in comparative philology; whilst Japetus Steenstrup, Kröyer, Schiödte, C. F. Lütken, Rudolf Bergh and Boas are all renowned in Zoology; Bergh has chiefly studied molluscs and Schiödte's great speciality is entomology. In Botany: J. W. Hornemann and Schouw ("Geography of Plants"), J. Lange, Warming and Vaupell ("Danish Forests"). In Physics: the great name of H. C. Örsted (died 1851), discoverer of electro-magnetism ("Soul in Nature") and Lorenz. Geology: Forchhammer and Johnstrup. Chemistry: Julius Thomsen, Barfoed and S. M. Jürgensen. Physiology: Eschricht and Panum. Medicine: Oluf Bang, Fenger, C. Lange, Engelsted, Saxtorph, O. Bloch etc.; and the Medical-historian Julius Petersen. Mathematics: Ramus, Zeuthen ("Theory of conic sections in Antiquity"), Julius Petersen ("Theory of Equation", "Problems in geometrical construction"; translated into German, French, English and Italian), J. P. Gram and C. Juel. Astronomy: d'Arrest, Schjellerup, Thiele and Pechüle. Statistics: Falbe-Hansen, M. Rubin, W. Scharling, and H. Westergaard.

H. Schwanenflügel.

II.

Danish Art

There is nothing left from the heathen period in Denmark deserving the name of architecture; and its figured remains, excepting pieces of Roman origin, brought into the country, are most imperfectly executed. On the other hand objects of daily use (household utensils) and jewelry merit especial attention from an artistic point of view, both as to shape and ornament; characteristic of the Bronze Age is its use of geometrical lines, while in the Iron Epoch we have figures of animals together with interlaced and ribbon work.

With Christianity came to Denmark (notably thro Germany) the so-called Romanesque style in all its perfection. It was a development from ancient Roman art, and retains essential evidences of its origin. To this class belong the most ancient monuments, nearly all of them however later than the year 1100. Our oldest Cathedrals — those of Ribe and Viborg — are more or less imitations of those in the Rhine countries, and the really primitive parts of Ribe minster are built of tufa, imported from the same districts. The Danes value greatly, and with reason, these their earliest structures, not only as beautiful and venerable in themselves but also as replete with historical memories. To strangers they of course cannot afford the same interest, as compared with similar edifices abroad, in which the Romanesque style have displayed still more originality and richness of decoration. These temples, as well as a large number of village churches, dating from the same period, are chiefly built of hewn stone.

In the latter half of the 12th century, under the rule of Valdemar I and Archbishop Absalon, a great change took place in Denmark. The island of Sealand now gained, politically speaking, the prominent position hitherto occupied by Jutland; thus the influence formerly exercised by the Rhine countries was succeeded by that of the German lowlands south of the Baltic. A new building material, brick, was then introduced and was almost exclusively used until the close of the Middle Ages. The Cistercian church in Sorö and that of the Benedictines at Ringsted are of brick, both being Romanesque, but of a gloomy, severe and inferior style. From the same time is Kalundborg church, remarkable for its ground-plan, a Greek Cross, its five towers and its granite columns inside. There are also beautiful village churches, some of them with a circular ground-plan.

About 1200 and in the first part of the 13th century the Cathedral of Roskilde was erected, in the bolder and lighter manner which had originated in north eastern France. The choir of course seems to be an imitation of the Cathedral in Tournai. By numerous additions during the Middle Ages and later, and because the tombs of the Danish Kings lying buried there, it has become the most sumptuous national monument in the country.

The Gothic style was introduced into Denmark towards the end of the 13th century. This epoch is marked by evil times, especially for the working classes, a state of things which lasted all thro the Middle Ages, notwithstanding the great increase of political power acquired by the country at home and abroad under Valdemar Atterdag and Margrethe. Thus the Gothic sanctuaries of that period — St. Knud's in Odense, the Cathedral in Aarhus, the Birgitine churches in Maribo and Mariager and others — are, on the whole, not to be compared with those of southern lands, altho some among them are very remarkable, and altho they have contributed not a little to the character of Danish scenery. They belong to the same type of brick edifices as those of the Baltic German provinces, but are not equal to the best of these either in delicate workmanship or in magnificence.

With regard to sculpture or painting, but few works of any note remain to us from this period. In the Old Northern Museum in Copenhagen is preserved a cross of walrus tusk with curious Christian figures in relief, carved by Liutger, a German artist for Gunhild, daughter of King Svend Estridsen. It is from the latter half of the 11th century. The frescoes discovered, hidden under coats of whitewash in the Romanesque churches, show rudeness and simplicity. Those from the later Gothic time are crude and overcharged. From the close of the Middle Ages we have many altar pieces carved in wood, painted and gilt, similar to those in Germany and probably for the greater part supplied therefrom. The most important work of this class is a large reredos at Odense, executed at the beginning of the 16th century by Claus Berg of Lübeck.

The Gothic was superseded in Denmark by the Renaissance, much about the same time that the Roman faith gave place to the Lutheran, in 1536. The Renaissance has left but slight traces as regards Church architecture, but we owe to it splendid secular piles. These date from about the year 1600, and were erected principally for the titled families and the last Danish Kings, who may be considered as the highest representatives of the national nobility. This renaissance also came to us from a North German source; it did not at once remodel architecture, which preserved its mediæval type, but brought in a more decorative exterior, partly borrowed from the antique altho somewhat more pretentious and artificial. The effect is bold and spirited, stately and rich even to excess. In this style is Kronborg Castle, built during the reign of Frederik II; Frederiksborg under Frederik II and Christian IV; Rosenborg and the Copenhagen Exchange both erected by Christian IV. The site chosen for these buildings adds greatly to the charm and characteristic effect. With the age of absolutism began a renaissance more classic, founded on French models and followed by the rococo of Louis the Fifteenth; but these styles have bequeathed to posterity no such first-rate monuments as those of the former epochs. Nor can any Danish painter or sculptor of merit be mentioned, as having flourished throughout this period; foreign artists were generally employed, among them especially the celebrated Dutch painter Carl van Mandern (died 1672).

In the year 1754 the Academy of Art was established, or more properly reconstituted, in Copenhagen. This school did not spring from the agency of the people themselves, but owes its existence to an imperative order of the government, on the pattern of others in Europe, especially in France. French artists were at first placed at its head; the transition from rococo to a purer antique, affords sufficient evidence of their influence. Among these masters we may mention Saly the sculptor, to whose genius is due the equestrian statue of Frederik V at Amalienborg, and Jardin, the architect. The latter began to build the Frederik's church ("Marmorkirken", the Marble Church) in Copenhagen, the construction of which was interrupted for about a century, and is not yet quite completed. After the lapse of a generation, Danish artists again took the lead, but the old traditionary form of instruction continued to be French, and in fact these men were far more European — Greek, Roman, Italian, French, — than Danish in their profession, tho national events were proposed as subjects to be treated by the students. But among them were artists of talent, who brought fame to the Academy. For instance Harsdorff, one of the first architects in Europe, who employed Greek motives of marked purity; Wiedevelt the sculptor honestly tried to embody the antique; Abildgaard was a many-sided and gifted Academic painter with great technical skill; Juel was a portrait painter of talent and refinement; Clemens produced admirable copperplates, and even abroad he ranked high in his calling.

The highly gifted painter and draughtsman A. I. Carstens (a native of South Slesvig) also studied for several years at the Academy under the teachers mentioned above; later on he went to Germany and finally to Rome, where he opened the way for the modern German school of painting. The Danish sculptor Bertel Thorvaldsen also received his early instruction at the Academy; he took up his abode in Rome in 1797, and for a space of forty years worked there with untiring energy. To the fruits of this labor may be ascribed the largest contribution which Danish art has furnished to the intellectual development of Europe. Far better than all his contemporaries, and especially between the years 1812 to 1830, he was able to interpret the human ideal in harmony with contemporary taste, reaping a harvest of thanks and honor from Italians, Germans, Poles, Englishmen and Scandinavians. And what was scarcely noticed at the time, tho clearly perceptible later on, in this all-triumphant ideal there was something really Danish, something taken from the blood of his nation and which was thus made to circulate thro the veins of Europe. As to the sources and subjects of his art, however, and the use he made of his inspiration, Thorvaldsen belonged far more to the great world than to his own little fatherland. Towards the close of his life and after his death his own people appropriated him once more, and raised a museum for his works. Constructed in the Antique style by G. Bindesböll, it was opened in 1848. This building, altho rich in both architectural and decorative art, must strike the beholder as somewhat of an alien in Denmark as to its form and contents. Thorvaldsen's younger brother-artist and fellow-worker H. E. Freund, attained distinction by his able rendering of subjects from Scandinavian mythology. The sculptor H. V. Bissen followed chiefly in the footsteps of Thorvaldsen during the first years of his career, but gradually struck out into a new and independent treatment of his material. To this group, who spent their days partly in the South and partly in the North of Europe, must also be reckoned the medalist C. Christensen and the decorative painter Hilker, as also in part the painter Constantin Hansen; after studies from the Antique, Hansen executed the mythological frescoes adorning the vestibule of the University, Hilker painting the decorations.

In the beginning of this century, which had opened with such political disasters for Denmark, dark clouds hung over both government and people. But the very destructive fires in the capital necessitated the construction of many important edifices, among them the palace of Christiansborg, the Cathedral Church of Our Lady, the Townhall and Courts of Justice. The architect C. F. Hansen to whom these works were entrusted, acquitted himself in a way which shows great lack of taste and resources. According to the style of the time, these buildings are an imitation of ancient Roman architecture. G. F. Hetsch, a German by birth, altho educated in Paris, followed Hansen's manner—the Empire style. In works of a higher class, the study of the Antique also inspired the labors of Bindesböll (spoken of above), and the brothers Christian and Theophilus Hansen. Of these, Christian established himself in Athens; Theophilus settled in Austria, where he has won a name of great repute. Christian Hansen subsequently returned to Denmark.

After Abildgaard's death in 1809, followed Kratzenstein-Stub, a gifted dilettante of the idealistic school; Gebauer, a spirited animal painter, who however studied more in the galleries than from nature; Fritzsch the flower painter, etc. But in 1816 C. V. Eckersberg, who had studied for some years in David's studio in Paris, and subsequently spent some time in Rome, returned to his home. He introduced into the Danish School the sound and thorough, if somewhat dry and prosaic method taught by his master. Altho not gifted with creative genius, he was endowed with remarkably pure and subtle feelings, which enabled him to portray faithfully scenes from real life on land and water. All these advantages were secured by an exceptionally trustworthy and solid system, which became a firm basis for the continued development of national art. Thro his ascendency, Danish painting escaped what elsewhere in Europe was known as romanticism; for the idealistic tendencies of his colleague, J. L. Lund, exercised but little influence on the younger generation. There were of course other artists who, each in his own particular branch, satisfied the requirements of the age; for instance C. A. Jensen, whose portraits now and again were most excellent; but Eckersberg alone founded a school.

Among his pupils Rörbye, Küchler, Constantin Hansen, Bendz, and Chr: Köbke are to be mentioned. The last two, especially Köbke, went still further in the genial treatment of the picturesque, but were on the whole as truly naturalistic as their master. To this same group belongs Roed, who more than others made the human form his chief study; his portraits have remarkable merit.

V. Marstrand also, the greatest of all Danish painters, was a member of the Eckersberg school. He was endowed with such fertility of conception, that his ideas, following each other in quick succession, allowed no time for his treatment to be determined by study. But he was singularly felicitous in composition, remarkably talented as a colorist, with an innate sense of the beautiful, full of feeling and dramatic power, and above all with a rich vein of humor. His life was partly spent in Denmark and partly in Italy. In him as in most of his contemporaries, who in Thorvaldsen's time made Italy their headquarters, æsthetic admiration for Italy and its people plays a great part. Besides the above, this is especially noticeable in the canvasses of Ernst Meyer, an eminent "genre" painter, J. A. Krafft, an intelligent observer (both from Holstein), Petzholdt, the landscape painter, and others. This intense worship of everything Italian was of long continuance, and culminates resplendently in Marstrand. On his return he produced a number of excellent compositions, principally those inspired by the comedies of Holberg, and the great historical scenes adorning the walls of Christian the Fourth's Chapel in Roskilde Cathedral. Marstrand, however, was not the founder of a school.

Meanwhile the great popular movement, which ended in the democratic Constitution and the war with Germany in 1848-1850, had worked great changes in Danish Art. N. Höyen, the intellectual Professor of the history of art, contended with all the power of his eloquence for a closer union between execution in art and the national life. The stirring scenes from the field of warfare were at once depicted by the two able painters, N. Simonsen and J. Sonne, both of them facile and clever in composition. Sonne, with his old-fashioned simplicity, displays in his panoramas of war and peace a richly poetic nature. After the battle of Fredericia, it was decided to raise a monument in honor of the victory; two sculptors entered the lists (1850): J. A. Jerichau, and H. V. Bissen. The former was already well known at home and abroad, having risen to fame by works displaying novel and excellent studies from nature as well as from the Antique. Bissen carried off the prize by his statue the foot-soldier (Landsoldaten), the first piece of Danish sculpture which took firm hold of the real life of the people and was in its real garments. This figure, which was hailed with enthusiasm, made Bissen for all the rest of his life the favorite, to whose hand were entrusted most of the plastic national monuments. Owing to the roused patriotism of the nation, these were in more general demand now than formerly. He afterwards produced a series of portrait statues and busts, remarkable for their faithful and profound grasp of individual character; but at the same time, like Jerichau, he continued to devote himself to more ideal subjects. Conradsen followed somewhat closely in Jerichau's steps, but Bissen had far more influence as leader of the younger generation of sculptors. These were chiefly Bissen's son (Vilhelm), Peters, Hertzog, Saabye, Stein, Evens and C. Freund. All show proofs of the powerful Thorvaldsen traditions, but V. Bissen and Saabye deviated most from this beaten track.

The poets had revived a loving admiration for the relics of antiquity; hence gifted men were eager to reproduce in marble or on canvas the denizens of the old Northern mythological world. Among the painters Constantin Hansen and Frölich more especially depicted these subjects, but on the whole it is far more the real, the occurrences and scenery of home, and every day life, to which their attention is directed. These subjects had proved most interesting to Eckersberg and his pupils, leading them by land and sea, far and near, from the peasant's cottage to the fisherman's hut. Naturally this tendency was strengthened by the rising democratic movement, as well as by the teachings of Professor Höyen.

Danish landscape had excellent interpreters in J. P. Møller, Buntzen and Kiærschou, but about 1840 there appeared a group of artists, who in fact first created a Danish landscape school. The first and most eminent was Lundbye, equally clever whether his subjects were landscapes or animals; he was followed by P. C. Skovgaard, Rump and Kyhn who each after his own fancy faithfully depicted the tones and harmonies of Danish scenery. They were pioneers and discoverers in this field; no wonder then that there is a vivid freshness and originality about their work, which shows no marks of either contemporary or retrospective art. It was the same at first with the men who ventured to depict episodes from peasant life, especially Vermehren, Exner and Dalsgaard. To all these artists the development of a truly national art is due; but its value does not depend upon the national programme alone, it is the result of a personal and intimate familiarity with its subject, the scenery and people of their native land. Technically speaking they were limited to their own resources and to subjects within their capacities; their execution was therefore naive, incapable of independent reputation, sometimes even awkward and clumsy. Their age too was not always in harmony with the national tendency. Many did not recognize the power and significance of this style; they thought it strangely one-sided, and preferred the freer and more dashing manner with technical "chic" characterizing the best works of Mrs. Jerichau who had studied in German studios; and the portraits of Gertner. The two parties were strongly opposed, and the contrast between them is more or less sharply defined throughout. It is worthy of remark that the marine painters after Eckersberg (excepting his pupil Emanuel Larsen) pursued a different way from that of the landscape painters, working mostly after the principles of the foreign schools; notably the most talented of these, Anton Melbye and Sörensen. The flower-painters Ottesen, who practised in Denmark, and Grönland, who worked abroad, also belong to this period. Our short sketch may be closed with the names of Heinrich Hansen of architectural fame, of Schiött, Olrik and Siegumfeldt following each other in the portrait line, whilst Dorph, F. C. Lund, H. J. Hammer and others were "genre" painters. Ballin the engraver and Kittendorf the lithographer are also worthy of honorable mention.

By degrees the antagonists laid down their arms, and the harsh contrasts were effaced; but on the whole, national art won the victory, gaining the most talented and efficient chiefs in both camps. The younger men who now successively follow, la Cour, Aagaard (both pupils of Skovgaard), Kölle, Frisch, Ed. Petersen, Foss, Friis and Thorenfeld worked more or less independently on the track marked out by the masters we have named. Haslund was influenced by Lundbye, but eventually made a name for himself as a painter of children. Neumann, Rasmussen and Blache succeeded Sörensen as Marine painters. Little by little the "genre" artists, who had so faithfully depicted scenes from peasant life, now set about the production of pictures from the middle-class. Carl Thomsen and Helsted particularly excelled in this style; the latter has also given us some excellent rural and everyday scenes from Italy. During this last period Carl Bloch occupied the highest position. He devoted himself since 1860 with extraordinary energy to great historical and religious subjects; and it is in this particular line, above all others, that he has replaced Marstrand and his contemporaries. Among a number of his achievements of a monumental character, there is a series of biblical pictures for the oratory at Frederiksborg. His etchings and smaller "genre" pieces, especially those of a humorous kind, and his landscapes, enjoy no less reputation. Whilst at Rome, Bloch was at first greatly influenced by foreign art; the same may be said of several other men of the same or a later period, such as L. A. Schou and V. Rosenstand, Hasselriis, the sculptor, and Harald Jerichau, the landscape painter. Otto Bache is also one of those who led the way to a new era for Danish art, thro a keen appreciation of the technical details of foreign schools, especially the French. An artist occupying a more solitary position is Zahrtmann, who has produced with great originality characteristic pictures from Danish history, especially from the life of the unfortunate Eleonora Christina Ulfeldt, daughter of King Christian the Fourth.

A certain distance separates the competitors who appeared after 1870 — men still in their prime — from the bolder and more vigorous principles proclaimed by the national school. But under no circumstances could this earlier tendency have withstood the weakening influence of the disastrous war of 1864, a calamity which affected the nation to its core. Besides this, the notable Eckersberg tradition was dying out, having scarcely more than one thoroughly competent and capable representative left in Roed. Nor was its place taken by any other energetic style, sufficiently well grounded to ensure cohesion and to be capable of resisting the pressure from abroad. Communication with foreign countries was now daily easier, and the frequent international exhibitions led to comparisons between native and foreign art. The obvious result was that the Eckersberg tradition, based on David's school in France at the beginning of the century, became out of date when brought into contact with the later European development. It was consequently incapable of solving the problems which were now the order of the day: richness and brilliancy of coloring, truthful rendering of picturesque phenomena and a thoroughly realistic interpretation of human life. This demanded light, air, nature, in short all the characteristics displayed with such brilliant ability by the powerful and flourishing French school.

Thus came an abrupt break in the national development; some of the cleverest and boldest of the younger painters, after elementary instruction at home, emigrated to the studios in Paris (especially Bonnat's). Foremost were Tuxen and Kröyer, but they were speedily followed by others, who had begun in the footsteps of the older party, the landscape artists Zacho, G. Christensen, Niss and Viggo Petersen, the animal painter Philipsen and Locher, the marine painter. The fate which undermined Eckersberg's school also befell Thorvaldsen's; several of the younger sculptors, such as Schultz and Carl Smith, abandoned the traditions of the great master for those of modern foreign art.

This was however but a transition; native talent was again drawn homewards. If the artists did not intend to leave their own country altogether, the claims of their home would return in full force, altho on a somewhat modified technical basis. Realism, above all things, demands that the objects shall be before ones eyes that they may be familiarly and intimately handled. Realism at a distance is an impossibility. Kröyer who had already produced scenes from the Danish coast life and fisher-folks' doings, now returned to this branch of painting with renewed vigor and success. His style had great weight with Michael Ancher, who has rendered with great breadth of style the Danish seaman; the same may be said of his wife Anna Ancher. Both had carried on their studies principally at home, as had Viggo Johansen and Julius Paulsen, painters of such great natural ability that they rose to the standard of foreign art with but little study in its schools. Among this later group, must be named the two brothers F. and E. Henningsen, and Engelsted, who all three have excelled in depicting Copenhagen and town life. To these must be added the portrait painters Jerndorff, Bertha Wegmann and Middelboe, the animal painters Therkildsen and N. Petersen Mols; while Brændekilde and Ring have made rural scenes and landscapes their speciality. Besides these are Irminger, the brothers J. F. and N. Skovgaard; the illustrators H. N. Hansen and Hans Tegner; and Aarsleff, the sculptor.

A few words may yet be said on architecture, taking it up where we left it, in 1850. From this time the employment of the Antique in Danish architecture ceases nearly altogether, altho it still continues to be taught in the Academy. The imitation of the Antique was followed partly by a purely modern style, devoid of historical associations and copied from foreign patterns, partly also by a severer type closely allied to the Mediæval and Renaissance, more especially resembling the older Italian and Northern styles. After the year 1850 a new generation of architects arose, first Herholdt and Meldahl, later on V. Petersen, Fenger, Hans Holm, Storck, Dahlerup, Klein, M. Nyrop and many others. The historical type was revived, and materially strengthened in a national direction, by the restoration or reconstruction of several of the most stately buildings of the past. Prominent among these are the Cathedral of Viborg, restored by the combined efforts of several architects, most successfully by Storck; and Frederiksborg castle in the hands of Meldahl, who has also undertaken to complete the Marble Church (Frederiks Church). Altho there are not any widely marked distinctions among these modern architects, Herholdt, Holm and Storck are more nearly allied in a severely historical aim, whilst the freer school is chiefly represented by Dahlerup, who built the Royal Theater.

Of no less importance than the actual building, is the artistic execution of each object and detail within its walls, everything connected with our human comfort, such as upholstery, wrought metal work, ceramic art, etc. These have of course kept pace with the general advance in every branch, more especially with that of architecture, and of late this branch of art has linked itself closely to the remains of Scandinavian heathendom. Many of the above-mentioned painters, sculptors and architects, recognizing the full importance of this question, have worked hand in hand with the craftsmen. Two especially, Abildgaard and H. E. Freund, were enthusiasts on this point, minutely investigating the commonest objects in daily use; following their wonted bias, they sought their models in the Antique. Among other men of merit, who in their own way have earned distinction in this direction, may be mentioned Hetsch, Bindesböll, Roed, Peters, Olrik, Heinrich Hansen, Dahlerup and A. Krogh, the architect.

Julius Lange.

III

Music

Music has been cultivated in Denmark from an early period. The Sagas mention minstrelsy and play upon the harp as arts practised by the bards, and even if such of the ballads as have descended to the present time cannot lay claim to any great antiquity, they bear internal evidence of a certain musical feeling, the result of gradual development. The ballad, simple and delicate in its uncultured growth, early found a favorable soil both in Denmark and the other Scandinavian lands. The art of music proper was an exotic brought from other climes and required a long period of cultivation before it could strike root in our country. Now however it is thoroughly at home, and we are justified in speaking of a Danish school of music, with a literature and distinctive features all its own.

Under the protecting wing of the Church, music at first found a firm footing and became an art. But for this shelter it would long have remained an alien it since; was only heard by accident, when some wandering bard passed on his way to the halls of the great, singing his lays.

Early in the 16th century, during the reign of Christian the Second, music rose to greater independence. From surviving records, we know that this king had his own musicians, and naturally the art gained something by this association with a permanent institution. Still, it did not receive systematic care until much later. Christian the Fourth, we are told, held music in honor. His private band during its best days consisted of about 70 performers, many of them foreign musicians of some note. It became the fashion to send for foreign celebrities, and to send our own young men abroad to study, particularly under the renowned Gabrieli in Venice. Queen Elisabeth's well-known composer of madrigals, John Dowland, acted as lutist to the King of Denmark for some years. Heinrich Schütz, an Oratorio composer, held the director's post for a short time. Dietrich Buxtehude, one of the first organists of the day, was born in Elsinore.

These were halcyon days for music, destined however soon to close, as the political troubles which now overwhelmed the country stopped all further progress until the middle of the next century, when some partial vitality was again apparent.

Opera was now introduced, after having held the rest of the civilized world under its sway for some time. The first opera performed in Copenhagen, in 1689, was "Der vereinigte Götterstreit". Later on, in 1721, a permanent German operatic company came over from Hamburg, under the leadership of the composer Reinhard Keiser. Italian opera soon became a rival, and gradually grew in favor with the Court until it finally took the lead during the greater part of the 18th century. During one season, (1748—49) the Royal Opera was under the direction of Gluck, then a young man. While he was in Copenhagen, he composed a festival-play. Guiseppe Sarti, Cherubinis teacher, was one among several of the later orchestral directors.

In spite of Court fashion, there was no lack of opposition to the unnatural and tasteless style of the Italian school. Adolf Scheibe, a German musician and author, especially labored for operatic reform. Gluck, afterwards in Paris, closely followed his suggestions in the changes which he introduced. Scheibe's first aggressive attacks were, oddly enough, aimed at Gluck himself, who was then director of the Italian opera and thus a natural enemy. Public taste gradually rose against the Italian company however, especially after the arrival in Copenhagen of a French opera comique troupe in 1750. This new school at once took hold among us and exercised considerable influence upon the national music. Primarily at least, we may trace the form of our dramatic inspiration to this source.

Until about 1750, foreigners had almost entire lead in our musical circles. From that time however, a national interest springing from within may be traced. At first this musical enthusiasm took the form of representations outside the theater. The opera, as we have said, virtually belonged to the Court, which still continued to favor all that was foreign. A number of private societies were founded about this time with the object of cultivating music for the common enjoyment, as well as for the performance of public concerts. We find no great musicians among these zealots, nor was it to be expected, this was the seed-time — fruition came later. There was a steady progress meanwhile, and from these small beginnings, the national movement at last reached the theater. The first musical piece "Gram og Signe" modelled after opera comique, still borrows its music from the Italians, but in 1776 the opera "Belsor i Hytten" appeared, the music by Zielche; and now the trammels are cast off.

As yet it cannot be called a national product. A permanent staff of Danish musicians had been gradually gathered; the general interest in music spread more and more among the educated classes. But, at this moment the real leaders were still foreigners. Chief among these was Johan Hartmann, who composed music to several of Johannes Ewald's works, and who was the ancestor of the renowned family of that name. And so with J. G. Naumann, who gave us the music to "Orpheus og Eurydice", the first important opera with Danish text. Later on J. A. P. Schultz, whose music to several operettas ("Höstgildet", "Peter's Bryllup") added much to the growth of national music, and L. C. Kunzen had a share in this the dawn of better days. Most of these foreign composers quickly became nationalized, and thus their labors helped on the local tendency and imparted the needful coloring. At the theater also Danish composers by degrees gained ground, notably Claus Schall and J. F. Fröhlich, in whose music the Danish element is distinctly perceptible.

The stirring period which commenced in Denmark at the beginning of the 19th century, with romanticism in literature under the guidance of Oehlenschläger, and the vigorous intellectual life which sprang up simultaneously, did not at once affect music, which was still in its infancy. The formation of the different societies and the activity with which concerts were arranged and given, are the best proofs that there was no backward tendency. At the same time that home powers were trained and matured, the stimulus from the great European centres was never wanting. The national characteristics are now strong enough to bear the friction, without being effaced.

Before all these new and conflicting elements could settle into shape, they required a certain amount of pliability, whereby the foreign and native tone-waves could blend into harmony. This transition stage is marked by the names of Weyse and Kuhlau. Both these men exercised paramount influence on our music, each in his own way. Weyse was the pioneer of the strictly national tendency; whilst Kuhlau was the channel through which the Beethoven current flowed down to us. Weyse (1774—1842) was born in Altona, but settled in Copenhagen in his youth, and by his intercourse with the most distinguished men of that time, as also by his own rare personal gifts, he exercised no inconsiderable power over the intellectual circles of the capital. By nature conservative, he had strong leanings to the Mozart school, whose pure classical lines are often met side by side with his own peculiar tones. His distinctive feature is a thorough "Danism"; thro his music ring the airs of the old ballads, giving their own sweet spirit and coloring to all he wrote. It is not the strength of the Wiking power; Weyse's harp had but few chords for the sterner moods of our Scandinavian nature; it is smiling landscapes, blue, breezy seas, waving cornfields of which we are reminded. All that is softly and dreamily harmonious and gently humorous, he renders melodiously complete. Having the faculty of giving expression to the characteristic feelings of the people, he sang himself into their hearts, with his ballads and ditties. From these songs, Weyse may be called the Schubert of Denmark. Moreover, his was a prolific genius, both as a composer of church and operatic music, tho according to our present ideas his style often appears cold and conventional. As organist and pianist he also occupied a distinguished position. Liszt, in one of his "Letters" mentions having heard Weyse improvising on the organ in Frue Kirke (Our Lady's Church) and expresses himself in terms of high eulogy, comparing the glow of his inspiration to that of Sebastian Bach.

F. Kuhlau's (1786—1832) European reputation was greater than Weyse's, whilst in Denmark the two composers were of well-nigh equal fame. Kuhlau was born in Uelzen near Hannover, and came to Denmark at the age of 24. The rest of his life he passed in Copenhagen. Abroad Kuhlau is mostly known as the author of a number of piano-sonatas, widely used in elementary instruction, and also by his compositions for the flute. But these, written only for a livelihood, give a very inadequate idea of his genius. His most important works, the operas he composed for our stage, are now unknown out of Denmark; yet these were of the greatest significance in our musical development.

Kuhlau was of a very different character from Weyse, the one conservative, the other representing all the progressive ideas of the day. Kuhlau's lively, impressionable temperament had absorbed much of the Romanticism of the age, long before it found its way, with Weber's "Freischütz", to the German stage. His opera "Röverborgen" (The Robbers' Castle) 1814, is quite a remarkable prototype of the era of romance. His gifts are full of variety, and he was a most fertile laborer. Tho no friend of the then raging Rossini mania, he was not always able to withstand the influence of Italian music. In great part it was his international style which made his music of such importance to our Danish school, since thro him every new thought came to our knowledge. Kuhlau cannot be said to possess Weyse's individuality, altho his imagination is as powerful. His works retain their freshness even now, in spite of the time which has elapsed since their production. A remarkable instance of this is his opera "Lulu"; composed to the original text of "Il Flauto Magico", it is well-nigh modern in character. His style is rich in coloring, charmingly varied in its flowing melodiousness and brilliant in orchestral handling. He was not touched like Weyse by what is so distinctive in the ballads, still he could use and develop the typical features skilfully. This is especially the case in his music to Heiberg's "Elverhöj" (Elfin Hill); the overture interweaves a series of Danish folk-songs, and is looked upon by the musical world as a national monument. With Weyse and Kuhlau terminates the period in which our music served its apprenticeship to foreign masters.

A series of composers of Danish birth now arose, whose labors follow closely the steps of the new national school. The leading features may be called the national, based on the ballad, and the international, which clings to the German Classics.

To understand what is meant by the folk-element in our music, we must dwell a moment on the Folk-song, or, as it is also called: the Scandinavian heroic ballad, the study of which only dates from this century. We are especially indebted to A. P. Berggreen for his researches, and for the collection of melodies which he made. With regard to their date, it is difficult to speak positively; some no doubt go back to the Middle Ages, whilst others are of more recent origin. The oldest Danish lay on record is contained in a manuscript of about the year 1300, the next is in a parchment from 1450, both are in the University Library of Copenhagen. Even if we have no folk-songs copied earlier, there is no doubt that many in Berggreen's collection are, at least, from the same time; the greater part cannot be later than the 16th and 17th century.

The Danish folk-song forms a link in the chain of ancient Scandinavian lore; many of the melodies show nothing especially Danish, but are common to the three lands, which just at that time formed a national, even partly a political unity. These ballads are quite equal to any in the world for originality, powerful rhythm, lyrical beauty and grace; for the expression of sad pathos and melancholy they are not surpassed. Marked peculiarities are found in the closing cadence, a frequent use of the intervals of the third and the key-note, omitting the second; and in the rhythm there is often a prolongation of the air, by introducing syncopes and by emphasizing the unaccented parts of the bar, thus giving a character of firmness. Another salient point is the burden, a concluding phrase which is intended to be sung in chorus, and which in its unvarying repetition serves to express a leading idea or an important point in the song. The burden is an inherent part of the whole, and was used in guiding the dance; for in olden times, when instruments were little used, they danced to ballads, alike in the king's hall and at the revels of the peasantry.

The cosmopolitan levelling process of modern civilization has swept away all this; the old strains are now only heard in out-of-the-way corners in the far North; in the Færöes alone they are preserved with many other relics of an older time. There the heroic ballad still takes the place of instruments on festive occasions, and no merry-making is considered complete without a set or two of their characteristic country-dances to the tune of the old airs. The Færöes ballads are so numerous, that in some places it is the law not to sing the same more than once a year. Among the most remarkable is a cycle relating to Sigurd Fafnersbane — the subject which Richard Wagner has used in his "Siegfried".

The composers J. P. E. Hartmann and Niels W. Gade, are the most distinguished representatives of the school sprung from the Danish ballad. This is however far from being their only claim to eminence, as both are gifted with a dual artistic physiognomy, one pointing to the national, the other belonging to the cultured world of music.

J. P. E. Hartmann, born in Copenhagen 1805, claims descent from the Johan Hartmann mentioned above, whose family has given Denmark four generations of composers. Hartmann made his mark at an early age; during a long life he has continued to work, and still produces pieces of great vigor and merit. As a young man he was easily influenced by the various schools. His early compositions, chamber music, symphonies, organ pieces, songs and the opera "Ravnen" (The Raven) show traces of Spohr, and Rossini, Auber, and Weber. Luckily he had great original strength of his own, and this soon silenced foreign echoes, and gave us pieces in harmony with the influences that surrounded him. In the music to Oehlenschläger's "Guldhornene" (The Golden Horns) 1832, the transformation was perfect. The same may be said of the opera "Liden Kirsten" (Little Christina) with words by Hans Christian Andersen. This was at one time performed in Weimar, under Liszt's leadership. In it the very spirit of the ballad has become incarnate. Already in these earlier compositions we find examples of the double nature of the national tendency in Hartmann's productions. In "Liden Kirsten" as in the ballet "Et Folkesagn" (A Folk-legend) and in the concerted piece "En Sommerdag" (A Summer's Day) the mellow and joyful tones of the homeland predominate as its first phase. Its second, which may be called Scandinavian, is weird and wild and serious, grandly inspired by tales of the olden Gods. It is in "Hakon Jarl", in the two beautiful Ballets "Valkyrien" and "Thrymskviden", in the Drama "Yrsa" and lastly, in the deep-colored Tone-poem "Völvens Spaadom" (The Sibyl's prophecy, taken from the Edda) that this darker mood is most powerfully expressed. It is not because Hartmann is only a local celebrity that he is so little known abroad. The reason is to be found in his personality as a retiring, modest man, one who never stirred to make himself popular. Besides, the strongly National character of his compositions renders them less easily understood or appreciated by strangers. Hans von Bülow remarks, in his correspondance, "that Hartmann is most certainly a National writer, but by no means merely local". He further adds: "I have seldom seen so distinguished a presence, or one so little affected by old age, tho so venerable in appearance. A thorough patrician in mind and morals, few illustrate better the noble words of Anton Rubinstein: Music is an aristocratic art. Nor has Hartmann ever written a trivial line".

The same affinity which existed between Weyse and Kuhlau, repeats itself in certain respects with regard to Hartmann and Gade. Weyse and Hartmann are essentially national, Kuhlau and Gade have as decided international traits, mingling with the former.

Niels W. Gade, born in Copenhagen 1817, spent some years of his early life in Leipzic, attracted thither by the wealth of its musical talent, as well as by Mendelssohn's personality. There he wrote his first works, the Ossian Overture and the Symphony in C minor; these, tho composed abroad, are decidedly Danish in tone and feeling. In fact during his youth he belonged entirely to this school. Since then he has become cosmopolitan, and may now be claimed by either or both. Mendelssohn took great interest in Gade, and more especially admired the Symphony with its novel and original musical subjects. A kind of mystic radiance surrounded Gade's person. In his name of four letters — comprising the four strings of the violin — which can be written with one single note in four keys, there seems a secret summons from the ideal world. In person and features he resembled Mozart; and in Paris the story was told of how he wandered from Copenhagen to Leipzic and back again, carrying his violin. His talent expanded under most advantageous conditions in Leipzic. For several years he shared with Mendelssohn the honor of conducting the famous "Gewandthaus Concerts"; at that time there was much which seemed to indicate, that he was lost to his fatherland. But in 1848 the Slesvig war aroused his patriotism, and he returned to devote his life to Denmark. Gade now became the director of the "Musik-Forening" (Mucical association), the Concerts of which Society he still conducts. To the works of his first "Danish" period must be added the cantata "Comala", with words from Ossian, and "Elverskud" (The Elfshot), also one act of the Ballet "Et Folkesagn" perhaps the most typical of this Romantic-Danish era; it is airy and graceful, without any of the usual heavy mysticism common in describing Chivalry. Also his two Symphonies in A minor and G minor partly belong to this class. Meanwhile, the merely national range became too narrow for his genius; in his fourth Symphony in B flat major, he reaches at one stride — universal humanity! In a series of Concert Dramas he unfolds this idea further thus: The Creeds of the Nations — Man groping after light and heavenward aspirations; "Zion", the people of Jehova; "Psyche", the beautiful myth of the Hellenes; "Kalanus", the Indian seer wrestling with the worldliness of Alexander and his triumphs. Again, in the "Crusaders", are united the passion and enthusiasm of Christian Romance and Chivalry. Gade has also written many other pieces, chamber music, numerous songs and a solitary opera "Mariotta". Nowhere perhaps is the characteristic tone peculiar to his Muse more perfectly exhibited, than in that little gem "Frühlingsphantasie" (Spring Fantasia).

The school founded by Hartmann and Gade has been of

crowning importance to Danish music of the present day; thro them it has won a place in the literature of the musical world, and stamped its own style as a link in the Scandinavian chain. Many younger composers have followed the footsteps of these masters, and on the whole musical life in Denmark, during the last decades, has risen rapidly and mounted higher than ever before. It would lead us too far to name those who have attracted public attention in this Art. We must be contented to specify only the few who are associated with the Institutions established for its cultivation.

The Opera at the Royal Theater, under the leadership of Johan S. Svendsen, a Norwegian, favors no one School, but impartially brings forward all foreign dramatic works of any value. Among the vocalists are effective performers, some even may be called artists of eminence, whilst both the Orchestra and Chorus are admirable. During the last few years our modern Danish school has produced several operatic composers of note, Heise and Emil Hartmann representing the elder section, while Lange-Müller (whose opera "Spanske Studenter" has made its way both into Germany and Sweden), V. Kalhauge, A. Grandjean, J. Bartholdy, F. Rung, and C. F. E. Horneman range among the workers of the present day.

Concerts occupy a prominent place with us. There are many large musical societies, which give excellent orchestral and choral concerts during the winter seasons. The "Musik-Forening" has the pre-eminence both as to age (founded 1836) and powers. As led by Gade, it has had great educational influence, and may be said to have the position in Copenhagen which the "Gewandthaus Concerts" have in Leipzic. It may be regarded as a kind of musical college for home production, as it has performed compositions, not only of the Danish masters already spoken of, but of Barnekow, Bechgaard, Victor Bendix, Bohlmann, Gerlach, Gerson, Grandjean, Asger Hamerik, C. J. Hansen, Emil Hartmann, Heise, Carl Helsted, C. F. E. Horneman, Liebmann, Lövenskjold, Otto Malling, Matthison-Hansen, Paulli, Ravnkilde, F. and H. Rung, Erik Siboni, Sick and

Winding. The "Cecilia-Forening", conducted by F. Rung, cultivates chiefly the older Masters, particularly old Italian and Church music. The "Concert-Forening" under the guidance of Otto Malling makes known modern composers, foreign or native; among the last the names of Jacob Fabricius, Robert Hansen, Gustav Helsted, Krygell, G. Matthison-Hansen, Leopold Rosenfeld, Steenberg and Wiel-Lange, figure worthily with those above. As composer for the piano L. Schytte has acquired a name, known also by foreigners. The "Philharmoniske Concerter", set on foot by Johan S. Svendsen and under the sway of his baton, reproduce great orchestral compositions, and introduce the most renowned foreign artists. Also the "Kammermusik-Forening", whose leading spirit is the Violoncellist Franz Neruda, must not be omited. Finally, there is the Copenhagen conservatory of music, founded 1865 with the assistance of a legacy from P. W. Moldenhawer, where the rising generation is instructed under the supervision of Gade, Hartmann and H. S. Paulli.

During the summer months the famous Tivoli Gardens keep alive musical interest by daily concerts. The orchestra is most select, and was first made widely known when led by H. C. Lumbye, the famous composer of sparkling dance-music — his "Champagne-Galop" is familiar everywhere. After his death, Balduin Dahl succeeded to his staff, and gained a name by bringing forward many novelties at the Saturday Symphony Concerts.

Angul Hammerich.

IV

The Stage and its Actors

To the specialist on this subject before the days of Holberg, we recommend Birket Smith's exhaustive and elaborate studies. The general reader need only begin with Holberg.

As is well known, chance has often been the means of enriching the world. So with regard to Holberg's comedies. Two members of a French troupe, at that time acting before the Court, wished to bring their plays before the general Copenhagen public. For this purpose a small theater was opened in a side-street, but their efforts were unsuccessful. One of them, Montaigu, whose wife was a Dane, fancied that Danish comedies might be tried. For the purpose he applied to the learned and influential Frederik Rostgaard. By his marriage with the half-sister of the Queen, this gentleman was in a way King Frederik the Fourth's brother-in-law. Rostgaard had lately had a conflict with Holberg on account of the satirical poem "Peder Paars", but was highminded enough to know that Holberg was gifted and competent to write what was required. The petition was not refused, and thus, in less than four years, most of his immortal pieces saw the light. Some of the comical figures were already to his hand in "Peder Paars", but to produce so much, incessant labor was necessary, and thus one after the other these masterly productions flowed from his pen.

At first the public did not understand the value of a national stage as an educational medium, nor were they aware that a great genius was working in their midst. The result was, that the small theater in Grönnegade was closed for debt, and every effort to reopen it was unavailing. Then came the terrible fire of 1728, and immediately after the Pietist period of Christian the Sixth. The Court as usual gave the tone, and it now became a sin to see a play; every pleasure was invented by the Devil for evil — all was vanity.

With the advent of Frederik the Fifth, there was a reaction. Holberg was once more authorized to open his theater, and luckily there were clever actors ready to play the parts — not only of Holberg's pieces but of Moliere's, Lesage's and Reynard's. The most notable among these artists were: Londeman, Clementin and Rose. Londeman was a clever comic actor, but chiefly relied upon impulse, without going deeply into his characters; he always succeeded in amusing his audience, and was a capital delineator of

Holberg's intriguing valets (Henrik), as well as a first-rate "Tartuffe". The Pietistic age which had just passed away gave plenty of these types. Altho a great sufferer and in constant trouble, he forgot all when on the boards, and was happy in giving others pleasure. Wessel wrote at his death:

> "Man græder, for han er ej mer,
> Man husker, hvad han var, og ler." [1]

Clementin, also a humorous player, gave Holberg's old men in a superior manner. In contrast to Londeman's superficial style, Clementin studied every detail, with his speaking eyes and mobile features giving a perfect whole. Rose was a serious dramatist of great intelligence. His handsome face and noble action made him especially fitted for such characters as Orosmane in Voltaire's "Zaire".

It was chiefly as students of nature that these first actors made a mark. Holberg we know encouraged this, for we have an anecdote to the point. When Clementin was rehearsing "Den Stundesløse" (The Busy-body) Holberg interrupted him: No, no, that won't do; you think too much about being very busy; run to the Treasury Offices, look at Mr. N. N.! This advice was followed, and next time the piece was on, Holberg was delighted with the result.

Thus, thanks to "Father Holberg's" genius and eye for the requirements of the stage, dramatic art was founded. His school was based upon a rigorous observance of nature and the study of particular types. Nothing coarse or overdrawn, no clown's tricks were allowed, but an independant examination of the character belonging to each part. Reality and truth became the standard for the Danish national scene.

Holberg's only imitator was Wiwet. The general public still found entertainment in seeing Holberg's comedies, but the fine

---

[1] Sure weep we; for he's dead, alas;
Yet smile, remembering what he was!

people already considered them vulgar. Suhm the historian, who dabbled a little in poetry, complained that: "In Holberg we never find educated persons, only the commonality." Then Goldoni and Destouches were brought on the stage, as also the feeble imitations of Charlotte Biehl. N. K. Bredahl, at one time director of the theater, was anxious to perform heroic melodramas, but Rosenstand-Goiske's criticism made this variety for ever impossible. In fact, the critics of the day would only allow the school of Plautus and Holberg for comedy, and the classical writers of Louis XIV's time for tragedy. However not even this last could live long. J. N. Brun's "Zarina", modelled on the classics, was entirely destroyed by the bitter satire of Wessel's "Kjærlighed uden Strömper" (Stockingless Love), which pulled the sentimentalists to pieces.

The moment had now arrived for hailing the first original Northern tragedy with delight. Johannes Ewald's "Balders Död" was written in iambics of five feet, instead of the alexandrines of the elder tragedies. This versification was henceforth employed by the Danish tragic writers. It was a private company who had the honor of bringing this striking piece on the boards. At their head was Schwartz, who combined great enthusiasm with good histrionic gifts. The best pupil of this "Dramatic Company" (1777) was the Norwegian Michael Rosing; Schwartz continued the school created by Londeman and Clementin; Rosing was the father of a new tragic embodiment. Rosenstand-Goiske, severe in his strictures, upbraided Rosing for his "convulsive movements and dancingmaster steps", but by great diligence and burning ardour he got over these drawbacks. It was in the part of "Hother" in "Balders Död" that he gained the public entirely. Mrs. Rosing, as Nanna in the same piece, was much admired. She was one of our first really great actresses, and was celebrated for womanly grace. Later on, she became as successful in "noble mothers".

Order and regularity, at first unknown in theatrical affairs, came in gradually; and with an improved theater built in 1748 by Eigtved on Kongens Nytorv, a new era commenced. In 1761 Royal support from the King's Privy Purse began, and in 1772 it became the Royal Danish playhouse. A first-rate administrator was found in Warnstedt; by his unusual culture, taste and humanity, coupled with strict justice, he succeeded in making himself respected by his capricious and unstable staff. Formerly, when the stage was despised, the lives of actors became despicable. Now, with discipline from within and interest increasing from without, their self-esteem was roused and a great change took place. K. L. Rahbek, one of the most important writers of the tender middle-class drama, says in his excellent dramaturgic study ("Letters from an old Comedian to his son"), that only a moral man can become a true actor. Rahbek's friends, Rosing and his spouse made good this paradox by living worthy lives, and showing a good example to their comrades. Rosing and Schwartz were decorated with the Order of the Danebrog, and even this was a useful lever in raising the calling. From that day until the present moment, good society has been glad to honor the artist.

With Ewald's "Fishermen" the national lyric drama was admitted to the stage. This piece led the way for Thaarup's "Höstgildet" (Harvest Home) and "Peter's Bryllup" (Peter's Wedding), two dramatic idyls with melodious music by Schultz. They were written in 1790, to commemorate the wedding of the popular Crownprince Frederik (the Sixth). P. A. Heiberg wrote very differently. His plays were polemical, and threw out their satirical allusions broadcast among the audience; and as the time was full of opposition, every hint was received with thundering applause. The real character-comedy however suffered by this. Only one piece can be said to belong to this category, "The golden Casket" (1793), in which Rosing had one of his best parts, while Miss Winther was excellent as the Vixen.

At this time pathetic plays were much in vogue, such as Samsöe's "Dyveke", a tragedy in prose, which had a run with Schwartz, the Rosings and Miss Alstrup, the latter a most imposing person. Miss Marie Smith, later so well known as Mrs. Heger, was greatly admired as the heroine. This actress was a child of her time; the very personification of the sentimental, she entranced her public by visionary dreaminess, grief of the most tear-distilling order. Shortly afterwards however, stronger food was presented on the scene in Sander's "Niels Ebbesen" — an echo of Göethe's "Götz". National instincts and sympathies running very high just then, this piece made its mark, especially as it was backed by most excellent acting. Each of the chief characters was nobly portrayed by Schwartz and the Rosings. This was in 1796.

With the beginning of this century, there was a change of taste, and show-pieces were now in favor. The literary value of such things is always doubtful, and whether it was "Hermann v. Unna", or burlesques and sentimentalities in the Kotzebue manner, such as "Misanthropy and Repentance", made no difference. Not even such a masterpiece as Oehlenschläger's "Hakon Jarl" could at first make its way. Rosing who ought to have been the tragic actor, was now a gouty invalid, and Schwartz had retired. Only melodramas and comic operas flourished. Falsen's "The flying Kite" (Dragedukken), Dupuy's "Youth and Folly" (Ungdom og Galskab), with the foreigners Mozart, Cherubini etc. In these, the sympathetic voice and hearty humor of Chr. Knudsen created quite a sensation. Not until 1813 did the theater succeed in finding a perfect delineator of Oehlenschläger's great Northern heroes in Johan Christian Ryge. He was already Doctor of medicine and a married man, head physician of the district, a citizen of distinction — but he left all to follow the call of his genius. He had great difficulties to surmount, a rather ordinary voice, a large head on a short neck, and weak legs to a powerful body. But, driven on by his art and enthusiasm, he gained the victory, and made Oehlenschläger's creations living realities on the Danish stage. A contemporary critic says: "Ryge was not possessed of the classic calmness necessary to high-tragic art, and yet his impersonation of Northern Wikings was marvellous: they became coarse, sharp realities, shrouded in a shade of romantic spirit, with the very scent of the Ocean-mist hanging around them, full of heathendom and sacrificial blood. His "Hakon Jarl", "Palnatoke" and "Stærkodder" were true to the life, and their words fell like blows on a copper-shield." In the comic opera and lighter pieces Frydendahl was thoroughly competent. By his gentlemanly demeanor, patrician figure and graceful manner, he was able to do justice to every kind of personality. His fine perception of irony enabled him to modify any extravagance in his parts. Lindgreen was a great contrast to Frydendahl, his comic vein was strongly flavored and drastic, and in farce he inspired roars of laughter. Thus in Holberg's "Gert Westphaler", "Den pantsatte Bondedreng" (The peasant in pawn) and especially in "Jeppe paa Bjerget" he has never been equalled.

By this time Iffland's and Kotzebue's dramas had to give way to Scribe, here as elsewhere. The new style however was scarcely better for the public taste than the old, and it was a most useful counter-balance when J. L. Heiberg wrote his vaudevilles. Heiberg defined the vaudeville as: "situations with lightly sketched characters, where the dialogue at certain effective points is supported by couplets to popular airs." The Swedish poet-musician Bellman is often traced in these melodies. Heiberg depicted types of the day, Copenhagen originals well known to all; thus the audience had ample opportunity of seeing the weaknesses of the living people around them. Of course the older dramatists thought lightly of this new style, and Rahbek called it mere Mountebank fun. But the Copenhagen public were never tired of seeing their own foibles so amiably scourged. The first-rate way in which these figures were made to live by such interpreters as the elder Rosenkilde, Miss Jörgensen, and Foersom jun:, naturally added greatly to their success. Rosenkilde sen: was, both as author and actor immensely humorous. His "Autobiography" and other sketches, in two volumes, is most entertaining. He needed scarcely any change of dress or voice; it was by his inimitable mimicry alone and by the power of his eyes, that his wonderful comical effects were produced.

Boye and Sötoft were imitators of Oehlenschläger. The former,

especially, wrote plays that were appreciated for a time. They were
but weak however, owing to pomp of words and bombast their
chief attraction. It was about 1820 or later, when the great
tragedian Nielsen' gained his first laurels. He was perfect when
declaiming these sonorous iambics. He had his chief parts in
Oehlenschläger's tragedies, and in these perhaps his finest was Axel
in "Axel og Valborg". Nielsen continued a great favorite —
sharing with his distinguished wife the general admiration — until
after 1850. Mrs. Nielsen also took Oehlenschläger's historical
heroines, one of her creations being Queen Margaret in "Dronning
Margrete".

J. L. Heiberg holds a considerable place in our literature, both
as critic and poet. He followed Baggesen in demanding regularity
of thought and clearness of perception in every poetic work. Henrik Hertz was a very distinguished pupil of this school. He renewed
the Holberg comedy in "Sparekassen" (The Savings-bank), wrote
charming blank verse comedies, as "Amors Genistreger", and
romantic dramas as "Svend Dyrings Hus", "Ninon", "Kong René's
Datter", "Den Yngste" etc. In "Sparekassen" Phister had one of his
best comic figures. Johanne Louise Heiberg, the poet's wife, as
Ragnhild in "Svend Dyrings Hus", as "Ninon", the celebrated
French courtezan — who in the hands of the Danish poet became
a very different person to what history has made her, a graceful,
refined and loveable woman—made a mark in the annals of histrionic Art. Rosing's grandson, Michael Wiehe, the young Chevalier
in love with Ninon (his Mother tho he knew it not), has never had
his equal as the romantic ideal lover. These three artists worked
together, making a perfect whole, and long held sway as first
favorites with theater-goers. Phister was always surprising
with new transformations, and created at least three hundred comic
types. In voice, walk and mask, he was never to be recognized
from one character to another. Michael Wiehe fascinated by the
perfect nobility of his romantic eroticism — the chevalier sans peur
et sans reproche, "the lover and Minnesinger from the days of the

Troubadours." Mrs. Heiberg enchanted all beholders by her graceful plastique, the perfect treatment of her sentences, and the brilliant conception of every detail; in Conversation pieces especially, she still stands unequalled.

Between 1840 and 1850 a new star arose on the dramatic firmament. Hostrup's comedies were inspired by the students and college life, and give a whole gallery of student-types. He has also represented many imperishable pictures from the middle-class, as in "Æventyr paa Fodrejsen" (Adventure on the walking-tour), "Tordenvejr" (A thunderstorm), "Mester og Lærling" (Master and Apprentice), etc. He is however at his best in pieces like "Gjenboerne" (The neighbors), and "En Spurv i Tranedans" (A sparrow in the crane's nest), where the complication is solved by præternatural means. Hostrup was also lucky in finding good representatives of his imaginary beings; no one could have suited better than Hultmann for his ideal student, and Mrs. Södring (a daughter of the elder Rosenkilde) worked out his honest, active, goodnatured housewives to perfection. She had before this won the ear of the audience, and long kept her place as a clever and useful actress. Hostrup's friend and brother-in-law, Kr. Mantzius shone by the perfect types he made in some of the plays mentioned. In spite of having to compete with so many excellent rivals as the theater then boasted, he succeeded beyond expectation. Unfortunately his arrogance and temper kept him in constant feuds with his superiors and comrades; and in consequence, after many unpleasantnesses, he was at last obliged to withdraw.

Another very great loss to the Royal Theater was the retirement of Höedt, a very great capacity, and highly accomplished man. He was independant in means and a learned student; it was his love of acting which brought him on the boards. Höedt's motto was Hamlet's: "for in the very torrent, tempest and whirlwind of passion, you must acquire and beget a temperance, that may give it smoothness — o'erstep not the modesty of nature." It was this he wished to carry out. The imitators of Nielsen, led on by the poetry of Oehlenschläger — which tempts to exaggeration — had now introduced a noisy unnatural declamation, which was a parody on true taste. After a long and careful preparation, Höedt made his first appearance in "Hamlet", and was warmly received; soon after he proved a very capable light comedian also even useful in general humor. He was anxious to come out in "Richard III", but J. L. Heiberg, now an old man, was the director, and as he did not care for Shakespeare, and moreover considered it an impertinance for an actor to claim a part for himself, the request was denied. Höedt left, but some time afterwards returned; a journal of some note had stirred up bitter feelings against him, a few silly youngsters hissed — Höedt was profoundly hurt, and now finally retired.

With the appearance of the two Norwegian poets, Björnson and Ibsen, a new era commenced at the Royal play-house. Vilhelm Wiehe, a brother of Michael, came from the Christiania stage, with all the routine necessary for this style, and at once took the chief part in Björnson's "De Nygifte" (The newly married) and Ibsen's "De Unges Forbund" with much success; whilst another brother, Johan Wiehe, was a masterly Bothwell in Björnson's "Marie Stuart". After these eminent men had withdrawn, the brothers Olaf and Emil Poulsen and Mrs. Hennings have been well-nigh alone in keeping up the prestige of the scene. Emil Poulsen showed himself a superior actor of character-pieces, in Ibsen's "Kongsemnerne" (The Pretenders), and in "Et Dukkehjem" (A dollshouse) by the same author. Olaf Poulsen has not only inherited Phister's place, but been able to invent new comic figures, and act excellently in graver styles. Mrs. Hennings has borne her share of the burden most ably.

Among the plays which of late have succeeded, may be mentioned Ernst von der Recke's "Bertran de Born" (music by Heise), with Emil Poulsen as the Warrior-Minstrel, and Molbech's "Ambrosius", in which the author tries to give a picture of the first lyrical poet of our country. In this part also Emil Poulsen's success was a perfect ovation, especially as to the fair sex. Of late, Drachmann's "Der var engang—" (Once upon a time) has filled the House, and even a new dramatic author Ejnar Christiansen, has arisen. No doubt all these pieces will share the same fate, and will soon be forgotten, whereas for the best of the social-problem-plays of Edward Brandes, there may perhaps be some future.

It must not be forgotten that our Royal Play-house has a three-fold object. The Opera, the Drama and the Ballet have their home under its roof. The most renowned Danish composers are of German descent, whilst others have been greatly influenced by this school, so that we can scarcely say we have a distinctly national opera; tho, as shown in the article on "Music", we have something to boast of in such pieces as Kuhlau's "Elverhöi", Hartmann's "Liden Kirsten" and Heise's "Drot og Marsk". We have however a Ballet all our own, created by August Bournonville. Generally speaking ballets are merely for the eye, but Bournonville aimed higher. He made the picturesque and poetic the chief interest, and in his country-dances and national airs, costumes and myths, created a Northern Ballet not known elsewhere. The "Corps de Ballet", formed by him, will hand over to coming generations the master's choreographic principles as a healthy and noble tradition.

Besides the Royal House, Copenhagen possesses three other theaters, the Casino, the Folketheater and the Dagmartheater. These employ many talented artists, but their existance is precarious, as the Royal stage has the privilege of making every classic play her own, reducing the secondary Houses to light comedy; this is no doubt an injustice not known elsewhere.[1]

H. Schwanenflügel.

[1] Rectified in great measure since the above was written.

Among works concerning "Language and Literature" we cite: Dansk Ordbog (Danish Dictionary), edited by the Royal Academy of Science, Copenhagen 1793—1863. Ch. Molbech, Dansk Ordbog, 2nd edition Cop: 1859, 2 vol.; Dansk Glossarium eller Ordbog over forældede danske Ord (Danish Glossary or dict: of obsolete words), Cop: 1857—66, 2 vol.; Dansk Dialektlexikon (Dict: of Danish dialects), Cop: 1841. Kalkar, Ordbog til det ældre danske Sprog (Dict: of olden Danish), Cop: 1881 and fol:. H. F. Feilberg, Ordbog over jydske Almuesmaal (Dict: of Jutland dialects), Cop: 1886 and fol: P. E. Müller, Dansk Synonymik (Danish Synonyms), 3rd ed: Cop: 1872. E. v. d. Recke, Principerne for den danske Verskunst (The Principles of Danish poetry), Cop: 1881, 2 vol. G. Stephens, The Old Northern Runic Monuments of Scandinavia and England, Lond: and Cop: 1866—84, 3 vol., abreviated edit: 1884. N. M. Petersen, Det danske, norske og svenske Sprog under deres historiske Udvikling af Stamsproget (The historical development of Danish, Norwegian and Swedish from the Mother language), Cop: 1829—30, 2 vol: R. K. Rask, Undersøgelse om det gamle nordiske eller islandske Sprogs Oprindelse (Researches into the origin of the Old Northern and Icelandic languages), Cop: 1818. Broberg, Manuel de la langue Danoise, Cop: 1882. N. M. Petersen, Bidrag til den danske Literaturs Historie (Studies on the history of Danish literature), 2nd ed: Cop. 1867—71, 5 vol: (contains the Middle Ages and Modern times until 1800). R. Nyerup and K. L. Rahbek, Bidrag til den danske Digtekunsts Historie (Contributions to the history of Danish poetry), Cop: 1800—28, 6 vol.; R. Nyerup, Historie af Danmarks, Norges og Islands Literatur i Middelalderen (History of literature in Denmark, Norway and Iceland in the Middle Ages), forms the 2nd part of his work: Historisk-statistisk Skildring af Tilstanden i Danmark og Norge i ældre og nyere Tider (A historical-statistic sketch of the situation in Denmark and Norway in olden and modern times), Cop: 1803—6, 4 vol:. Ch. Molbech, Indledning til Forelæsninger over det danske Sprog og den danske Nationalliteraturs Historie (Introduction to lectures on the Danish language and history of National literature), Cop: 1822; and Forelæsninger over den nyere danske Poesi (Lectures on Modern Danish poetry), Cop: 1832, 2 vol:. C. A. Thortsen, Historisk Udsigt over den danske Literaturhistorie indtil Aar 1814 (Historical view of Danish literature until 1814), 6st ed: Cop: 1866. C. Rosenberg, Nordboernes Aandsliv fra Oldtiden til vore Dage (Intellectual life in the North from the earliest times until our days, Cop: 1878—85, 3 vol:. P. Hansen, Illustreret dansk Literaturhistorie (Illustrated History of Danish literature), Cop: 1887, 2 vol:. F. Winkel-Horn, Den danske Literaturs Historie (History of Danish literature), Cop: 1881; Geschichte der Litteratur des skandinavischen Nordens, Leipzig 1880. Marmier, Histoire de la littérature en Danemark et en Suède, Paris 1839. Fürst, Briefe über die dänische Litteratur, Wien 1816, 2 vol.; Strodtmann, Das geistige Leben in

Dänemark, Berlin 1873. Ph. Schweitzer, Geschichte der skandinavischen Litteratur von ihren Anfängen bis auf die neueste Zeit, Leip: 1886—87, 2 vol:. Danmarks gamle Folkeviser (Ancient Danish popular Ballads), ed: by Svend Grundtvig, 1853—78, 5 vol: (the work was stopped by the death of the author, but is being continued by Olrik). G. Brandes, Ludvig Holberg og hans Tid (L. Holberg and his time), Cop: 1884 (in German, Berlin 1885). Kr. Arentzen, Baggesen og Oehlenschläger, literaturhistorisk Studie (B. and O., an historical literary study), Cop: 1870—78, 8 vol:.; Adam Oehlenschläger, literaturhistorisk Livsbillede (Ad: O. Historical-literary life), Cop: 1879; Danske Digtere i det 19de Aarhundrede (Danish poets in the XIXth Century), Cop: 1864. P. Hansen, Nordiske Digtere i vort Aarhundrede (Northern Poets in our Century), 2nd ed: Cop: 1880. R. Nyerup and J. E. Kraft, Almindeligt Literaturlexikon for Danmark, Norge og Island (General literary Dictionary for Denmark, Norway and Iceland), Cop: 1820. Th. H. Erslev, Almindeligt Forfatterlexikon for Kongeriget Danmark med tilhörende Bilande fra 1814—53 (General dictionary of Authors for the kingdom of Denmark and its dependencies from 1814 to 1853), Cop: 1843—68, 6 vol:.

Works relating to "Art": Worsaae, Nordiske Oldsager i det kongelige Museum i Kjöbenhavn (Antiquities in the Royal Old-Northern Museum in Copenhagen), new ed: Cop: 1859. Kornerup, Om den tidligere Middelalders Trækirker (On the wooden churches from the earliest Middle Ages), and, Materialet i de ældste danske Kirkebygninger (The material of the oldest Danish churches); these two Memoirs are in Aarböger for nordisk Oldkyndighed og Historie (Annals of Northern Archæology and History), Cop: 1869 and 1870. L. de Thurah, Den danske Vitruvius (The Danish Vitruvius), Cop: 1746—49, 2 vol:. (Descriptions in Danish, German and French of Churches, Castles and other public buildings with illustrations). Tegninger af ældre nordisk Arkitektur (Drawing of ancient Northern Architecture) ed: by V. Dahlerup, H. G. Holm, H. B. Storck and others, Cop: 1871. Danske Mindesmærker (Danish Monuments). Cop: 1869—77, 2 vol:. Julius Lange, Nutidskunst (Art of our time), Cop: 1873; Billedkunst, Skildringer og Studier fra Hjemmet og Udlandet (Plastic Art, descriptions and studies at home and abroad), Cop: 1884. Sig. Müller, Nyere dansk Malerkunst (Modern Danish painting), Cop: 1884. F. J. Meier, Efterretninger om Johannes Wiedewelt og om Kunstakademiet paa hans Tid (Notices on J. W. and the Royal Academy in his time), Cop: 1877. J. M. Thiele. Thorvaldsen og hans Værker (Thorv. and his works), Cop: 1842—57, 4 vol: (in German, Cop: 1854—57, 2 vol:); Thorvaldsens Biographie — under various titles (History of Thorv: youth; Thorv: in Rome; Thorv: in Cop:) 1851—56, 4 vol: (in German, Leip: 1852—56, 3 vol:). M. Hammerich, Thorvaldsen og hans Kunst (Thorv: and his Art), 2nd ed: Cop: 1870 (in German, Gotha 1876). Eugène Plon, Thorvaldsen, sa vie et son œuvre, 2nd ed: Paris 1874.

Julius Lange, Sergel og Thorvaldsen, Studier i den nordiske Klassicismes Fremstilling af Mennesket (S. and T., Description of Northern classical reproductions of the human form), Cop: 1886. Ph. Weilbach, Maleren Eckersbergs Levned og Værker (Life and works of Eck. the painter), Cop: 1872. V. Freund, H. E. Freunds Levnet (The life of H. F. Freund), Cop: 1883. Eug: Plon, Le sculpteur danois Vilhelm Bissen, 2nd, ed: Paris 1871. N. L. Höyen, Skrifter udgivne af J. L. Ussing (Works of, edit: by J. L. Ussing), Cop: 1871—76, 3 vol:. Ph. Weilbach, Dansk Konstnerlexikon, indeholdende korte Levnedstegnelser af Kunstnere, som indtil Udgangen af 1876 have levet og arbejdet i Danmark eller den danske Stat (Dict: of Danish Artists, containing short biographical notices of artists, who until the end of 1876 have lived and worked in Denmark or the Dan: state), Cop: 1878. Tidsskrift for Kunstindustri (Review of Art-Industry), Cop: 1885— . Kunstbladet (Art Journal), Cop: 1888—89.

Works about "Music": V.C. Ravn, Koncerter og musikalske Selskaber i ældre Tid (Concerts and Musical Societies in olden times), Cop: 1886. Angul Hammerich, Musikforeningens Historie 1836—86 (Hist: of the Musical Soc:), Cop: 1886. C. Thrane, Danske Komponister (Danish composers), Cop: 1875. V. C. Ravn, the article entitled "Skandinavische Musik" in the Musical Dict: ed: by Mendel-Reissmann, new edit: Berlin 1885. P. A. Berggreen, C. E. F. Weyses Biographie, Cop: 1876. H. V. Schytte, Nordisk Musiklexikon (Dict: of Northern music), T. 1. Copenhagen 1888.

Works on the Theater: S. Birket Smith, Studier paa det gamle danske Skuespils Omraade (Studies concerning the ancient Danish Theater), Cop: 1883; also excellent editions of older Danish dramas by the same author. Th. Overskou, Den danske Skueplads i dens Historie fra de første Spor af dansk Skuespil indtil vor Tid (History of the Danish Stage from the earliest beginnings until our time), Cop: 1854—76, 7 vol:. Af Jonas Collins Papirer, Bidrag til det kongelige Theaters og dets Kunstneres Historie (From the papers of J. C., Contribution to the History of the Royal Theater and its Artists), Cop: 1871. Rosenstand-Goiske, Kritiske Efterretninger om den kgl. danske Skueplads 1778—80, udgivne af C. Molbech (Critical account of the Danish Stage 1778- 80), Cop: 1839. F. Schwartz, Lommebog for Skuespilyndere (Pocketbook for Amateurs), Cop: 1784—86, 3 vol:. K. L. Rahbek, Om Ludvig Holberg som Lystspildigter og om hans Lystspil (Concerning Ludv: Holb: as a dramatic author and his Comedies), Cop: 1815—17, 3 vol:; En gammel Skuespillers Breve til hans Søn (Letters from an old Comedian to his son), Cop: 1782. Ed. Brandes, Dansk Skuespilkunst (Danish dramatic Art), Cop: 1880.

DANISH LAW.
THE CONSTITUTION. THE LAW OF SUCCESSION

Danish Law

The relationship between the teutonic tribes, a reflection of which is seen in the affinities between their languages, has left permanent traces in their judicial conditions. The teutonic languages may be genealogically grouped according to their nearer or remoter kinship, and similar analogous conditions may be traced between the laws of the teutonic races. In the same way therefore that the Danish tongue is allied to the north teutonic (Scandinavian) stock of language, so is Danish law (beside Swedish, Norwegian and Icelandic) one of the ramifications into which the north teutonic law has gradually branched out. The relationship in which Danish law stands to that of the other Northern states, as also to that of the various south teutonic (Saxon, Frisian, Anglo-Saxon, Franconian, etc.) races, becomes more and more apparent the more remotely its origin can be traced.

At the earliest period of its existence, Denmark could not boast of a legislature common to the kingdom in general; the country was divided into a number of regions, the size of which was determined more or less by certain geographical boundaries, each division having a "Landsthing" as the centre from which legislation was carried on and justice administered in that special territory.

Neither do the most ancient records of Danish law furnish any one code common to the whole realm. They consist principally of traditionary usages which were formulated as enactments valid in the larger or smaller parts of the kingdom. In the provinces of Scania, Halland and Bleking, as also in the island of Bornholm, the "Scanian law" (preserved in Latin and Danish) prevailed; the Danish text is also found in a manuscript written in Runic characters and preserved in the University library; a curiosity of which a photolitographic facsimile has lately been published. For Sealand, Möen, Laaland and Falster, the "Sealand Laws" held good, a minor code known as King Valdemar's, and one of greater volume bearing the name of King Erik. These collections are however only the work of private individuals; they comprise records of certain customs, a few royal decrees, answers to or information on points of law by the assembly of the people at the "Things", and probably fragmentary portions of legal discourses held at the "Things" by men versed in jurisprudence and specially appointed for the purpose. As these documents are not dated, and the most ancient codices can scarcely be traced further back than the year 1300, it is difficult to say with certainty to what epoch they belong, whether they have come down to us in their original form or have been compiled from still more ancient manuscripts. This last conjecture is not improbable; they presumably first saw light in the course of the 12th century.

On the other hand the so-called "Jydske Lov" (Jutland law) which was in force in Slesvig and the North of Jutland, Fyn, Langeland and the surrounding isles, is a veritable code, and was adopted by a "Danehof" at Vordingborg in 1241. Besides these secular enactments, there are ecclesiastical ordinances holding good for Scania and Sealand (the Scanian and Sealand Canon law) dating from the end of the 12th century. All these texts are in Danish; and they are the oldest monuments extant of the Danish written language. But by degrees statutes having reference to other matters were enacted. More especially must be mentioned those touching the kings bodyguard, and later on those regarding the estates of the nobility —

landed property acts, "Gaardsretter". The earliest of these, the penal code or "Vederlagsret", dates from the time of Knud (Canute) the Great. Professor Wimmer derives the word "Vederlagsret" from "Withærlagamannalagsræt", that is to say "law for the society of the men of Criminal code". After these followed municipal laws, originally regulations or rules voted by the citizens themselves or formulated by the burgomaster and municipal council, with reference to the special interests of the market towns as opposed to those of the country districts; and as time went on, it became a custom to have these confirmed by the king. From the fact that Danish commerce during the Middle Ages was in the hands of the Hanseatic league, and that there was a marked admixture of the German element in the population of the market towns, not only were a number of German law-terms introduced into Danish legal phraseology, but also many foreign regulations and phrases were adopted in the municipal laws, whence they eventually made their way into the law of the land. But the origin of the State-laws is especially to be sought in the coronation-charters ("Haandfæstninger"); for from the year 1320 the Danish kings were forced to sign these pledges, before allegiance was sworn to them.

By degrees, as the influence of the royal prerogative on jurisprudence increased at the cost of the people's power, it became the centre of a legislative activity comprehending the whole of the kingdom. This in the course of the 13th century gave rise to a number of ordinances and minor decrees; and this tendency was largely developed from about the 16th century. At the same time attention was turned towards compiling a statute-book common to the whole nation, a reform effected in Norway in 1274 through the medium of the code of King Magnus, and in Sweden about the middle of the 14th century by Magnus Eriksson. Christian II had two general ordinances drawn up, one for the country and one for the towns, but these were set aside after his expulsion in 1523. Christian III then commissioned counsellor Erik Krabbe to compile a code from ancient statutes, but happily for the national character of Danish institutions, this led to no result. Roman law had just made its triumphal entry into several European states, and a short time before, had been adopted in Germany. As a scientific Jurist Erik Krabbe by no means escaped this influence, and the draft still preserved of his proposed code, proves that it was his intension to model Danish to some extent upon the principles of the Roman law, as also to introduce its terminology. Later on, no possible opening was left for Roman law in Denmark. Meanwhile Christian III in 1558 by the name of the Kolding Recess had codified a number of the laws made in the preceeding generation. Christian IV on two occasions undertook similar minor codifications — the Recesses of 1615 and 1643 — but in no case fell back on the Kolding Recess. In 1590 a revised edition of the "Jydske Lov" (Jutland law) was published thro the instrumentality of the government. Tho it was not intended to be put in force outside its original province, still in its new form it became practically of great importance, to the detriment of the other provincial lawcodes. Of these however, with the exception of Valdemar's Sealand law (which had never been printed) only old and inferior copies were to be found. So it was first formally turned to account by the Supreme Court of the period (the king and the state-council) and continued to be employed in the courts of law elsewhere in the land. Conjoined with the Kolding Recess and the Coronation-charter of Frederik II ("the Law, the Recess and the Charter") it was therefore subsequently looked upon as the very substance of right and justice. As the most important legislative work of the 16th century must also be mentioned Frederik the Second's Maritime Act of 1561, which was an independent revision of the Hanseatic and Dutch maritime law essentially adapted and strongly modified according to Danish requirements. The Church ordinance of 1539, which regulated ecclesiastical affairs in accordance with the introduction of the Reformation, also deserves mention.

As was the case with regard to so many other political problems, the form of government at this period in Denmark had shown itself most inefficient in dealing with the need for a general lawcode for the state. But on the establishment of absolutism in 1660, measures were taken with this object in view, and after various commissions had worked for a score of years towards its realization, "Christian the Fifth's Danish code" ("Danske Lov") was finally promulgated in 1683. This was to be a monument in memory of the king; not only did it bear his name, but it was dated on his birthday, the 15th of April. It was immediately printed, a fair copy being at the same time transcribed on parchment, and this latter, bound in thick plates of silver, is now preserved in the Royal Archives. The work is altogether a classification and remodelling of the ancient Danish lawcodes and statutes; but foreign sources have also here and there been drawn upon, as in the section on maritime Law, notably the Swedish Maritime Act of 1667. It abrogated all previous regulations in so far as these did not fall within the range of police law or contain special privileges for certain orders or corporations. The contents are divided into six books. Book I Procedure; Book II Ecclesiastical law; Books III and V Civil law; Book IV Maritime law; Book VI Penal code. With the "Danske Lov" ended the efforts so strenuously made to lay a common foundation for a code valid over the different parts of the country. More recently this code has been employed as a basis for further additions, and tho certain portions have since dropped out, from the enactment of more recent statutes, it still forms the firm groundwork of Danish law, especially in civil cases. In the 18th century efforts were made to revise it, but after a generation of fruitless labor the attempt was given up.

Among the older sections which remained in force, must be specially mentioned the "Kongelov" (Royal Law) of 1665, which regulated the constitution of the realm and settled the order of succession to the throne. It was drawn up by P. Griffenfeldt, subsequently known as chancellor of the kingdom; an original copy on parchment in the handwriting of Griffenfeldt himself, with artistically executed marginal designs and bound in heavy silver plates, may be seen among the curiosities of the Royal Archives. The "Kongelov" remained in force, until it was rendered null and void by the Ground-law (Constitution) of 1849 (revised 1866) and the Law of Succession of 1853.

The development which has taken place in Danish law since the code of 1683, and which in the course of time has manifested itself by the promulgation of a great number of minor rules, owes its importance principally to the fact, that since 1732 it formed the subject of constant enquiry at the University lectures; whereas before that time Roman and Canon law had paramount sway in these discussions. For years however the learned mode of treating such matters had consisted in formulating and reducing legislation into a system, and an independent Danish jurisprudence was not created until the first half of the present century, thro the literary exertions of A. S. Örsted. The work begun by Örsted has been carried on by various talented and astute writers, who have successively subjected the different parts of the judicial system to a careful and scientific revision. In more recent days efforts have been made to lead the expansion of Danish law into a new channel, an attempt which will prove of the greatest importance as regards its future prospects. Since 1872 the lawyers of the three closely connected Scandinavian kingdoms, at intervals of few years, have met in union to discuss questions of jurisprudence and legislation in general. Their chief aim has been, to work together for the introduction of as complete a uniformity as possible into the laws of each individual kingdom. One of the results of this movement was the "Vexellov" (relating to bills of exchange) for the Scandinavian countries, which was promulgated in 1880; since then combined efforts have been made towards drawing up a maritime code equally advantageous to the interests of the sister kingdoms. To facilitate the attainment of this, efforts are being made to diffuse all over the Northern lands a better knowledge of their laws by the publication of an "Encyclopedia of Scandinavian law", a concise account of the laws, under distinct heads, actually in force in each of the three lands, prepared by various experts in Northern law. These advances towards unity will gain fresh support through the instrumentality of a Scandinavian jurisprudential journal commenced in 1888.

V. A. Secher.

II

The Ground-Law
(Fundamental Law, Constitution)
of the Kingdom of Denmark
of the 5th of June 1849

Revised

and promulgated the 28th of July 1866

We Christian IX,

by the Grace of God King of Denmark, the Wends and Goths, Duke of Slesvig, Holstein, Stormarn, Ditmarsch, Lauenburg and Oldenburg, hereby make known, that the Rigsdag (Parliament), in the manner required by § 100 of the Ground-Law of the 5th of June 1849, having three times read the same, and that We, having temporarily approved it after the second reading, now confirm with Our Royal consent the Grundlov (Ground-Law) of the Kingdom of Denmark, of the 5th of June 1849.

I.

§ 1. The form of government is a limited Monarchy. The Royal power is hereditary. The order of succession is that established in the Law of Succession to the throne, of July 31st 1853, articles 1 and 2.

§ 2. The legislative power is vested in the King and the Rigsdag jointly. The executive power is in the King. The judicial power is ledged in the courts of justice.

§ 3. The Evangelical Lutheran Church is the Danish Folke-Kirke (National Church), and is aided as such by the State.

II.

§ 4. The King cannot rule in other countries without the consent of the Rigsdag.

§ 5. The King must belong to the Evangelical Lutheran Church.

§ 6. The King is of age when he has completed his eighteenth year. This is also the case with the Royal Princes.

§ 7. Before the King enters upon the government, he is to give in the State Council a written assurance on oath, inviolably to observe the Constitution of the Kingdom. Of this act two exactly corresponding originals are to be prepared, one of which is to be delivered to the Rigsdag to be kept in its archives, the other is to be deposited in the privy archives. If on account of absence, or for any other reason, the King cannot take the oath immediately after coming to the throne, the Council of State shall carry on the government until this is done, unless it be otherwise decided by law. If the King has already taken the said oath as successor to the throne, he shall undertake the government immediately after his accession.

§ 8. Regulations as to carrying on the government in case of the King's minority, illness or absence, shall be made by law. Until such a law is passed, the government is to be carried on temporarily in the aforementioned cases by the Council of State. The Council shall at once convoke the Rigsdag, which in a united assembly (§ 67) shall pass a resolution as to how the government is to be carried on until the King can enter upon it. If upon the vacancy of the throne there should be no successor to the crown, the united Rigsdag shall choose a King and establish a future order of inheritance.

§ 9. The King's civil-list is fixed by law for the term of his reign. Therewith shall also be determined what palaces and other state-property shall belong to the civil-list.

The civil-list cannot be charged with debt.

§ 10. Appanages may be appointed by law for members of the Royal family. No appanage can be enjoyed out of the kingdom, without the consent of the Rigsdag.

III.

§ 11. With the restrictions laid down in this Ground-law, the King has supreme authority over all affairs of state, and exercises the same thro his ministers.

§ 12. The King is without responsibility; his person is sacred and inviolable. The ministers are responsible for the conduct of the government; their responsibility shall be more particularly determined by law.

§ 13. The King appoints and dismisses his ministers. He determines their number and the division of business among them. The King's signature to the laws and the resolutions relating to the government gives them validity, if accompanied by the signature of one or more of the ministers. Every minister who has signed, is responsible for the resolution.

§ 14. The ministers can be called to account by the King or the Lower House (Folkething) for the discharge of their duty. The State Court (Rigsret) decides in actions against the ministers relative to the way in which their duties have been carried out.

§ 15. The ministers as a body form the Council of State; the successor to the throne, if of age, takes his seat among them. The King acts as president, except in the cases mentioned §§ 7 and 8.

§ 16. All proposed laws and important government matters are discussed in the State Council. Should the King in particular cases not be able to preside in the Cabinet, he can have the question examined in a Council of Ministers. This consists of all the ministers under the chairmanship of the minister whom the King has appointed as president (premier). Each minister shall then enter his vote on the minutes, and the resolution is agreed to by the vote of the majority. The president shall lay before the King the protocol of the proceedings, signed by the ministers present, and the King decides whether he will immediately sanction the proposition of the Council, or have the business brought before him in the Council of State.

§ 17. The King shall appoint to all offices, to the same extent as hitherto. Alterations herein may be made by law. No one can obtain any public appointment who is not a native or naturalized citizen. Every servant of the state, whether civil or military, shall take an oath to adhere to the Ground-law.

The King can dismiss the officers of the state appointed by him. Their pensions are fixed in accordance with the pension law.

The King can remove public servants without their consent, but in such wise that they do not lose in official income, and that they have the choice between removal and retirement, with a pension according to the general rules.

Exceptions for certain classes of functionaries, besides those fixed in § 73, are settled by law.

§ 18. The King declares war and makes peace; he also enters into and dissolves alliances and commercial treaties, but he cannot, without the consent of the Rigsdag, cede any part of the country, or enter into any engagement which changes the existing international relations.

§ 19. The King convokes an ordinary Rigsdag every year. Without his consent it cannot remain assembled for more than two months.

Alterations in these regulations may be made by law.

§ 20. The King can summon the Rigsdag for extraordinary meetings, the duration of such meetings depending upon his decision.

§ 21. The King can prorogue the ordinary meetings of the Rigsdag for a certain time, but without its consent, not for a longer period than for two months and not more than once in the year, in the interval between two ordinary sessions.

§ 22. The King can dissolve the whole Rigsdag or one of its divisions; should only one of the Things (Houses) be dissolved, the meetings of the other Thing shall be adjourned until the whole Rigsdag can meet. This shall take place before the lapse of two months after the dissolution.

§ 23. The King may cause bills and other resolutions to be laid before the Rigsdag.

§ 24. The King's consent is necessary to give a decision of the Rigsdag the force of law. The King orders the promulgation of the law, and sees that it is carried out. If the King has not confirmed a bill passed by the Rigsdag, before its next meeting, it is considered as lapsed.

§ 25. In specially urgent cases the King may, if the Rigsdag is not assembled, issue provisional laws; but these must not be at variance with the Ground-law, and must always be laid before the next Rigsdag.

§ 26. The King can pardon and grant amnesty; but he cannot, without the consent of the Lower House (Folkething) free ministers from the punishment awarded to them by the State Court.

§ 27. The King, either directly or thro the government authorities concerned, sanctions such grants or exceptions from the laws as are in force, either according to the regulations made before the 5th of June 1849, or for which authority is contained in an act passed since that time.

§ 28. The King has the right to coin money, according to the law.

IV.

§ 29. The Rigsdag consists of the Folkething (Lower House) and of the Landsthing (Upper House).

§ 30. Every man of good reputation, native or naturalized, who has completed his 30th year, has the right of voting for members of the Folkething, unless he:

a. Is in private service without a household of his own;
b. Is or has been in receipt of poor-law help, which has not yet been written off by the authorities or repaid by him;
c. Has not the disposal of his own estate;
d. Has not had a fixed residence for a year in the electoral district, or the town where he is staying at the time when the election takes place.

§ 31. Every man of good reputation, who has the rights of a native and has completed his 25th year, may be chosen to the Folkething, with the exceptions named in a, b and c of § 30.

§ 32. The number of the Folkething shall be in the proportion of approximately one member to 16,000 inhabitants. The elections take place in electoral districts; their division and the mode of election are fixed by the electoral law. Every electoral district chooses one member from amongst the candidates.

§ 33. The members of the Folkething are elected for three years. They receive a daily remuneration, the amount being regulated by the electoral law.

§ 34. The number of the members of the Landsthing is 66. Of these 12 are nominated by the King, 7 are elected in Copenhagen, 45 in the larger electoral districts, comprising country and commercial towns; 1 in Bornholm, and 1 by the Lagthing of the Færöes Islands.

§ 35. No one can take part, directly or indirectly, in the election of the members of the Landsthing, unless he fulfill the general conditions for electing to the Folkething; but residence is only required, in one of the commercial towns or in the country district within the Landsthing centre concerned, during the last year before the election.

§ 36. In Copenhagen all the voters (§ 35) elect one elector for every 120 voters, a surplus of 60 being reckoned for a full 120. An equal number of electors is chosen by the voters whose last year's taxable income was assessed at 2000 rixdollars (4000 kroner) at least. All the electors together then choose the members of the Landsthing for Copenhagen.

§ 37. In the country all the voters (§ 35) select one elector in every parochial district. For the commercial towns, among which are included Frederiksberg, Frederiksværk, Marstal, Silkeborg, Lögstör and Nörre Sundby, half as many electors are chosen as there are parochial districts; if the number of electors is not equal after this, one more must be chosen. One moiety of the electors of the commercial towns is nominated in every town, by all entitled to vote; the other moiety is chosen by the town voters who in the last year have been assessed on a taxable income of at least 1000 rixdollars (2000 kroner), or have paid at least 75 rixdollars in direct taxes to the state or commune. The distribution of the whole body of electors among the several towns in proportion to their voters is fixed by the government, whenever there is a general election to the Landsthing, but in such manner that every town shall receive at least one elector from each class of voters. With the electors in each Landsthing division, meet as many of the country voters as there are parochial districts, such as during the last year have paid the highest contribution to State and Provincial revenue; they together choose the member of the Landsthing.

§ 38. Any one is eligible to the Landsthing who is eligible to the Folkething, provided he has lived in the electoral division during the last year.

§ 39. The King's appointment of members to the Landsthing is for life, from among those who are, or have been, elected members of former or existing representative assemblies of the kingdom. But every member is at liberty to resign his seat in the Landsthing; whereas, if he lose his eligibility, he is bound to resign.

The other members of the Landsthing are elected for 8 years, but one half of these retire every 4th year.

The members of the Landsthing receive the same daily remuneration as the members of the Folkething.

§ 40. The elections to the Landsthing take place according to the rules for proportionate numbers. The electoral law determines the details relative to the elections.

V.

§ 41. The ordinary Rigsdag assembles on the first Monday in October, if the King has not summoned it earlier.

§ 42. The seat of government is the place of the Rigsdag's meeting. In extraordinary cases however, the King can summon it to meet in another place in the kingdom.

§ 43. The Rigsdag is inviolable. Whoever assails its security and freedom, or issues or obeys any order for that purpose, is guilty of high treason.

§ 44. Each Thing (House) is entitled to propose and pass laws for its own administration.

§ 45. Each of the Things can present addresses to the King.

§ 46. Each of the Things can appoint committees of its members to enquire into subjects of general importance. Such committees are empowered to demand information, verbal or in writing, from public authorities and private citizens.

§ 47. No tax can be imposed, altered or abolished except by law; nor can any levy be decreed, any State loan made nor any domains belonging to the State be alienated, except by law.

§ 48. At every ordinary Rigsdag, as soon as it is in session, is submitted the ways and means (a financial law) for the following financial year, containing the estimate of the State receipts and expenditures. This finance-bill and the additional grants asked for, are first considered in the Folkething.

§ 49. No taxes can be collected before the budget is accepted. No expenditure must be incurred which is not warranted by the budget, or by a law for an additional grant.

§ 50. Each Thing appoints two paid auditors, who examine the yearly State accounts and take care that all the State receipts are brought therein, and that no expenditure has taken place without the sanction of the budget. They can demand all necessary explanations and documents. The yearly State account, with the remarks of the auditors, is then laid before the Rigsdag, which passes a resolution thereon.

These provisions may be altered by law.

§ 51. No foreigner can be naturalized except by law.

§ 52. No bill can be finally carried, before it has been three times considered by the Thing.

§ 53. When a project of law has passed one Thing, it must, in the form in which it has been passed, be laid before the other Thing; if it be altered there, it goes back to the other House; if changes are again made there, the bill is returned to the other Thing. If unanimity is not then attained, and if either Thing demand it, an equal number of members shall be chosen by each Thing, to meet in committee, which shall give its opinion on the points of difference, and make a proposition to the Things. Each Thing finally decides for itself in reference to the proposition of the committee.

§ 54. Each Thing decides for itself on the validity of the election of its members.

§ 55. Every new member takes oath to the Ground-law, when the validity of his election has been acknowledged.

§ 56. The members of the Rigsdag shall follow only their own convictions, and not any instructions from their voters or electors.

Functionaries who are elected as members of the Rigsdag, do not require the permission of the government to accept the election.

§ 57. So long as the Rigsdag is assembled, no member, without the consent of the Thing to which he belongs, can be imprisoned for debt, or arrested or prosecuted, unless he be taken in the act. No member of the Rigsdag can, without the consent of his House (Thing), be made responsible outside of the assembly for his utterances within its walls.

§ 58. If any one duly elected falls into a position which precludes his eligibility, he loses the rights accruing from his election.

It remains to be more precisely determined by law, under what circumstances a member of the Rigsdag who is appointed to a paid State office, must be re-elected.

§ 59. The ministers have access to the Rigsdag by virtue of their office, and are entitled to speak on the matters under discussion as often as they wish, provided they otherwise observe the established rules. They only vote when they are also members of the Rigsdag.

§ 60. Each Thing elects its president, and the person or persons who are to preside in his absence.

§ 61. Neither of the Things can pass any resolutions, unless more than half of its members are present and take part in the voting.

§ 62. Every member of the Rigsdag can, in the Thing to which he belongs and with its consent, bring any public matter under consideration, and demand from the ministers an explanation thereof.

§ 63. No statement can be submitted to either of the Things, except thro one of its members.

§ 64. Should the Thing not see fit to pronounce upon such application, it may refer it to the ministers.

§ 65. The meetings of the Things are public. But the president, or the number of members prescribed in the rules may demand that all strangers withdraw, whereupon the Thing decides whether the matter shall be discussed in public or in secret meeting.

§ 66. Each of the Things prescribes the special regulations for the transaction of its business and the preservation of order.

§ 67. The united Rigsdag is formed by the Folkething and the Landsthing meeting together. To pass a resolution it is necessary that more than half of the members of each Thing be present, and take part in the voting. It elects its own president, and otherwise draws up the special regulations required for its proceedings.

VI.

§ 68. The State Court (Rigsret) consists of the ordinary members of the Supreme Court of the Kingdom, and a corresponding number of judges elected by the Landsthing for four years, from its own members. If in any particular instance the full body of the ordinary members of the Supreme Court cannot take part in the treatment and decision of the case, a corresponding number of the members of the State Court, from among the last elected by the Landsthing, or who have received the least number of votes, retire. — The Court elects its president from among its own members.

Should the Landsthing be dissolved after any accusation has been brought before the State Court, the members elected by the dissolved Thing retain their seats in the Court as to the question before it.

§ 69. The State Court decides the cases brought by the King or the Folkething against the ministers.

The King can also bring other persons to trial before the State Court, for offences which he considers especially dangerous to the Commonwealth, if the Folkething gives its consent thereto.

§ 70. The exercise of the judicial power can only be regulated by law.

§ 71. The administration of Justice shall be separated from police functions, according to rules enacted by law.

§ 72. The tribunals have the right to decide all questions concerning the limits of the competence of the authorities. But no one by bringing a case before the tribunals can relieve himself from temporary compliance with the orders of the authorities.

§ 73. The judges have only to regulate their functions by law. They cannot be dismissed except by legal sentence nor be removed against their will, unless in case of a reorganization of the tribunals. A judge who has completed his 65th year may, however, be discharged, but without loss of income.

§ 74. Publicity and oral process shall be carried out as soon and as widely as possible, throughout the whole judicial administration.

In criminal cases and in questions arising from political offences, trial by jury shall be introduced.

VII.

§ 75. The constitution of the national Church (Folkekirke) shall be regulated by law.

§ 76. Citizens have a right to assemble in community to worship God according to their convictions, but so that nothing be taught or done contrary to good morals and public order.

§ 77. No one is bound to render personal contributions to any other form of Divine worship than his own; but every one who does not prove that he is a member of a religious community recognized by the state, shall pay to the educational funds the personal taxes ordered by law for the Folke-Kirke (National Church).

§ 78. The position of religious communities differing from the national Church shall be regulated by law.

§ 79. No one can be deprived of full civil and political rights, on account of his religious belief; nor can he for that reason decline to fulfil any general civil obligation.

VIII.

§ 80. Every one who is arrested shall be brought before a judge within 24 hours. If the prisoner cannot at once be set at liberty, the judge shall order his imprisonment by a sentence containing the reason, to be issued as soon as possible, at latest within three days; if he can be released on bail, the judge shall determine the kind and amount of that bail.

Against the sentence given by the judge, the party concerned may at once appeal to a higher court.

No one can be committed to close imprisonment for an offence which is only punishable by a fine or simple confinement.

§ 81. The domicile is inviolable. Searching a house, or the seizure and examination of letters and other papers, can only take place after a legal order to that effect, unless special exception be authorized by law.

§ 82. The right of property is inviolable. No one can be compelled to give up what he owns, unless the common weal require it. This can only take place in accordance with law, and on full compensation.

§ 83. All restrictions as to the free and equal requirement of a livelihood, unless based on the general weal, shall be abolished by law.

§ 84. Every person who cannot support himself, or those belonging to him and whose maintenance is not incumbent on another, shall be entitled to receive public aid; but he must submit to the conditions prescribed by the laws.

§ 85. Children of parents lacking means to provide for their education, are to be taught without cost in the primary schools.

§ 86. Every one has a right to express his opinions thro the press, but with responsibility to the tribunals. Censorship of the press, and other preventive measures, can never be re-introduced.

§ 87. Citizens have a right, without previous permission, to form associations for any lawful purpose. No association can be dissolved by a government decree; it may however be temporarily forbidden; but in cases of this kind an action shall immediately be brought against the association, for its dissolution.

§ 88. Citizens have a right to assemble unarmed. The police are entitled to be present at public meetings. Open air assemblies may be prohibited, if there be reason to fear danger to the public peace therefrom.

§ 89. In case of riot the armed force, unless attacked, cannot interfere until the crowd has been thrice summoned to disperse, in the name of the King and the law, without effect.

§ 90. Every man able to bear arms is bound to assist in person in the defence of the country, according to the particular regulations prescribed by law.

§ 91. The right of the communes to manage their affairs independently, under State supervision, shall be regulated by law.

§ 92. All legal privileges connected with nobility, title or rank are abolished.

§ 93. No feudal, entailed or feoffment in trust estates can hereafter be created; the manner in which those now existing may be converted into free property, shall be determined by law.

§ 94. The provisions in §§ 80, 87 and 88 apply to the army and navy subject to the restrictions arising from the precepts of military law.

IX.

§ 95. Proposals for alterations in, or additions to the present Ground-law (Constitution) may be made both in an ordinary and an extraordinary Rigsdag.

If such proposal for a new regulation in the Ground-law be accepted by both Things, and the government is in favor of the same, the Rigsdag shall be dissolved, and a new general election take place to the Folkething and the Landsthing. Should the resolution be accepted unaltered by the new Rigsdag, thus chosen, in ordinary or extraordinary session, and it be confirmed by the King, it becomes a law.

Temporary Arrangements.

1. The present members of the Landsthing of the Rigsraad chosen by the King shall, as such, take their seats in the Landsthing of the Rigsdag for the period of 12 years from each of their several appointments. The validity of such appointment does not cease with the dissolution of the Landsthing.

2. With regard to the mode of procedure in the State Court (Rigsret), until a new law is issued, that of the 3rd of March 1852 shall remain in force, with the modifications made necessary by its altered composition and the direction in the last part of § 68.

3. The rule in § 73, that judges cannot be dismissed except by legal sentence, nor removed against their wish, shall not be

applicable to Judges in office who also exercise administrative functions.

4. Until new regulations for criminal process are carried out, the appeal from a sentence of imprisonment mentioned in § 80 will take place as from a private action, but with extra legal notice, the complainant being also exempt from the use of stamped paper and the payment of judicial fees. On occasion of such a complaint, the plaintiff shall be allowed access to counsel for consultation, and fresh information may be laid before the superior court.

5. (This section, regulating the elections, was abolished by the law of July 12th 1867.)

The condition laid down by the Constitutional provision of November 17th 1865, having been completely fulfilled, and whereas We have this day likewise confirmed the provision of the Constitution passed by the Rigsdag, in the manner appointed by the Ground-law as to the abolition of the Constitutional provision of August 29th 1855, the Ground-law of November 18th 1863 is hereby repealed, and the Ground-law of the Kingdom of Denmark in its present revised form comes again into force for all the affairs of Our Kingdom.

Given at Our palace of Amalienborg, the 28th of July 1866.

By Our Royal hand and seal.

CHRISTIAN R.

(L. S.)

C. E. Juel-Vind-Frijs. Th. Rosenörn-Teilmann.   Neergaard.   Grove.
Leuning.   C. A. Fonnesbech.   J. B. S. Estrup.

III.

The Law of Succession to the Throne of Denmark

of July 31st 1853.

We, Frederik VII,

by the Grace of God King of Denmark, the Vends and Goths, Duke of Slesvig, Holstein, Stormarn, Ditmarsh, Lauenburg, and Oldenburg, make known: The Rigsdag has adopted, and We have given Our Sanction to, the following Law.

It has been considered by Our predecessors on the throne a fundamental principle of the government, that the countries which are subject to the Danish sceptre should not be disunited or separated from each other.

In accordance herewith, Our well-beloved father His Majesty the late King Christian VIII, of glorious memory, when He found Himself constrained to make some declaration respecting the state of succession to the Danish Monarchy, gave to all His faithful subjects, in the open letter of the 18th of July 1846, signed by Us as Crown Prince at that time, the assurance that His constant efforts had been and should be directed to cause the integrity of the Danish Monarchy to be fully recognized, so that the different parts of the country united under His sceptre should never be separated.

During the convulsions, soon after Divine Providence had called Us to the throne of Our forefathers, which in several European states threatened to overthrow the foundations of civil society, and subsequently penetrated the boundaries of Our Monarchy and placed its integrity in the greatest peril, We considered it Our duty to maintain this integrity with unshaken constancy, its realisation and preservation having been transmitted to Us by Our predecessors as one of the chief duties of the Kings of Denmark.

But as this result necessarily presupposes a common succession to all parts of the Monarchy, and We and Our well-beloved father have in vain endeavored to secure the legal establishment of the female succession in Our Danish Kingdom to be extended to Our Duchy of Slesvig, as being indissolubly united with the Danish crown, and likewise undoubtedly in the other parts of the Monarchy, recognized as binding on the whole, if, by the inscrutable will of Providence, the male line of the late King Frederik III should become extinct, — We submit that the most suitable means to prevent the eventual dissolution of the Monarchy will be to promulgate a new Law of Succession valid for all its parts and repealing the arrangements in the Royal Law, We causing the same to be acknowledged by the other European Powers.

After Our efforts to this end were facilitated, partly by the friendly goodwill with which His Majesty the Emperor of Russia, as head of the oldest line of the house of Holstein-Gottorp, renounced in favor of His Highness, Prince Christian of Slesvig-Holstein-Sonderburg-Glücksburg, and his male descendants, the hereditary claims to a part of Our hereditary dominions which His Imperial Majesty assumed to belong in the above-mentioned event to the aforesaid line; and partly by the magnanimous readiness with which Our relatives nearest the throne have relinquished their right of succession to the same to promote this object, — We have determined, with the full concurrence of Our well-beloved uncle His Royal Highness the hereditary Prince Frederik Ferdinand, in case the male line of succession from Frederik III should fail, to abrogate all rights of succession by the Royal Law, and, excluding the female line, to call as successor to all the countries subject to our sway Our well-beloved kinsman His Highness Prince Christian of Slesvig-Holstein-Sonderburg-Glücksburg and his male offspring by his spouse, our well-beloved cousin, Her Highness Princess Louisa Wilhelmina Frederica Carolina Augusta

Julia, of Slesvig-Holstein-Sonderburg-Glücksburg, born Princess of Hesse.

Whereas also, by the treaty concluded in London on the 8th of May 1852 and afterwards ratified between His Majesty the Emperor of Austria and King of Hungary and Bohemia, the Prince President of the French Republic, now Emperor of the French, Her Majesty the Queen of the United Kingdom of Great Britain and Ireland, His Majesty the King of Prussia, His Majesty the Emperor of Russia and His Majesty the King of Sweden and Norway, and by the adhesion to the same of most of the European Powers, given when article IV of the treaty was laid before them, We have procured the acknowledgement of the indivisibility of the Danish Monarchy as a perpetual maxim of European public law, with the recognition of the succession established by Us; and finally whereas the United Danish Rigsdag, in accordance with § IV of the Constitution of the 5th of June 1849, has, by its decision of June 24 1853 assented, as far as it is concerned, to Our proposal addressed to it upon this subject; — We are now enabled to publish a Law of Succession applicable to Our whole Monarchy, and thus to complete a work which has so long been the object of Our patriotic efforts.

We therefore ordain and make known as follows:

Article I.

In case the male descent from King Frederik III, by the Royal law of November the 14th 1665 empowered to succeed to the Danish throne, should by God's inscrutable will become extinct, — then all rights according to articles 27—40 of the above law shall be abrogated, and only male from male, with the exclusion of females, shall have the right of succession in the countries united under Our sceptre. This right shall then pass in all these countries to Our well-beloved kinsman His Highness Prince Christian of Slesvig-Holstein-Sonderburg-Glücksburg, to whom from this time We have given the title of Prince of Denmark, and to his male offspring by His Consort, Our well-beloved cousin Her Highness Princess Louisa

Wilhelmina Frederica Carolina Augusta Julia of Slesvig-Holstein-Sonderburg-Glücksburg, now Princess of Denmark, born Princess of Hesse.

Article II.

The Crown shall pass in this descent, male after male, begotten in lawful wedlock, according to the right of primogeniture and the agnatic line.

Article III.

In the event, which God forbid, that danger should arise of this male descent becoming extinct, — then Our successor who may occupy the Danish throne, shall take steps to regulate the Royal succession in such way as shall be most efficacious for maintaining the independence and integrity of the Monarchy and the rights of the Crown, and for obtaining the recognition of this succession by the European Powers, in conformity with article II of the treaty concluded in London on the 8th of May, 1852.

In consequence whereof, We hereby publish and sanction this Law of Succession, which We have had drawn up in Danish and in German, the same being signed by Our well-beloved Uncle H. R. H. Prince Frederik Ferdinand, as well as by all the other members of Our privy council; and We order that the original shall be preserved in the archives of the Kingdom.

To this all shall obediently conform, whom these presents may concern.

Given in Our palace of the Hermitage, the 31st of July 1853.
By Our Royal hand and seal.

FREDERIK R.

(L. S.)

Frederik Ferdinand. *Örsted.* *Reventlow-Criminil.* *C. Moltke.*
C. F. Hansen. *C. A. Bluhme.* *W. C. E. Sponneck.* *Steen Bille.*
W. A. Scheel.

ECONOMICAL AND SOCIAL CONDITIONS

Economical Legislation

The economical legislation of Denmark, during the last hundred years, has been conducted in the spirit of that liberal movement which sprang up in France at the close of the 18th century, and has since swept over all Europe.

It must however be said, that as regards several essentials every thing was not overthrown, and there have moreover been lasting pauses in the work. As a consequence, the endeavors in a contrary direction, towards limitation and restriction, have not been so intense as in many other countries, and at all events have been followed by few positive results.

1. With regard to Agricultural legislation. During the last decades of the 18th century a complete re-arrangement was made in whatever concerned farmers. By the statute of Partition (1781) every owner who cultivated a share in conjunction with others, was permitted to demand the separation of the land in such a manner, that he got his lot or lots collected in one place or at the most in two, while the rest of the proprietors were obliged to pay their part in the costs connected herewith.

But these regulations had no practical result till (in 1792) they were put in connection with others, giving to the landlords greater liberty than formerly to dispose of the land, on condition of their joining and conducting the allotment. This ended in the abolition of "joint cultivation", an event of the most decisive importance to the agriculture of modern times.

It was moreover ordered, that the Socage ("Hoveri") — the obligation of the tenant to do work for the manor — should be clearly specified (1799), so as no longer to be casual or arbitrary, an injustice by which the cultivation of the tenant's own farm was frequently neglected or made impossible.

At the same time successful efforts were made to get rid of socage; but this was not fully accomplished till the law of 1850 stipulated terms of commutation. Payments in kind have now virtually ceased.

Tithes in kind have been similarly treated. Also several statutes (at the end of the last century) regarding fences and the drainage of water, have been of the greatest importance for the advancement of agriculture.

As to the person of the tenant, a new era was inaugurated by the statute of 1788 abolishing "Stavnsbaand", the obligation of the tenant to remain on the manor to which he belonged. This regulation, made in the first third of the century, had been associated with the militia. It resulted in giving to the landlord, who was compelled to furnish a certain number of soldiers from his estate, power to claim the stay of every male from his fourth year; still later, it authorized him to pick out whomever he chose for a soldier, and at the close of his service to force the discharged man to lease whichever of his farms he chose.

The reforms thus carried out and continued in this century did not stop with the socage and payment in kind. Further steps were taken. For instance, the abolition of the old gamelaws; a new assessment of taxes, doing away with the difference between "privileged" and "unprivileged" land; fresh detailed regulations for the protection of fields and roads and for the drainage of hurtful water; and the establishment of credit-associations. Thus in the last ten years two such associations for cottagers have been guaranteed by the State, one for Jutland and one for the isles.

As to disposal of land, we point out in the first place, that the ordinance of Sept. 27th 1805 and later laws have largely protected woods and forests, and limited their being realized. As to other land, the law as a rule forbids the discontinuance of peasant-farms. The chief ordinance hereon dates from 1769, and is a continuation of earlier laws; as to division of farms, there is a fixed minimum for the area to be left (Dec. 3d 1819) and for the parcels separated. Here are then limits as well to the liberty of accumulation—preventing the destruction of the middling properties — as to the right to parcel out, for such separated lots must be large enough for the support of one family.

Connected with the prohibition against discontinuing farms, is the obligation to lease them to the country people, instead of cultivating them under the manor. The laws to this end are parts of the complicated leasehold legislation of the former century, whose tendency and result may be thus summed up: They encourage the transfer to the peasantry, where possible, of farms, as freehold property (or, which is very near to this, as heritable lease, with right to sell and mortgage); all this in such a way that the proprietor, by such a transfer of a certain part as not fully disposable by him, obtains a right, as leases die out, freely to dispose of as much of the land left him, as corresponds to $1/9$ of that sold (statutes of Febr. 19th 1861 and March 9th 1872). At the same time provision was made for securing to the lessees under certain circumstances repayment of a part of the sum given when entering upon the lease, and compensation for improvements.

In this manner the state has endeavored to create as many peasant freeholds as possible — as statistics show with most favorable results—and enable leasehold-farmers to cultivate without too great hazard in a rational manner. It has also set bounds to the formation of "latifundia" and to the crushing of the land to dust.

It may yet be added, that the later agrarian movements also have obtained some sympathy in Denmark. They have not however, as will be mentioned below, had any protectionist character; rather they have accomplished an enlargement of the state-support already given to agriculture (such as prizes for land and cattle, credit for country-people, etc.).

At present the claims grow higher. There is a wish that farmers shall obtain veterinary scientific assistance, that the state shall establish mutual loan-associations, and that producing or at all events exporting artificial butter shall be forbidden, in order not to injure the chief export, natural butter. A law of 1888 strictly regulates the trade in margarine and allows, among other things, that the export of artificial butter may be altogether prohibited.

An alleviation of the Hartkorn-tax, resting on the land, has also been asked for. A new registration of the land was made in the first half of this century, which has almost driven out the earlier system. By this registration all the land in Denmark was divided according to a rate, that fixed a certain area ($5^1/_1$ Tønde Land[1]) of the best soil, found in the "Amt" (County) of Copenhagen and estimated to the value of 24, as being equal to 1 Tönde Hartkorn (making use of the nomenclature of the old taxation). According to this all other land was registered in classes in such a manner, that the lower the class the more "Tönder Land" was calculated to one "Tönde Hartkorn". On the basis of this division — in which were separate arrangements for the registration of the forests by Hartkorn and of the island Bornholm — the groundtaxes are assessed pr "Tönde Hartkorn", ("the old tax" however according to the old register). The amount of the tax depends accordingly not only on the size of the area, but also on its presumptive quality, estimated in "Tönder Hartkorn". It is clear however, that by the great changes in the course of the century in the quality of the soil, this division is at present far from satisfactory, especially as the large areas at an earlier period not or scarcely cultivated (f. inst.

[1] 1 Tönde Land, "Danish acre", = 1,4 acres.

in Jutland), and in the register valued at a very low Hartkorn, now represent far greater values, tho they still pay tax according to the old registration In this and similar ways are many inequalities in the land-tax. Some consolation is sought in the fact, that these taxes ("the old tax", "the land-taxes" and "the assessed taxes") have partly passed into mortgages or charges on the ground, as allowance has long been made in buying and selling for the circumstances named, and owing to this there is no necessity for making a new registration as a basis for taxation. Even if such an analogy between the ground-taxes and fixed charges on the land may only be drawn with regard to the "old tax", the Hartkorn-taxes do not upon the whole amount to any very considerable sum (in all 17^1/$_2$ Kroner pr Tönde Hartkorn). But the complaints chiefly apply to the municipal taxes etc., which rest on the Hartkorn. It is looked upon at all events as impracticable to assess new state-taxes of any importance on the basis of the existing registration.

In the kingdom as a whole 17^1/$_2$ Tönder Land go to one Tönde Hartkorn, which gives for the tax of Hartkorn a mean of 1 Krone on every Tönde Land, in the isles on an average 1 of Hartkorn to a mean of 10 Tönder Land, in Jutland 26^1/$_2$ Tönder Land go to one Tönde Hartkorn.

Besides the Hartkorn-taxes, buildings in the country in no way pertaining to agriculture (dwellings, lodging-houses belonging to factories, inns, etc.) must pay a house-tax according to the area built on and the number of the stories (ordin: Oct. 1st 1802 and later statutes). This tax is also levied in the towns and especially has been raised several times with respect to Copenhagen. On real property in the towns are also levied the assessed taxes, as charged by the ordinance of June 20th 1850 partly on Copenhagen with a fixed amount, partly on all the other towns together with a fixed amount, apportioned among the latter according to population and the insurance-sum of the buildings; this must now be regarded as a tax on the communes (but not resting on the country-communes).

2. Coincident with the reforms on behalf of agriculture, were published new regulations of the customs, strongly influenced by the liberalistic political economy of the end of the 18th century, which had found its chief advocate in Adam Smith. By two ordinances of 1788 the trade in corn and cattle was made free, and it was settled that in future everybody might freely import and export bread-stuffs on payment of a slight import-duty, the export of cattle being allowed. But the decisive step was the custom's law of 1st Febr. 1797, which is yet the basis of the Danish tariff, and by which the former system with oppressive rates of duty or even prohibitions (150 prohibitions against import and 12 against export) was reorganized in the direction of a moderate system of protection. However excellent this statute was for its time, the Danish customs legislation has only slightly kept pace with the process of development. The first reform of the statute of 1797 was in the ordinances of 1838 and 1844, both going somewhat further in the direction of free trade. They lowered the duties, abolished several of the still existing prohibitory rates, and left others still standing. It was first by the statute of July 4th 1863, which is yet in force, that all prohibitory rates were abolished, while at the same time the tariff was simplified and the import-duties sank to a generally moderate amount.

The tariff of 1863, whose rates on a few articles were somewhat raised by the war-duty of 1864, and which has now for near 30 years been the basis for the production and trade of Denmark, is in several particulars irrational. It lays a duty on the import of raw materials of which the country has great need (timber, iron), on an article important for its own production (coal) and on food-stuffs (salt, rice). Its rates being calculated by weight (f. inst. as to dry-goods) it taxes cheaper (heavier) goods proportionally far more heavily than valuable things. It also contains rates on a series of industrial products, by reason of which has been nursed an industry not always successful, hampering free trade and the consumption of the population at large.

But it has no duty on the most necessary articles of food (corn, cattle, provisions), and gets its chief revenue in good objects of taxation (groceries), the import of which in proportion to other countries is taxed moderately (war tax included, 50 pct. of the original duty, coffee pays now a duty of 12 Öre pr pound, tea 33 Öre, sugar from 8,2 to 13 Öre, and raw tabacco 14 Öre pr pound[1]).

The present protectionist current in Europe has only so far influenced the custom-bills proposed by the ministry and the agitation for tariff reform, as these in general do not wish to abolish the protection for the small handicrafts or for branches of industry likely to prosper in the country, when sheltered in some degree from the overproduction of foreign countries, especially the German factories. But no one, not even a fraction of the farmers, cries out for an agrarian duty. In general, all desire a simplification of the tariff and juster rates (especially as to dry-goods) and to abolish the duty on raw materials and on auxiliary materials most important to industry. As however any revival of the customs would affect many contending interests, and as the financial administration will accept no lowering of revenue from the customs without a fair compensation from some other source, and as the political complications for many years have thrown obstacles in the way of peaceful agreement, it cannot be said that a new Danish customs tariff is immediately at hand.

Some of the obstacles the tariff throws in the way of free transactions are partly remedied by the provisions for repayment of the duty on re-exportation of foreign goods, by bonded warehouses, transit-warehouses and credit-warehouses, etc. Lately it has been proposed to make Copenhagen a free port, and the government has lately laid before the Parliament a bill for that purpose.

In connection with the customs must be mentioned the law of harbour duties, now reduced to a duty only on ingoing vessels in foreign trade, the tax on the manufacture of beet-root sugar, a stamp-tax on playing cards, and a tax on distillation of spirits.

[1] 1 pound = $\frac{1}{2}$ Kilogramme.

The last in proportion to the duty in other countries is very low (by statute of April 1st 1887 according to the yield of the production ordinarily 18 Öre pr Pot[1]). A tax on beer has not yet been carried thro.

3. With regard to inland production and commerce, new and liberal provisions for town and country were made by the statute of Dec. 29th 1857. This abolished the guilds, and instead made handicraft free with no compulsory trial of skill, but only asking burghership (freedom of the city), in the country a licence. This important law contains in its second paragraph (compare the statute of May 23d 1873) the conditions for obtaining the freedom of a city or a licence ("Næringsbevis"). They are: that the party concerned must be of age (i. e. 25 years; by a law of the same date any unmarried woman, who has reached the age of 25, is to be considered as of age); that he must not be insolvent; that he must be of unspotted reputation (defined at length in the statute); and that, if not a native of Denmark or entitled (by a stay of 5 years) to parochial relief from the commune, in which he is going to settle, he must be able to guarantee, that he and family in case of being in need, will be relieved elsewhere.

In connection with the trade-law ("Næringsloven") may be mentioned acts for the registration of firms issued in 1862 and 1889, and an insolvency act (1872). On the other hand Denmark is still in want of a special law for joint-stock societies. With regard to these must be applied the general provisions of the legislation relative to the participation of several shareholders in one and the same firm, but the want of a law directly providing for joint-stock companies cannot be relieved in this way.

Among acts of taxation relative to the home-trade must be mentioned the duty of $1/4$ percent on the buying and selling of real property and on sale by auction, and the act on the use of stamped paper for all documents affecting money or money's worth and foreign stocks (statutes of Febr. 19th 1861 and March 25th 1872). As

[1] 1 Pot = 0,966 lit.

a similar class in a broader sense may be mentioned the inheritance-duty, fixed at 1 percent on property passing to the surviving spouse, heirs of the body or parents; 4 percent on what is claimed by sisters and brothers and the children of such (first cousins), and 7 percent on every other inheritance. No one having legal heirs can dispose by will of more that $1/3$ of the property; sons and daughters succeed to equal shares; heirs may renounce inheritance and debts; the wife may retain undivided possession of the estate, etc. (See the Danish code of Christian V, book 5, chapter 2, the laws of 1845 and 1857, and that on division of inheritance given in 1874, etc.).

4. The abolition of the guilds (trade corporations) in 1857 of course gave rise in Denmark as elsewhere to a liberty, that later produced unhappy consequences. In many trades, corporations still exist, but they have an altered character, and frequently only represent the master-workmen, the journeymen having formed socialistic-democratic unions. Any return to the old relations is naturally out of the question, tho legislation as opportunity offers will endeavor to remedy the serious inconveniences caused by the existing liberty (especially as to apprenticeship).

There are no labor-laws proper in Denmark. Relative to work in factories and shops employing children the statute of May 23d 1873 has forbidden the employment of children under 10 years of age, but permitting young persons from 10 to 14 years to work for 6 hours and a half (out of which must be given half an hour's interval for rest, with no night work), and young people from 14 to 18 years of age only for 12 hours (minus 2 hours for rest, and with no night work). Two inspectors with about 12 deputies have the superintendence of the carrying out of this, and the laws for the inspection of steam-engines and for preventing accidents from engines (statutes of 1875 and 1889; according to the latter persons selected by the communes have the inspection of other machinery than steam-engines).

Some years since, the government proposed a bill for assisting workmen in their old age. It was not important and was not accepted by the Rigsdag. Quite lately it has prepared comprehensive measures for statehelp to sick-clubs and for the insurance of laborers in perilous branches of industry against accidents during their work. These questions have been treated by a special commission, and are now placed before the representation.

The present summary must be limited to this mention of some of the most important economical laws. Of course there are in existence very many others touching the different sides of economical life. For instance laws on the transfer of real property, mortgage-laws, and relative to bills of exchange, to navigation, coinage, rail-roads, savings-banks, insurance, etc. Others similar are in preparation, and there is an evident tendency in the three Scandinavian lands to adopt a common economical system, wherever it can facilitate their mutual intercourse, without compromising the interests of any one of them.

With regard to fiscal legislation we refer to the different direct taxes touched on above (on Hartkorn, on buildings, etc.), and to the indirect (customs, navigation, duty on spirits, stamp duty, etc.). The income derived from these sources will be given in the chapter "Statistics".

II

Statistics

A. Population

Density of the population; its distributions in town and country; according to sex, age, single or married. Marriages, births, deaths. Immigration and emigration. Foreign nationalities. Dissenters.

1. The kingdom of Denmark (Denmark proper) at the last general census (Fbr. 1st 1890) numbered 2,172,205 inhabitants;

besides these the Færöes had 12,954 souls. According to the census of 1880 — information from 1890 has not appeared yet — Iceland had 72,445, Greenland 10,000, the Danish West-Indies 33,763. In what follows we shall confine ourselves to the population and industry of Denmark proper.

The area of Denmark was estimated in 1890 at 696 geogr. ☐ miles (about 38,300 ☐ kilom:), which gives to each ☐ mile 3121 souls. This is a density of population of good mean average, compared with other European countries. It surpasses neighboring states. Sweden has only 568, Norway 313, Greece 1583. The great civilized States, however, stand much higher. Austria, France, Germany, Great-Britain number from four to six thousand inh: pr ☐ mile, while such countries as Saxony, England proper and Belgium have about 10,000.

As to density of population the various parts of Denmark differ not a little. In 1890 the isles had an average density of 5200 inhabitants pr ☐ mile, Jutland only 2100. In the isles Copenhagen, as a matter of course plays an important part in giving this large number. But even outside Sealand, in Fyn for instance, there is an average of about 4200, nearly three times that of the south-west of Jutland (1450), the poorest part of Denmark as to population.

2. The town population in 1890 was 663,121, to 1,509,084 in the country districts. This division, however, more than $^1/_4$ town-people and nearly $^3/_4$ country people, is only a purely administrative classification. If we number among the towns-people those settled in nominally country communities, but in fact belonging to the cities (such as in the suburbs of the capital), the urban population will reach a much higher figure. In fact we find that the population in 1890 was distributed as follows. To every 1000 inh. there were:

In Copenhagen and its suburbs	173
In other towns	167
In the country	660
	1000

The real town density thus reached 340 p. mille, or more than ⁵/₁₀, the real country-population 660 p. m. The following table will show how this has been modified of late.

	1840	1860	1880	1890
Copenhagen	96	104	139	173
other towns	111	133	147	167
country	793	763	714	660
	1000	1000	1000	1000

Consequently the population of the capital and the towns becomes an ever greater, that of the country an ever smaller, part of the whole. The proportionate increase for the capital takes place chiefly from 1860 to 1880, that for the population in other towns from 1840 to 1860. From 1840 to 1890 the urban population has relatively increased more than $1/3$ at the expense of the country-folk.

In spite of this Danish migration from country to town — a feature found everywhere in Europe — Denmark has not many large towns. It has (1890) only one with more than 100,000 inhabitants, 7 (not counting the suburban communes of Copenhagen) with from 10,000 to 40,000 inh., 40 with from 2000 to 10,000, among the rest none with 2000. The absolutely leading city is Copenhagen; in 1890 it had 312,387, and with its environs 375,251. This makes the capital to hold $1/6$ of the whole Danish population, which shows Copenhagen to be relatively the largest capital in the world.

The seven towns of more than 10,000 inh. in 1890 are:

Aarhus	33,308
Odense	30,277
Aalborg	19,503
Horsens	17,290
Randers	16,617
Helsingör	11,082
Fredericia	10,044

3. Denmark in 1890 numbered 1,059,222 males and 1,112,983 females, or 1000 males to 1051 females. This predominance of females prevails in most other countries, in these as a rule still more marked. In spite of more boys being born than girls, and altho in the first years of age there are more males than females, the work and way of living of the men swallow up more lives than that of women (see lower down); at an advanced age the latter are in a great majority. In the class "below 1 year" were in 1880 — no information is on hand of later date than 1880 relative to the classification of the population according to age and married or single state — only 770 females to every 1000 males, even from 15 to 20 only 980 to every 1000; but at 20 to 25 there were 1067 females to every 1000 males, at 30 to 35 lived 1083, at 60 to 65 were 1093, at 80 to 85 1409, and so on.

4. Classified by age, the population for every 1000 is:

Below 15 years	338
From 15 to 20	90
„ 20 · 40	285
„ 40 · 60	191
60 years and above	96
	1000

Consequently more than ⅓ of the whole belongs to the years of childhood, in which there is no productive labor, or at all events not sufficient for support. The same applies, tho to a smaller extent, to the class above 60, or nearly $1/10$ of the population. The most vigorous group, 20 to 40 years, which works hardest and continues the race, numbers nearly $3/10$ of the whole, and in a broader sense the productive classes (15 to 60 years) count $6/10$ (57 percent).

As the towns attract a large number of able-bodied men, who later on often return and marry, as also many are forced for a time to stay there (soldiers and others), the age of 20 to 40 is relatively best represented, especially in the capital, but least in the country, which inversely influences the other ages. Again women from 20 to 40 are more numerous in the towns than men, also because they can better get work there (see below). In the towns are 1133, in the country only 1011, females to every 1000 males.

5. According to Danish law no woman can marry before her completed 16th year, no man before his 20th, and in 1880 of 341,000 married women in Denmark were not 1000 below the age of 20. Only after this age does the question of the population single or otherwise offer any interest.

Of every 1000 persons of each sex above 20 years there were in Denmark in 1880:

	Males	Females
Single	303	277
Married	628	581
Widowed	64	136
Divorced	5	6
	1000	1000

So that only $3/5$ of the adults lived together with spouses, while $2/5$ were celibates, widows or divorced.

Over 40 years marriage is so infrequent (especially as to women), that it may be considered as the limit to wedlock. Even after this age, 8 pct of men and 10 pct of females are single. The unmarried are far more numerous in the towns than in the country, particularly the capital counts many single persons, 13 pct of the men and 22 of the women above 40.

6. From 1870 to 1879 the yearly number of marriages in Denmark was 156 to every 1000 persons ($15^1/2$ pct). This corresponds to the state of things in the other European countries; any how the difference is not greater than the variations in Denmark itself from decade to decade. The average age for wedlock in 1880—84 was for men 30,1 years, for women 27,1. Altho the mean is somewhat lower than in the preceding five years, it is still higher in Scandinavia than in the other European countries, the maturity being later the higher we travel northward.

7. The mean number of yearly births from 1880 to 1889 was 329 for every 10,000 souls. For 1800 to 1880 the variation, with rare exceptions, is between 3 and 3½ pct. The actual birth-rate (still-born deducted) is about 3,1, which is a little higher than Sweden, rather less than Norway (3,3) and most other European countries. In Germany and Austria the birth-rate is about 4 pct., in England 3⅓, in France only 2,6.

For every 1000 girls are born in Denmark on an average 1006 boys, a proportion usual in the rest of Europe, and which undergoes no material change, if we take long periods.

Scarcely 3 percent of the babes are still-born, and this number is ever diminishing.

On the other hand Denmark differs greatly from other lands as to legitimate and illegitimate births. In Denmark about 10 pct., or every tenth child, is a bastard. Apparently the number is proportionately greatest in Copenhagen, but this is because the Lying-in hospital ("Födselsstiftelse") is in the capital. Otherwise the country-districts have rather a greater than a smaller number of illegimates than the towns; reaching their maximum in Fyn, where every eighth child is born out of wedlock.

Austria gives the same number of base births as this province, thus more than Denmark as a whole. All other countries have a smaller number of base-born than Denmark (Sweden 10,6, Germany 9,0, Norway 8,7, France 8,0, England 4,8, etc.). It must be remembered, however, that the number of illegitimates is no conclusive standard as to immorality; this shows itself in many other and in certain respects more objectionable ways than illegitimacy; but this kind of debauchery cannot be registered statistically, as can births out of wedlock.

8. The number of deaths 1880 to 1889 has annually reached 196 out of every 10,000 persons. If we take the period from 1800 to 1880, we find far greater deviations than for the births, the variation being between 3 and 3½ percent, while the mean mortality

has been below 2 and above 3 percent, but in general with a tendency to decrease.

Deducting the still-born, the present percentage of deaths for Denmark is 1,9; this is somewhat more than for Sweden and Norway (1,8), but less than in most other European countries (England 2,1, France 2,2, Prussia 2,6, Austria 3,1 Hungary 3,6, etc.).

The mortality of the very young is in Denmark as elsewhere far greater than that of the later ages. By our death-statistics from 1870 to 1879 about $1/5$ of all born alive die within the year from their birth, but of $5/6$ left only $1/6$ will be dead at the age of 20 years. Then it will take about 25 years before $1/6$ of those living at the age of 20 will have passed away; after that quickness of death increases. As elsewhere, in Denmark the mortality of males is greater than that of females. Excluding puberty and child-bearing, this holds good at all ages, and may be registered so, that the average life of men is 45,6 years, that of females 47,4. The females die quicker from 5 to 20 and 25 to 40 years, males die quicker at all other periods.

The mortality is different also according to the different classes of society and the different social circumstances. Avoiding particulars we point out, that the mortality is greater in towns than in the country, for in 1870 to 1879 in the country districts died 19,3 pro mille (incl. still-born), in the towns (outs. Copenhagen) 21,0 pro m., in Copenhagen even 26,1 pro m. (1880—89 in Copenhagen 24 p. m.), resulting from the different composition of the population, the different trades, manner of living, means of subsistence and lodging. The mortality of children born out of wedlock is greater than that of legitimates (in Copenhagen the first year even twice as large); this results evidently from neither mother nor child obtaining as much care and nursing outside wedlock as in marriage. As to the causes of death, we have only statistics with regard to the towns, not to the country at large. As to adults, the most frequent cause of death is phtisis. Of violent deaths, one great cause is suicide, as in Denmark annually 255 suicides take place for every million of people, which both in itself and relatively is a very considerable number (France has annually 155 self-murders pr million inh:, Prussia 143, Sweden 86, Norway 72, England 68, Italy 37, and so on).

9. In Denmark as in all old civilized countries the increase of the population is chiefly from excess of births over deaths. Between 1880 and 1889 it amounted yearly to 1,3 percent of the population, and as a general thing and excepting times of war and epidemics, it has distinctly increased from period to period in this century. This may be seen from the circumstance that in the period 1800 to 1880 the excess of births was on an average only 1,0 pct.

This advance has also arisen from the general decrease of mortality, there being no important variation in the frequency of births. As seen above, this frequency in Denmark is lower than in most other parts of Europe, but the mortality is also lower. To see whether the excess is higher or lower than in other countries, we point out that the excess of births in Denmark (1,3) is lower than in Norway and England (1,4), and not a little higher than in France (0,3), where the frequency of births is so small, and than in Hungary (0,2), where the mortality is so great.

10. But as the sum of the population is to some extent affected by immigration and emigration, the proportional percentage does not always coincide with that of the simple increase. In the first half of this century, however, this movement to and fro about balanced, and was never considerable. Then follows a change for some years; but in the last 20—30 years the outgoers far exceed the incomers. From 1880 to 1889 about 73,000 persons emigrated from Denmark above those immigrating, so that increase of population was only 0,99 percent, tho the excess of births was 1,3 percent. However in this way can only be stated the difference between the number of immigrants and emigrants (calculated by the figures relating to the census for births and for deaths), no statements being before us as to the absolute number of incomers and outgoers.

With regard to emigration we only remark that the chief stream is to the transatlantic countries, to which from 1888 to 1889 emigrated about 77,000 Danes. This is proportionally a far smaller ratio than from the other Gothic-German lands (Norway and Sweden, Germany, above all Great-Britain and Ireland); but it is greater than from the Romance countries.

The immigration is chiefly from the Duchies (Slesvig and Holstein) and from Sweden. We get good help for all this from the following list, which tells us how many persons had settled in the country previous to 1880, and had remained there.

In 1880 to every 10,000 inhabitants in Denmark proper, there were born in

Denmark proper	9678
The Færöes, Iceland, Greenland, the colonies, etc.	6
Sweden	123
Norway	14
Slesvig	112
Germany proper	57
Other foreign lands	10
	10,000

The most numerous immigrants are therefore Swedes, Slesvigers and Germans proper (but many in the last two groups had come in before the loss of the Duchies by Denmark, and thus were Danes by birth). The absolute numbers of these three classes is about 24,000 Swedes, 22,000 Slesvigers, and 11,000 Germans proper. On the whole, all this however is of little importance, for we see that only 3 perc. of the inhabitants were born out of the country. This does not of course exclude the significance of this movement in districts or neighboring towns, or in some branches of employ; for instance in Copenhagen there were very many Swedish servants, and not a few Swedish and German artisans.

11. Some who have settled from abroad are dissenters, but they are few. By the census of 1880 there were 3687 Baptists, 2985

Romanists, 1363 German and French Reformed, 1036 Irvingites, 746 Methodists, 125 Anglicans, 117 Quakers, 3946 Jews, 1722 Mormons, 1074 with no positive religion, and 558 scattered among diverse sects. The whole does not make 1 pct. of the population, which adheres to the national Church of the country (Evangelical-Lutheran confession).

B. Employments

The distribution of the people according to employments, generally in Denmark as a whole, more especially in the towns and in the country. The different employments: Agriculture, Industry, Commerce, Import and Export (comsumption), Navigation and the Mercantile marine. Other means of communication.

1. According to the Census of 1880 the Danish population was officially classified as follows:

1. Public officers, functionaries, men of science, artists, liberal professions	131,684
2. Pensioners, capitalists and the like	44,347
3. Farmers, etc.	925,152
4. Sailors and fishermen	53,905
5. Industry, manufactures	451,219
6. Trades people	134,272
7. Day-laborers and workmen	174,471
8. Porters, messengers, servants, others with no settled employment	21,000
9. Persons in hospitals, houses of correction, paupers and the like	32,989
In all	1,969,039

It appears from this that nearly half the people (47 perc.) maintain themselves by agriculture; nearly one fourth (23 perc.) in branches of industry, including the 9 perc. laborers; 7 perc.

are engaged in commerce; 7 perc. are "immaterial producers"; 3 perc. follow the sea and fishing; the rest (about 5 perc.) live on their means or are supported by the public or in some other way without employment.

Of course all these classes are distributed very unequally in town and country. Out of every 1000 inhabitants there belonged to

	Copenhagen	Other towns	Country districts
1. Immaterial producers..	130	123	46
2. Pensioners, capitalists, etc...	71	45	10
3. Agriculturists	8	45	627
4. Sailors and fishermen ..	19	48	25
5. Manufacturers and mechanics	396	390	171
6. Trades people	195	180	26
7. Day-laborers, etc.	115	138	75
8. Porters, messengers, etc.	55	14	3
9. Persons in hospitals, etc.	11	17	17
	1000	1000	1000

In the towns therefore industry, in the country agriculture, plays the chief part, to both belonging many laborers. But persons employed in manufacture only form $2/5$ of the town population, while agriculturists amount to nearly $2/3$ of the country people. In the country the second rank is taken by industrial classes, in the towns by traders. Then come in the towns the functionaries and the liberal professions, thereafter capitalists and pensioners, particularly in Copenhagen, after them other employments or no fixed occupation. Sailors and fishermen are proportionally more numerous in the other towns, but even here they only constitute about 5 perc.

Of all who provide for themselves, 456,527 are males, 101,559 females. In addition to these however must be counted the class of servants, above considered as part of the household of the providers and treated as "provided for"; but on the other hand they must be considered as self-maintaining. Their number was 102,541 males and 121,181 females. The persons really provided for (wife and children) amounted to 393,607 males and 760,635 females.

If we take towns and country by themselves, the number of providers and persons provided for are distributed in the following manner (paupers and the like deducted).

Of every 1000 of each sex were:

	Providers		Servants		Family	
	Males	Females	Males	Females	Males	Females
Copenhagen.......	640	202	19	115	331	672
Other towns	532	130	33	113	417	743
Country districts....	435	78	133	124	417	778

What strikes us is the considerably greater number of male providers in Copenhagen than in the rest of the land; this is partly because there is on the whole a constant and strong influx to the capital of able-bodied men, and partly because many, who in the country belong to the servant's class, in Copenhagen look for other employments. And then in Copenhagen women are frequently more self-maintaining than in the other towns and especially than in the country, a phenomenon connected with the great number of single women in the capital, while the household in the country more entails marriage and the assistance of the women. This shows among other things, that the term "provider" relating to the wife is frequently merely formal. Male servants are only slightly represented in Copenhagen, and partly in the other towns, while they are numerous in the country, helping to cultivate the soil. "The family" is explained by the other rubrics, the number of males and females being smaller in Copenhagen than in the other towns and there still less than in the country.

2. More nearly examining the branches of employment, agriculture naturally claims first our attention. From the facts at our disposal hereon, we add as follows.

Of the Danish area, 696 ☐ miles (38,300 ☐ kilom:), deducting the lakes (1,1 perc.), 80 perc. are cultivated, viz. 34 perc. as arable land (and gardens), 40,6 as meadows and pastures, and 5,4 as forests. Of the 20 perc. not cultivated, 12½ perc. or ⅛ of the area of the country is covered with heaths (especially in western Jutland). The remaining 7 à 8 perc. is bogs, fens, quick-sand, etc., or roads and fences, building grounds and court-yards, etc. Tho Denmark therefore relatively out-strips its mountainous neighbors in cultivation, much remains to be done, particularly in once more re-covering the heaths with forests, whose extermination greatly hastened the formation of these heaths. Of the present wood-covered area, or about 320,000 Tönder Land (32 ☐ miles), about 70,000 Tönder belong to the state.

Of the arable land was sown in 1881:

With wheat	4,42	perc.
,, rye	21,20	,,
,, barley	25,10	,,
,, oats	31,84	,,
	82,56	,,
,, buck-wheat	1,60	,,
,, peas, vetches, beans, etc.	2,26	,,
,, mangcorn (maslin)	7,28	,,
,, potatoes	3,54	,,
,, roots and marketable plants	2,76	,,
	100,00	perc.

The crops and values of the different cereals were:

1889

	Tönder of Grain	Value, Kroner	Yield of every Tönde pr. Tönde Land
Wheat	1,260,860	15,834,902	12,4 fold
rye	4,389,503	47,274,883	9,0 ,,
barley	5,049,286	53,764,199	8,8 ,,
oats	6,730,753	52,814,725	9,2 ,,

Average of 1885—1889:

	Value, Kroner	Yield of every Tönde pr. Tönde Land
Wheat	16,100,000	12,8 fold
rye	39,900,000	8,7 ,,
barley	54,700,000	10,0 ,,
oats	54,200,000	11,0 .,

To obtain the total value, we must add that of the crops of the above mentioned pulse and roots, etc. (46,2 millions Kroner in 1889 and 41,3 mill. Kr. on an average in 1885—1889) and the hay crops (respectively 58,6 and 52,6 mill. Kr.). Altogether the estimated value of all the crops amounted in 1889 to 274,4 mill. Kr. and on an average 1885—1889 to 258,8 mill. Kr.

By the live-stock list of 1888, the number of horses was 375,533, horned cattle 1,459,527, sheep 1,225,196 and swine 770,785. Horned cattle and pigs are constantly increasing, from the turn now taken by Danish farming, it having withdrawn somewhat from the extensive culture of cereals towards an intensive dairy-farming and production of provisions. This is proved by the fact, that Denmark at present imports more cereals than it exports, while it has developed a large surplus export of provisions and live-stock. The particulars will be found in the tables given below.

The tolerably equal distribution of property in Denmark, with only a few excessively large properties, but with a very large middling class, also shows itself by the way in which the landed property is distributed. The 1st of April 1885 the number of landed properties and the size of each was as follows:

			Number	Tdr. Hartkorn
Manors and farms	more than 12 Tdr. Hartkorn		1954	55,187
	,, ,, 8—12 ,, ,,		3718	34,871
	,, ,, 4—8 ,, ,,		24,220	137,411
	,, ,, 2—4 ,, ,,		23,131	67,095
	,, ,, 1—2 ,, ,,		20,609	29,590
Houses (cottages)	,, ,, ¼—1 ,, ,,		67,773	34,150
	less than ¼ ,, ,,		82,487	6,226

It will appear from the above (excluding the isle of Bornholm, which has a peculiar rate of Hartkorn), that agriculture on a large scale does not play any overwhelming part, for its characteristic Hartkorn only amounts to half that of the middling-sized farms (farms of 4—8 Tdr). This does not signify, that the landed proprietors of the country do not possess considerable social influence (now also political), but with regard to wealth they do not occupy the same predominance as in many other countries. It must be remembered however, that the figures above only treat of the size of the single properties; of course several may be collected under one proprietor; this holds good of the great proprietors, and several estates had from 1000 to 2000 Tdr. Hartkorn, a few even more. It is the class of farmers, that gives its stamp to the Danish landed interest. As to the cottagers, they work for the farms and manors, besides cultivating their own lot. This holds good still more as to the owners of the 35,329 cottages without land, not to speak of "Indsiddere" (lodgers), who have neither house nor land, but lodge with the cottagers.

Finally must be mentioned, that the farms and the houses in the middle of the preceding century were generally on lease from the lords and the manors; legislation and custom since then have made freehold property the rule. In 1884 of the collective Hartkorn about 243,000 Tdr. was freehold (or heritable lease with right of selling and mortgage), and only 26,000 Tdr. on lease. In the same way with most of the "houses" (cottages); the greatest part are freehold property (153,000 Tdr.), tho the change has not proceeded as quickly as with the passing of the farms into freehold.

3. Manufacture and industry. Denmark is no industrial country. Of course great numbers are occupied in manufacture (shown above), and from of old remains some domestic industry (such as the making of "Jydepotter", a pottery peculiar to Jutland, wooden shoes, woollen goods), but manufacture on a large scale has too few chances. A land without timber, iron, coal or rivers, wanting large capital and with no great market, could not create any industry of importance. In the later decades however several branches of industry have made considerable progress, especially as to textile goods, engines, sugar refineries, beer-breweries, tobacco, china and crockery; besides mills and other industries connected with agriculture, which at present is itself largely managed as a branch of industry.

No industrial statistics, comprising the whole country, now exist; for that reason we cannot know the extent of the activity in the different branches, still less the amount of production. From the reports of the supervisors of those factories and workshops, in which children and young persons are occupied, it appears that the number of such businesses in 1889 was:

	Number of businesses	Number of children (10-14 years)	Young persons (14-18 years)	Adults		In all
				Males	Females	
Copenhagen	252	672	1,013	5,729	2,267	9,681
The rest of the country	501	1,737	1,789	10,629	2,892	17,047
In all	753	2,409	2,802	16,358	5,159	26,728

About the year 1880 the number of industrial establishments in this country, employing steam or gas, was 720, with an aggregate horse power of 10,000 and about 21,000 hands.

As the production of beet-root sugar and of spirits is taxed, the following can be given as to their extent.

Beet-root sugar:

1884	23,156,000	Danish pounds
1885	33,898,000	—
1886	36,530,000	—
1887	42,242,000	—
1888	30,115,000	—

Spirits:

1884	35,062,000	Potter
1885	33,145,000	—
1886	32,651,000	—
1887	32,271,000	—
1888	31,353,000	—

This production of spirits is very great. As only little is exported, Denmark appears to consume spirits largely in proportion to its population; the decrease of late is therefore not to be regretted. Among the causes of this decrease must be mentioned the immensely increased production of beer, which not reckoning "Hvidtøl" (white or pale beer), certainly consumed to an equal extent, reaches yearly more than $1/2$ million of Tönder. This augmentation is chiefly owing to the highly perfected "Carlsberg breweries", which have made the drinking of beer quite common in Denmark, especially in the towns.

4. Commerce. The traffic of Denmark with other countries comprised during the five years 1884—88 on an average:

	Imports	Exports Danish produce	Exports Foreign produce	Total exports	Aggregate traffic
Weight in millions of Pounds..	4873	727	361	1088	5961
Value in millions of Kroner ...	252	150	28	178	430

So that the import as to value has been perceptibly in excess of the export, a fact not to be accounted for in the usual way only by differing calculations and so on, but especially is owing to a real diminution of export from Denmark.

This traffic is principally with Germany, England and Sweden. In 1882—86 the entire import and export, calculated according to value, amounted to:

	Import from: pCt.	Export to: pCt.
Germany	36,4	28,9
Great Britain	22,6	45,2
Sweden	14,2	12,7
In all...	73,2	86,8

So that about ⁴/₅ of the trade is with these three states. Then follow Russia, America, Norway and the rest of Europe. Denmark's greatest customer is England, which receives more than ³/₅ of the goods; its greatest supplier is Germany, furnishing more than ¹/₃ of the foreign goods consumed here.

The most important articles of import and export are:

1884—88 annual average		Import	Value in Kroner	Export	Value in Kroner	Surplus import Value in Kroner	Surplus export Value in Kroner
		Mill.	Mill.	Mill.	Mill.	Mill.	Mill.
Coffee and its substitutes	Pounds	16,8	8,6	5,6	2,9	5,7	
Sugar and molasses	—	42,9	5,9	18,2	1,4	4,5	
Tobacco	—	7,3	4,4	0,6	0,5	3,9	
Rice	—	30,1	2,0	14,1	1,1	0,9	
Tea	—	0,8	0,6	0,07	0,06	0,6	
Wine	Potter	3,2	2,0	0,5	0,3	1,7	
Spirits	—	2,8	2,0	2,9	1,3	0,7	
Drygoods (tissues):							
Cotton, linen and hempen goods	Pounds	14,9	14,9	1,8	1,4	13,5	
Silk goods	—	0,3	4,0	0,02	0,4	3,6	
Woollen goods and the like	—	5,6	18,8	0,7	2,9	15,9	

1884—88 annual average		Import	Value in Kroner	Export	Value in Kroner	Surplus import Value in Kroner	Surplus export Value in Kroner
		Mill.	Mill.	Mill.	Mill.	Mill.	Mill.
Metals, unworked	Pounds	33,5	1,8	16,0	0,4	1,4	
Metallic goods	—	118,0	20,9	12,9	2,9	18,0	
Timber and woods, unworked	—	588,1	11,5	5,2	0,1	11,4	
Coals	—	2388,5	15,1	228,9	1,5	13,6	
Horses and foals	Heads	0,004	1,3	0,01	9,3		8,0
Bullocks and cows	—	0,02	2,6	0,09	17,8		15,2
Calves, sheep, goats	—	0,03	0,4	0,08	2,1		1,7
Hogs and pigs	—	0,02	0,8	0,02	13,0		12,2
Pork and hams	Pounds	4,5	1,4	46,2	18,5		17,1
Meat	—	2,4	0,6	3,3	0,8		0,2
Butter	—	9,7	7,9	43,5	37,3		29,4
Eggs	Scores	0,2	0,2	4,5	4,0		3,8
Grease and lard	Pounds	13,2	4,0	8,2	2,5	1,5	
Wheat, unground	—	110,5	7,4	43,0	2,9	4,5	
Rye, —	—	158,1	7,2	19,2	1,0	6,2	
Oats, —	—	60,0	3,0	5,0	0,3	2,7	
Barley, —	—	26,9	1,5	112,5	6,6		5,1
Indian corn, —	—	83,4	3,9	8,4	0,4	3,5	
Wheat, ground	—	6,0	0,5	71,0	6,4		5,9
Rye, —	—	1,2	0,08	13,8	1,0		0,9

Denmark's most important articles of import are consequently groceries (surplus import 15,5 mill. kr.)[1]. Then come drygoods (33,0 mill.), metals (19,4 mill.), unwrought timber and wood (11,4 mill.) and coal (13,6 mill.). — The chief articles of export are horses (surplus export 8,0 mill. kr.), horned cattle (16,9 mill.), hogs (12,2 mill.), pork and hams (17,1 mill.), butter (29,4 mill.), barley (5,1 mill.) and wheat-flour (5,9 mill.).

[1] From the amount of groceries imported (connected with the manufacture of beet-root-sugar) it will appear, that the annual consumption pr head in Denmark is on an average: of coffee about 5 1/2 Pounds, tea 1/2 Pd., tobacco 3 1/2 Pd., and sugar 27 Pd.

The figures for the surplus export confirm the opinion stated above, that the intensive management of agriculture is now chiefly studied. It is the raising of animals, the dairy production, that makes the largest profits. Of late years a surplus import of grain has been the absolute rule, and at the same time the export of the products of the intensive management of agriculture has risen enormously. In the year 1889 f. inst. were exported: 25,000 hogs and besides 70 millions pounds of pork. Of butter were exported 60 mill. pounds, of eggs — the export of which 25 years age only amounted to 50,000 of scores — more than 5 millions of scores. The export of garden-produce and the like is also increasing at a great rate.

5. Navigation and the merchant marine. The navigation and domestic trade, not counting the few ships under repair or passers-by, shows for 1885—89 the following average:

To foreign ports:

Inward and outward	Number of vessels cleared	Tonnage Reg.-tons	Stowage Reg.-tons
Sailing vessels	27,474	1,468,706	786,856
Steamers	20,216	5,038,157	1,467,887
Totals	47,690	6,506,863	2,254,743

Measured by stowage, Danish commerce abroad has been carried on partly under the Danish flag (49,9 p. c.), and partly under a foreign flag (50,1 p. c.).

Domestic trade (between Danish ports):

Inward and outward	Number of vessels cleared	Tonnage Reg.-tons	Stowage Reg.-tons
Sailing vessels	27,741	662,751	325,608
Steamers	17,292	1,816,634	461,510
Totals	45,033	2,479,385	787,118

Measured by stowage, the domestic traffic by sea takes place almost exclusively under the Danish flag (99 p. c.).

As to the carrying trade (between foreign ports), there entered and departed during the year 1889 12,817 Danish vessels, with an aggregate tonnage of 4,467,239 reg. tons.

The merchant marine of Denmark was January 1st 1890:

	Number	Tonnage Reg.-tons	Horse-power
Sailing vessels	2,938	177,438	—
Steamers	305	103,577	25,253
Totals	3,243	281,015	25,253

To these must be added, besides some steam-mud-dredges, about 11,000 boats of 4 reg. tons or under.

Of the sailing-vessels nearly $1/10$ (9,4 p. c.) belonged to Copenhagen, with 10,1 p. c. of the tonnage; of the steamers more than half (53,1 p. c.), with $4/5$ (80,5 p. c.) of the tonnage, also so belonged.

A tonnage of more than 10,000 register tons is owned in Copenhagen (101,189), Svendborg (28,551), Fanö (23,050) and Marstal (19,491).

6. Other means of communication. Railroads (1889) convey passengers and goods a distance of 261 miles, of which 207 miles belong to the state and 54 to private companies.

Letters dispatched (in the fiscal year $1887/88$):

    Inland letters 35,680,522
    Foreign to Denmark 5,637,386
    Foreign from Denmark 5,049,338
                  Together ... 46,367,246

Telegrams dispatched (in $1889/90$):

    Inland telegrams 533,585
    From and to other countries 544,829
    Transit telegrams 386,584
                  Together ... 1,464,998

C. Finance.

Revenue and expenditure. Assets and debts. National property.

1. The revenue of the Danish state during the five years $1882/83 - 1886/87$ (the fiscal year runs from April 1st to March 31st) on an average amounted to 55,1 mill. kroner annually, of which 52,8 mill. was income speaking strictly. Specified, the details are as follows:

			Kr.
1.	Profit from domains (Land, forests, oysterbeds)		908,100
2.	Interests on state assets:	Kr.	
	a. Interest on reserve funds	814,846	
	b. Net income from railways	2,927,870	
	c. Other assets	899,745	
			4,642,461
3.	Direct taxes:		
	a. The old tax	5,003,253	
	b. Landtax and assessed taxes	1,717,672	
	c. Assessed tax from the towns	214,947	
	d. Tax on buildings	2,420,895	
	e. Tax on titles	57,097	
			9,413,864
4.	Indirect taxes:		
	a. Revenue from stamped paper	2,755,361	
	b. Inheritance-duty	1,207,902	
	c. Tax on the transfer of property	746,212	
	d. Fees to courts of justice and public offices	2,062,264	
	e. Import duties (including the excise on beet-root-sugar)	23,838,392	
	f. Tax on spirits	2,742,862	

Lateris... 48,317,418

			Kr.	Kr.
		Transport...	48,317,418	
	g.	Harbor dues and duty on measuring of ships.............	962,712	
	h.	Other smaller duties.........	213,219	
				34,528,924

5. Various revenues:
    a. Mail- and Telegraph service:
       mail-service 318,067
       telegr. service ... minus 126,803
                191,264
    b. State lottery 828,982
    c. Revenue from the Færöes 63,665
    d. Interest of cash balance 1,711,620
    e. Coin-operation, other accidental revenues 523,704
                 3,319,235
6. Grants of assets 1,761,974
7. Deductions from salaries to provide for public officers, sums given as security 554,866
                 55,129,424

Setting aside items 6 and 7, the revenues proper are 52,8 millions kroner, of which taxes amount to $5/6$ (83,2 p. c.), direct taxes 17,8 p. c. (of these "old tax", land- and assessed tax 12,7 p. c. or $1/8$ of all the revenue), and indirect taxes 65,4 p. c. (customs 45,1 p. c. or nearly half of all the revenue). Then, profits from domains and assets make 10,5 p. c. and all other income 6,3 p. c. of the aggregate annual revenue.

2. The expenditure of the Danish state during the five years $18^{82}/_{83}$—$18^{86}/_{87}$ on an average amounted yearly to 51,4 millions kroner, of which the annual expenditure proper was 44,2 millions, thus in detail:

1. Higher state authorities:

		Kr.	Kr.
a.	Civil list	1,000,000	
b.	Appanages	224,786	
c.	The diet (Rigsdag)	379,000	
d.	Council of state	100,282	
			1,704,068

2.	Interest of the public debt	8,236,439
3.	Pensions	3,530,686
4.	Foreign office	369,012
5.	Home-department	2,804,011
6.	Justice-department	3,093,500
7.	Church and school department	2,097,655
8.	War-department	11,120,857
9.	Naval-department	7,290,393
10.	Ministry of finance	3,835,779
11.	Iceland	102,858
12.	Part-payment of national debt	2,130,268
13.	Public works	4,510,453
14.	Various works, loans advanced	614,348
		51,440,327

Items 12—14 set aside, the public expenditure proper is 44,2 millions kroner. It must however be added, that many salaries to clergymen and some officers of justice are not paid by the state, but are covered by tithes, offerings and accidental revenue. Several other branches have also separate funds (such as the polytechnic school, grammar-schools, the University, the Academy of Arts etc.). They are in the budget (under the Church and the School department) and receive grants from the exchequer, if such are thought necessary and useful, but only in that case are such grants put down among the expenses of the state. It must moreover be mentioned, that the expenses under article 13 by their nature belong to the home-department (5). We have to decide whether they are regular ex-

penses of the state or if they may properly be called increase of capital, as the assets obtained frequently appear to bear no interest.

3. The yearly revenue and expenditure for the quinquennium is:

	Revenue millions kr.	Expenditure millions kr.
$1882/83$	53,6	50,7
$1883/84$	56,4	50,3
$1884/85$	57,1	48,0
$1885/86$	53,8	50,2
$1886/87$	54,4	58,1

The high revenue $1883/84$ and $1884/85$ is partly from the greater profits from the railroads and the indirect taxes. (The two items "Interest of state assets" and "Indirect taxes" in 1883—85 amounted to 40 à 41 mill. kr., 1885—87 to 37 à 38 mill. kr.).

As to the large increased expenditure in $1886/87$ (nearly 8 mill. kr. above that of the preceding year), it must be remarked, that during this period was paid off more than 3 mill. kr. of the national debt above the preceding year, and the expenditure in the war and naval departments was upwards of 4 mill. kr. greater than the preceding year. In the year mentioned these amounted to 22,6 mill. kr. or about $2/5$ of this year's total expenditure.

4. The assets and debts of the Danish state at the expiration of the fiscal year amounted to

	$1866/67$ mill. kr.	$1876/77$ mill. kr.	$1886/87$ mill. kr.
Cash balance (reserve fund) bonds etc............	148,0	85,9	98,6
National debt...........	267,3	176,7	195,7
Balance...	— 119,3	— 90,8	— 97,1

Thus the national debt during the decade $1866/67$ to $1876/77$ was reduced by about 91 mill. kr., or more than $1/3$. It increases again by 19 mill. towards the end of the subsequent decade, but while in

1877 by far the greatest part of the debt paid an interest of 4 perc., in 1887 it was reduced to $3^{1}/_{2}$ perc.

In the assets, as we see, the state railroads are not included. If we add these with the expenses of construction, management or purchase (in 1880 the state bought the Sealand railways) we obtain the following result:

	$18^{66}/_{67}$	$18^{76}/_{77}$	$18^{86}/_{87}$
Balance (as above)	— 119,3	— 90,8	— 97,1
State railroads	25,1	66,7	148,4
	— 94,2	— 24,1	+ 51,3

According to this, the state should be in possession of a property worth more than 50 mill. kr. at the expiration of the fiscal year $18^{86}/_{87}$; this is an increase of about 150 mill. during the last 20 years. If the railroads are to be reckoned as a common interest-bearing asset, the above amount may be called too high. But on the other hand, neither domains nor royal edifices or other similar property of the state are included in the roll of the national property.

To the quinquennial summary — the last which has appeared — given in this section, must yet be added that in the fiscal year $18^{87}/_{88}$ the revenue amounted to 54,3 mill., the expenditure to 59,9 mill., and in $18^{88}/_{89}$ there was a revenue of 55,9 mill., an expenditure of 60,2. The constant deficit is chiefly owing to the expenses for military purposes (in $18^{88}/_{89}$ 26,1 mill. kroner), which are still increasing. March 31st 1889 the national debt proper amounted to $190^{1}/_{3}$ mill. kroner.

Marcus Rubin.

INDEX

OF THE MOST IMPORTANT NAMES

Aalborg 125, 236.
Aarestrup, E., 151.
Aarhus 79, 123, 158, 236.
Abel 8.
Abildgaard, N., 160, 169.
Absalon 7, 109, 119, 139.
Academy of Arts 159.
Ærö 88, 122.
Al 84.
Alexandra, Princess of Wales, 68.
Alhede 97.
Allen, C. F., 14, 153.
Amager 97, 116.
Amalienborg 114.
Andersen, H. C., 115, 151.
Anscharius, St., 5.
Ansgar 5.
Army 104.
Arrebo, A., 138, 142.
Arresö 87.

Bache, O., 166.
Baggesen, J., 138, 145, 147, 148.
Ballads, popular, 140, 175.
Belt, great and little, 80.

Berg, Chr., 66.
Berg, Claus, 158.
Berggreen, A. P., 140, 175.
Bergsöe, V., 152.
Berlin, peace at, 37.
Bernhard, Carl, 150.
Bernstorff, A. P., 22, 25.
Bernstorff, J. H. E., 21, 23.
Bernstorff palace 117.
Bible, Christian IIIs, 137.
Bindesböll, M. G., 161.
Birket-Smith, S., 153, 180.
Bissen, H. V., 123, 161, 163.
Björnson, Björnstjerne, 189.
Blaavandshuk 77.
Blicher, St. St., 98, 150.
Bloch, Carl, 166.
Bluhme, Chr. A., 41, 57.
Bödtcher, L., 151.
Bondevenner 48, 59.
Bolbjerg 77.
Bording, A., 138, 142.
Bornholm 92, 101, 104, 105, 120.
Bournonville, A., 190.
Bov, battle of, 33.

INDEX

Brahe, Tycho, 15, 115, 142.
Brandes, E., 153, 155, 190.
Brandes, G., 152, 153, 155.
Brochmand, J., 141.
Brömsebro, peace at, 16.
Brun, Malte, 96.
Bülow, F. R., 35.

Canute, see Knud.
Caroline Mathilde, 23, 24.
Carstens, A. J., 160.
Casino 32, 190.
Charlottenlund 117.
Christian I 12.
Christian II 12, 15, 110, 121, 170, 199.
Christian III 14, 100.
Christian IV 15, 110, 170.
Christian V 19.
Christian VI 22.
Christian VII 23.
Christian VIII 28.
Christian IX 42, 52, 68.
Christian of Augustenburg 30.
Christiansborg palace 23, 113, 161.
Christianshavn 113.
Christopher I 8.
Christopher II 9.
Christopher III of Bavaria 11.
Clausen, H. N., 39, 154.
Clemens, J. F., 160.
Clementin, N., 182.
Climate 93.
Conservatory of music 180.
Constitution, see Ground-law.
Copenhagen, see Kjöbenhavn.
Criminal and Police Court 103.
Criminal code 51.
Customs 230.

Danes 96.

Danish code of Christian V 19, 201.
Danish language 137.
Dahlerup, J. V., 168, 169.
Dampskibsselskab, Forenede, 102.
Danebrog, flag, 8.
Danebrog, order of, 21.
Danevirke 6, 54.
Danske Lov, see Danish code.
Dansk Tunge 96, 137.
Djursland 79.
Downs 78.
Drachmann, H., 152, 189.
Dramatic Company 183.
Drogden, 81, 85.
Dybbøl 34, 55.
Dyrehave 117.
Dyveke 14.

Ebbesen, Niels, 10.
Eckernförde, engagement, 35.
Eckersberg, C. V., 162.
Egede, Hans, 131.
Ejer Bavnehöj 89.
Elephant, order of, 21.
Elsinore, see Helsingör.
Erik Ejegod 7.
Erik Glipping 9, 125.
Erik Menved 9.
Erik of Pommerania 11.
Erik Plovpenning 8.
Erlandsen, Jakob, 9.
Esbjerg 125.
Esquimaux 131.
Estrup, J. B. S., 62.
Ewald, Johannes, 138, 144, 172, 183, 184.

Færöes 96, 127, 175.
Falster 87, 120.
Farmers 100, 248.
Fischer, Olfert, 25.

Flinterende 81.
Folk-songs, see Ballads.
Forchhammer, J. G., 83, 156.
Forests 94, 100, 227, 246.
Fredensborg 68, 117.
Fredericia, battle of, 36.
Fredericia, town, 98, 122, 236.
Frederik I 14.
Frederik II 15.
Frederik III 16.
Frederik IV 20.
Frederik V 22.
Frederik VI 24, 27, 28.
Frederik VII 31, 50, 51.
Frederik, Crown-prince of Denmark, 68.
Frederik, Hereditary Prince, 24, 128.
Frederik of Augustenborg 46, 52.
Frederik of Noer 30.
Frederiksberg 111, 116.
Frederiksborg 118, 159, 166, 168.
Frederiksborg, peace at, 21.
Frederikshavn 79, 101, 126.
Frederiksstad 38.
Frederiksværk 101, 118.
Freund, H. E., 161, 169.
Frijs, E., 60.
Frijsenborg 124.
Fröbjerg Bavnehöj 88.
Frölich, I..., 164.
Frydendahl, J. P., 186.
Funen, see Fyn.
Fyn 88, 120.

Gaardmænd 100.
Gaardsretter 198.
Gade, N. W., 177.
Georgios I, King of the Hellenes, 68.
Gerlach, G. D., 54, 55.
Gluck 171.

Goldschmidt, M., 152.
Gorm den Gamle (the Old) 6.
Gram, F. T. G., 153.
Grand, Jens, 9.
Great Northern War 20.
Greenland 131.
Greisdal 89.
Grevens Fejde 14.
Griffenfeldt, P., 20, 201.
Ground-law 39, 60, 102, 203.
Grundtvig, N. F. S., 148, 149, 154.
Grundtvig, Sv., 139, 140.
Grundtvigianism 154.
Gudenaa 89, 90.
Guilds 232, 233.
Guldberg, O. H., 24, 153.
Gyldenlöves Höj 86.
Gyllembourg, Mrs., 150.

Haandfæstning, see Charter.
Hall, C. C., 44, 45, 46, 47, 53.
Hammershus 92, 120.
Hans, king, 12, 121.
Hansen, C. F., architect, 161.
Hansen, Chr., architect, 161.
Hansen, Constantin, painter, 161, 162, 164.
Hansen, Theophilus, architect, 161.
Hanstholmen 77.
Harald Blaatand 6.
Harald Klak 5.
Harsdorff, C. F., 160.
Hartkorn 228, 229.
Hartmann, Emil, 179.
Hartmann, J. P. E., 176, 190.
Hartmann, Joh., 172.
Hauch, C., 150.
Heaths in Jutland 84, 91, 94, 99.
Hedemann, H. C. G. F., 33.
Heger, Mrs., 184.
Hegermann-Lindencrone 55, 56.

Heiberg, J. L., 148, 149, 150, 152, 186, 187, 189.
Heiberg, Louise, 187, 188.
Heiberg, P. A., 184.
Heise, P., 179, 190.
Helgesen, H., 38.
Helgesen, Povl, 141.
Helgoland, engagement of, 56.
Helsingör 117, 236.
Hemmingsen, Niels, 141.
Hennings, Mrs., 189.
Herholdt, J. D., 168.
Hertz, H., 150, 151, 187.
Hetsch, G., 161.
Hilker, G. C., 161.
Hilleröd 118.
Himmelbjerg 89.
Himmerland 99.
Hirshals 77.
Hjörring 126.
Höedt, F. L., 188.
Höjesteret 103.
Höyen, N., 153, 163.
Hof- og Stadsret 24, 103.
Holberg, L., 119, 138, 143, 181, 182.
Hollænderdyb 81
Horns Rev 77.
Horsens 123, 236.
Hostrup, C., 152, 188.
Hoveri 226.
Husmænd 100.
Hveen 81, 141.
Hvitfeldt, Arild, 142.

Ibsen, Henrik, 189.
Iceland 128.
Ice-transport 80, 94
Indfödsret 24.
Ingemann, B. S., 149.
Inheritance-duty 233.

Isefjord 79, 101.
Isted, battle of, 37.

Jacobsen, C., 99.
Jacobsen, J. P., 152.
Jægerspris 118.
Jættestuer 3.
Jammerbugt 78.
Jellinge 5, 123.
Jerichau, J. A., 163.
Joint-stock societies 232.
Juel, J., 160.
Juel, Niels, 20, 113, 114.
Juliane Marie 24.
Justice 103.
Jutland, see Jylland.
Jydske Lov, 8, 198, 200.
Jylland 77, 89, 122.

Kaalund, H. V., 152.
Kæmpeviser 140, 175.
Kallebodstrand 81.
Kalmar Union 11.
Kalmar War 15.
Kalö 123.
Kalundborg 119, 157.
Kattegat 79.
Kiel, peace at, 26.
Kierkegaard, S., 154.
Kingo, Thomas, 138, 143.
Kjöbenhavn 93, 94, 98, 101, 102, 103, 104, 105, 108, 236.
Kjöge 120.
Kjöge, bay of, battle, 20.
Kjökkenmöddinger 3.
Klampenborg 117.
Klitter 78.
Knud VI 7.
Knud the Great 6, 199.
Knud the Saint 7, 121.
Knud Lavard 7.

Kolberg, battle of, 16.
Kolding, battle of, 35.
Kolding, town, 122.
Kongeaa 75, 91.
Kongedyb 81.
Kongelov 18, 20, 201.
Korsör 119.
Krabbe, Erik, 199.
Kröyer, P. S., 167.
Krogh, C., 37.
Kronborg 117, 159.
Kuhlau, F., 173.
Kunzen, L., 172.
Kyhn, P. V., 164.

Laaland 87, 120.
Labor-laws 233.
Lange, Julius, 153.
Langebek, J., 153.
Langeland 88, 122.
Lange-Müller, P. E., 179.
Lehmann, Orla, 32.
Leire 5, 119.
Licence 232.
Limfjord 78, 101.
Lindgreen, F. L. V., 186.
Londeman, G., 181.
London, treaty of, 42.
Louise, Queen, 42, 68.
Lumbye, H. C., 180.
Lundbye, J. F., 164.

Madvig, J. N., 39, 155.
Mandern, Carl van, 159.
Mantzius, Chr., 188.
March Ministry 32, 39.
Margrethe, Queen, 10, 119.
Maria Feodorovna, Empress of Russia, 68.
Mariager 124, 158.
Maribo 120, 158.

Marienlyst 117.
Maritime and Commercial Court 51, 103.
Marstrand, V., 162.
Martensen, H. L., 154.
Melbye, Anton, 165.
Meldahl, F., 168.
Meza, de, 54.
Middelfart 101.
Middelgrund 81.
Möen 83, 87.
Molbech, K. F., 152.
Mols 123.
Moltke, A. W., 32.
Moltke, C., 30.
Monrad, D. G., 32, 43, 53, 57.
Mors 91, 92.
Musik-Forening 178, 179.
Mynster, J. P., 146, 154.
Mysunde 38, 54.

Næringsbevis 232.
Næstved 119.
Nansen, Hans, 117.
National Bank 27.
Naumann, J. G., 172.
Navy 105.
Nielsen, N. P., 187.
Nobility 100.
Nörrebro 116.
Norröna 96.
North-sea 76.
Norway 6, 10, 13, 26, 28.
Norwegian Society 145.
November Constitution 50.
Nyborg 121.

Odense 120, 158, 236.
Oehlenschläger, A., 138, 146 f., 149, 176, 185.
Öresund 80.

Öresundstold, see Sound-dues.
Ørsted, A. S., 43, 146, 155, 202.
Ørsted, H. C., 115, 146, 156.
Østerbro 116.
Oldenburg Deed of Exchange 22.
Oversö 55.

Palladius, P., 138, 141.
Paludan-Müller, Fr., 151.
Peasants 22, 100, 226.
Pedersen, Chr., 137, 141.
Petersen, N. M., 139, 153.
Phister, L. J., 187.
Ploug, C., 152.
Poulsen, Emil, 189.
Poulsen, Olaf, 189.
Povl Vendekaabe 141.
Prague, treaty of, 58.
Provinsialstænder 28.

Rahbek, K. L., 140, 147, 184.
Randers 124, 236.
Rantzau, Daniel, 15.
Rask, R., 139, 155.
Recke, E. von der, 139, 152, 189.
Reykjavik 129, 130.
Ribe 101, 125, 157.
Richardt, Chr., 152.
Ringkjöbing 125.
Ringsted 119, 157.
Roed, J., 162, 169.
Römer, O., 142.
Rönne 120.
Rose, C. P., 182.
Rosenborg 114, 159.
Rosenkilde, C. N., 186.
Rosenstand-Goiske 183.
Roshage 77.
Rosing, M., 183, 184, 185.
Roskilde, peace at, 17.
Roskilde, town, 118, 157.

Roskildefjord 79.
Rostgaard, Fr., 181.
Royal family 68.
Royal law 18, 20, 201.
Rud, Otto, 15.
Rundkirker (Round Churches) 120.
Runes 4, 137.
Rye, Olaf, 36.
Ryge, J. Chr., 185.
Rytterknægt 93.

Sagas 4.
Sankelmark 55.
Sarti, G., 171.
Saxo Grammaticus 4, 119, 138, 139, 141.
Scandinavian seven year's war 15.
Scanian law 198.
Scanian war 20
Schandorph, S., 152.
Scheel-Plessen 45.
Schleswig, see Slesvig.
Schultz, J., 172.
Schwartz, Fr., 183, 184, 185.
Sealand, see Sjælland.
Sigbrit 14.
Silkeborg 124.
Sjælland 86.
Sjællandsodde 79.
Sjællandsrev 79.
Skagen 77, 126.
Skagerak 79.
Skamlingsbanke 89, 122.
Skanderborg 124.
Skarreklit 77.
Skodsborg 117.
Skovgaard, P. C., 164.
Slagelse 119.
Slesvig 9, 11, 12, 20, 28 f.
Slesvig, battle of, 34.
Slesvig-Holsteinism 29.

Slesvig war, the first, 34.
Slesvig war, the second, 54.
Smaalandsbugt 80.
Sneedorf, J., 138, 144.
Socage 226.
Södring, Mrs., 188.
Sörensen, C. F., 165.
Sophie, Queen, 141.
Sophie Amalie 16, 19.
Sophie Magdalene 23.
Sorö 119, 157.
Sound, the, 80.
Sound-dues 17, 51, 81, 117.
Sprogö 80.
Staffeldt, Schack de, 148.
Stavnsbaand 23, 25, 226.
Steamship Company, United, 102.
Steffens, H., 146.
Steinmann, P. F., 57.
Stendysser 3.
Steno (Stensen), Nicolaus, 142.
Stevns 83, 87.
Stjærneborg 142.
Stockholm, massacre of, 13.
Strib 121.
Struensee, J. F., 23, 24.
Succession, law of, 43, 218.
Suenson, E., 56.
Suhm, P. F., 153.
Sundbyer, 111, 116.
Sunesen, Andreas, 139.
Superior Courts 103.
Suseaa 87.
Svane, H., 17.
Svend Estridsen 6.
Svend Grade 7, 125.
Svend Tveskjæg 6.
Svendborg 102, 121, 254.
Svendsen, Johan, 179, 180.
Syv, Peder, 138, 142.

Taasinge 88.
Tater 97.
Tausen, Hans, 14, 124.
Tegnér, E., 148.
Telegraph Company, Great Northern, 102.
Thorshavn 128.
Thorvaldsen, Bertel, 99, 112, 113, 130, 160.
Thyland 91, 92.
Thyra, Duchess of Cumberland, 68.
Thyra Danebod 6.
Tietgen, C. F., 102, 114.
Tivoli 116, 180.
Topsöe, V., 152.
Tordenskjold, P., 20, 113.
Traventhal, peace at, 21.
Trolle, Herluf, 15.
Tscherning, A. F., 32, 33, 60.
Tuxen, L., 167.

Ulfeldt, Corfitz, 17, 19.
Ulfeldt, Eleonora Christina, 19, 120, 143, 166.
University, Copenhagen, 14, 98, 112.
Uranienborg 142.
Utterslev 111, 116.

Valdemar I the Great 7.
Valdemar II the Victorious 7.
Valdemar IV Atterdag 10.
Valdemar, prince of Denmark, 68.
Varde 125.
Vedel, Anders Sörensen, 138, 141.
Vederlagsret 199.
Vejle 123.
Vendsyssel 91.
Vesterbro 116.
Vesterhav (North-sea) 76.
Viborg 124, 157, 168.

Vienna, peace at, 57.
Vildmose, the great, 92.
Vildmose, the little, 90.
Villenage 25.
Vordingborg 119
Vornedskab 25.

Wessel, Joh. Herm., 138, 145, 183.
West-Indian Colonies, Danish, 132.
Weyse, C. E. F., 173.
Wiedewelt, J., 118, 160.

Wiehe, M., 187.
Wiehe, V., 189.
Willisen, W., 37.
Wilster, Chr., 150.
Winther, Chr., 150.
Wiwet, F., 144, 182.
Worm, Ole, 142.
Worsaae, J. J. A., 115, 153.

Zahrtmann, Chr., 166.

CONTENTS

	Page
A short summary of Danish history. By *H. Weitemeyer* ...	1
I. Denmark until 1660	3
II. Denmark until 1848	18
III. The Slesvig wars; Denmark as a constitutional state	31
Bibliography	69
Country and people. By *H. Weitemeyer*	73
I. The sea and the coasts	76
II. The country	82
III. The state and the people	95
IV. Topography	108
V. Dependencies and colonies	127
Bibliography	132
Literature and arts	135
I. Language and literature. By *H. Schwanenflügel*	137
II. Danish art. By *Julius Lange*	156
III. Music. By *Angul Hammerich*	169
IV. The Stage and its actors. By *H. Schwanenflügel*	180
Bibliography	191
Danish law. The constitution, The law of Succession	195
I. Danish law. By *V. A. Secher*	197
II. The Ground-law	203
III. The law of Succession	218
Economical and social conditions. By *Marcus Rubin*	223
I. Economical legislation	225
II. Statistics	234
Index	261

www.ingramcontent.com/pod-product-compliance
Lightning Source LLC
Chambersburg PA
CBHW031943230426
43672CB00010B/2031